Oct 22, 1995 Sunday, Homecoming C.N.D.
& had a lovely time.
Helen Rendon

Julie Billiart
Woman of Courage

THE STORY OF THE FOUNDRESS OF THE SISTERS OF NOTRE DAME

Roseanne Murphy, S.N.D. de N.

To Helen Toma Rendon '61
with love,
Sr. Roseanne Murphy, SND

PAULIST PRESS
New York/Mahwah, N.J.

The illustrations in this book were drawn by Sr. Genevieve de la Croix, S.N.D., and are taken from *The Charred Wood* by Malachy Gerard Carroll, published by Sands & Co Ltd, London, Glasgow.

Cover design by Christine Taylor of Wilsted and Taylor, California

Cover art by Arthur Poulin, O.F.M.

Library of Congress Cataloging-in-Publication Data

Murphy, Roseanne, 1932–
   Julie Billiart: woman of courage: the story of the foundress of the Sisters of Notre Dame / Roseanne Murphy.
     p.   cm.
   Includes bibliographical references
   ISBN 0-8091-3535-3
   1. Billiart, Julie, Saint, 1751-1816. 2. Sisters of Notre Dame de Namur—Biography. 3. Christian saints—France—Biography. 4. Christian saints—Belgium—Biography. 5. Sisters of Notre Dame de Namur—History. I. Title.
BX4700.B595M87   1995
271´.97—dc20
[B}
                                            94-25230
                                            CIP

Published by Paulist Press
997 Macarthur Boulevard
Mahwah, New Jersey 07430

Printed and bound in the
United States of America

CONTENTS

Contents

To my mother, Rose, and sister, Pat
two women of tremendous courage

and to another, Sister Catharine Julie Cunningham
whose love for Julie was contagious

Julie Billiart
Foundress of the Sisters of Notre Dame de Namur.

ACKNOWLEGMENTS

There are many people who have contributed to this book. It could not have been done without the generous help of Sisters Marie-Chantal Schweitzer (South Belgium) and Jean Bunn (Britain). I am grateful not only for all the materials they shared with me, but also for the friendship and support they extended to me when they heard that I had begun to write a new life of our foundress. During our Julie Conference in Namur, Sr. Mary Hayes suggested that, since I was the one who kept talking about needing a new life of Julie, I ought to do it. I thank her for the idea and the subsequent help she gave me by sharing her materials as well.

During the three years that I was working on the book, several sisters agreed to read the first drafts and comment on them. I am grateful to Sr. Joan Bland (Trinity College) and members of my community, Sisters Rosemarie Gavin and Ann Maureen King, Mary Emmanuel Donnelly gave me valuable suggestions and loving support. Sr. Mary Florence O'Rourke typed the manuscript for me when it had to be readied for the publisher and Sr. Ann Carmel Badalamente spent hours helping me with the edited version. Steve Furgus and Kathy Logan (College of Notre Dame) taught me things about the computer that I never knew existed.

Wherever I went, Sisters of Notre Dame gave me wonderful hospitality. The sisters in Namur, Belgium; at Speke Road, Liverpool, England; the House of Prayer, Carmel, and the Provincial House, Saratoga, California, made me feel so at home that it was hard to leave them when I had finished.

I am indebted to Paulist Press and especially to Larry Boadt, C.S.P., who was patient, encouraging and extremely helpful.

PREFACE

There is a strong tendency in all of us to lock saints into plastic images of perfection and store them safely away on the shelf. When we look carefully at the lives of truly holy people and attempt to relate their experiences to ours, we may feel very uncomfortable. We find out, if we are honest, that they have the same concerns that we do, but they were much better at bringing God's love to the world. Julie Billiart lived through some of the most terrifying periods of history. She reached out to the poor who were shamelessly neglected and inspired a whole movement in France and Belgium that reverberates around the globe today in the women who choose to follow her spirit. Born in the eighteenth century, she absorbed the faith of the culture surrounding her, tinged as it was with Jansenistic ideas about the "world." However, she was a woman ahead of her time when she knew that the Spirit was moving her to start a new kind of religious community. Her congregation would "go out to the whole world" wherever there were children who needed to be taught, especially those who had no one else to teach them. She was paralyzed for twenty-two years, hunted down by some radical revolutionaries determined to kill her, and suffered misunderstandings and rejection from members of the hierarchy and priests when she felt she needed to be faithful to the Spirit prompting her to look beyond national borders. Because we tend to quote the sayings of saints that demonstrate their deep faith and constancy in the face of suffering, we may overlook the fact that they did suffer immensely, which is the reason that we know how heroic they really were. Julie cried real tears, felt terror, experienced great loneliness, and was thoroughly confused when good people, especially her own sisters, seemed to turn against her.

The story of Julie Billiart is a wonderful one, that touches the hearts of many people today since our times are rife with some of the fears and confusions she faced. She lived through a period of great dissension in the church. Some priests signed the oath of allegiance to the Constituent Assembly, creating a schismatic church in France, while others fled for their lives. She had to hold on to her faith when those around her seemed to have abandoned theirs. And when she did what she felt was right, she was persecuted for it. Julie shows us how to grow through times that are painful for everyone. She was being shaped into a channel of grace for literally hundreds of thousands of people who have been touched because of her.

In this new biography, an effort has been made to let Julie and her good friend, Françoise, tell their own story. Whenever possible, Julie and Françoise's own words have been used to explain what was happening to them and the congregation. The modern reader has to allow for the fact that both women used the only language they had at their disposal, one which reflected the biases of their day. While Julie was obedient and reverent toward those in authority, she was profoundly moved by the Spirit of God within her. Compelled by grace, she held steadfast to what she felt God was calling her to do. In the end, those who knew her, including the very ones who resisted her most of all, came to admire her as a woman of great holiness and strength, one who carried out God's work in her day.

A few years ago, when I began to write Julie's story, a prayer group I had been facilitating asked that I share the story with them. Shirley, a member of the group, called me the afternoon of our first session to tell me how much she loved to hear about Julie and how excited she was to know of her. Shortly after our second session, Shirley discovered that she had terminal cancer. I called her immediately when I heard of the diagnosis. She said, "I keep thinking of Julie." Later, I brought her my statue of Julie which she kept at her side, asking for it whenever she was moved from her room. A close relationship had developed between

Shirley and Julie, one that gave the dying woman strength through her last days.

When I asked a young woman who knew nothing about Julie to read my manuscript and comment on it, her initial response was, "I love her. What a wonderful woman; I really feel that she is my friend now." Michele had been on retreat and said, "Julie was very present to me while I was there."

These two women demonstrated once again how alive Julie's spirit is today for those who come to know her. They have broken the plastic image of a saint, and have come to love the woman, Julie, whose contemporaries called her "The Saint Who Smiled." There is every reason to believe that Julie wishes to befriend all of us who face many of the conditions she knew.

Roseanne Murphy, S.N.D. de N.
College of Notre Dame
Belmont, California

St. Julie's house and garden, Cuvilly, Picardy, France.

Chapter I

ON THE ROAD TO FLANDERS
1751–1787

Cuvilly appeared to be an obscure French village in the mid-eighteenth century. The high road to Flanders passed by its homes that were settled in wheat fields stretching across the Picardy countryside. Travelers from Paris to Brussels often stopped in Cuvilly for rest or refreshment and spoke of changes in the large cities of Amiens, Beauvais, and Abbeville. The emerging textile industries were providing people with new opportunities; villagers could be carders, lacemakers or spinners and make a little money to improve their simple existence. But the rhythm of life in Cuvilly was mostly dictated by the change of seasons and the liturgical calendar. The soil was rich and the fields produced an abundance of grain and vegetables. Life appeared to be secure and predictable; at the day's end, most of the villagers gathered in their parish church of St. Eloi to pray evensong together.

The Billiart family had lived in Cuvilly for generations. They had been merchants, bakers, thatchers, stonecutters, weavers, cattle-dealers, masons and tillage farmers. A sizeable piece of land had belonged to the Billiart family for generations, and when Jean François, son of André Billiart, the "Lieutenant de Justice" of the village, married Marie Louise Antoinette de Braine from Maignelay in 1739,[1] the couple moved into a small cottage on the Rue Lataule located on a parcel of his ancestors' property. In addition to farming his section of the land, Jean François opened a draper's shop where he sold manufactured cloth and lace, along with the vegetables and fruits he had grown.

Their daughter, Louise Antoinette, was born during their first year of marriage, and the family "was provided with a comfortable living." According to the social positions of the times, the Billiarts belonged to the artisan and small business class.[2] But sorrow came quickly for the young couple. Little Louise Antoinette was only two years old when she died. Their grief was assuaged somewhat during the following years when three daughters were born to them. Marie Louise Angelique arrived in 1742, Marie Rose in 1743, and Marie Madeleine Henriette in 1744. Their first son, Bonaventure, came in 1747, followed by Jean Baptiste in 1749. But during 1750 the Billiarts suffered the loss of seven-year-old Marie Rose, and three-year-old Bonaventure. Undoubtedly that is why, when a baby girl was born to them on July 12, 1751, Marie Louise Antoinette's sister, Madeleine Demonchy, who had come to Cuvilly from Maignelay to help with the delivery, took the child immediately to St. Eloi to be baptized by Père Pottier, the pastor. Madeleine and Pierre Courtois, a distant cousin, were godparents for Marie Rose Julie, named for the child her parents had loved and lost, but given the name "Julie" to be her very own.

To the delight of the whole family, Julie was a healthy, robust child who seemed to be born smiling. She was affectionate and good-natured, somewhat impulsive and blessed with a sense of humor. Her parents nurtured the beginnings of faith in her, and Marie Louise Antoinette taught Julie simple prayers as soon as she was able to talk. The child responded to her mother's lessons easily, and loved to go to the garden where she found a quiet corner to talk to God in her own familiar way.

When Julie was three years old her brother, Louis François, was born. He was a sickly boy, crippled almost from birth; and as she got older, Julie helped to care for him. Sometimes Louis François would tease Julie about "talking to God." Occasionally, she would be cross with him, scolding him for interrupting her. But her sensitive heart would intervene, and almost before she finished scolding him, she would ask his forgiveness if she

Evening in Cuvilly.

thought she had hurt him. As brother and sister Julie and Louis François remained very close throughout their lives.

Julie grew strong and healthy. Her curiosity and love of learning encouraged her parents to send her to the village school where her uncle, M. Thibault Guilbert, was the schoolmaster. Since Cuvilly could not afford separate schools for boys and girls as was required by law, Julie received what would be considered a good education for a girl of her time and social position. Those who knew her said:

> She began her schooling when she was very young and quickly learned to read and write. But above all, she applied herself to her lessons in religion with an ardor that was extraordinary, so that at the age of seven, she had learned the entire catechism by heart, and understood what she had learned better than others much older and more gifted.[3]

Delighting in the stories of the gospels, Julie would often gather around her children too poor to go to school, and spend some of her time teaching them to read and write, along with the lessons of the catechism she loved. God was not boring to Julie. The gospel stories came alive for her, and when she shared them with other children it was as though a wonderful secret were being given to them. Julie's outgoing personality, enthusiasm, humor, and most of all her gentle love, attracted the children. What was a testimony to her charm was the fact that the children *wanted* her to teach them. Even at an early age, Julie won her students' attention and devotion.

Because Louis was crippled and her older sister, Marie Madeleine was nearly blind from birth, Julie was needed to assist her parents in the fields along with her older brother, Jean Baptiste and sister, Louise Angelique. What leisure time she had, was spent reading, and sharing what she had learned with the other children in the village.

At the time, there was a beggar boy in the village who was crude in his speech and shunned by the other children who were repulsed by his grimy appearance. Julie's heart went out to him and she began to teach him reading and writing along with instructions on how to behave. She coaxed him to adopt more refined manners and gradually he was able to find work. From these early beginnings, he was eventually able to set up his own business and wrote to Julie thirty years later to thank her for helping him get started on his way to a modest but comfortable life. He acknowledged that he could not have achieved anything without her help.

When she was eight, Abbé Dangicourt, the nephew of the pastor of St. Eloi, came to Cuvilly to help his uncle, Père Pottier, who was becoming increasingly lame, and finding it difficult to keep up the work of the parish.[4] Père Dangicourt was a well-educated priest, having completed a degree in theology at the Sorbonne, and had already acquired a reputation for holiness and spiritual insight. In reality, he "...was the counselor and director of the most fervent priests of the whole area around Cuvilly."[5] The villagers grew very fond of their new pastor. Wealthy persons who had chateaux outside the village began to seek him out for counsel.

Père Dangicourt marveled at the eager yearning for knowledge of God manifested by Julie. He recognized that this little girl had a special ability, almost an infused knowledge, to absorb the truths of faith in a way that gave her a delicate appreciation of the things of the Spirit. Her eyes would sparkle as she listened to the good priest speak of God's love for her. Her enthusiasm for what she learned made teaching her a pleasure. He began to tell Julie about mental prayer, and encouraged her to curb her natural impetuosity, which he saw might inhibit her spiritual growth. He advised her to make small sacrifices in order to strengthen her resolve, and to grow in discipline.

Julie responded so well to his promptings, that he felt confident enough in her understanding of the sacraments to allow her to receive her first communion when she was only nine years old. Ordinarily at that time, children had to wait until they were at least thirteen or fourteen before they could receive the eucharist. Abbé Dangicourt asked Julie to keep her privilege a secret for a while, knowing that others her age might be offended, since they had to wait longer. So in the early morning of some of the feast days designated for Julie to receive communion, she would walk the short distance from her home to the church to receive the eucharist, before any of the other villagers arrived in time for mass.

Of her first communion she wrote years later, "Never in my life have I experienced such wonder and joy as I felt that day."[6] Other spiritual practices began to be a regular part of Julie's day. No matter how busy she would be at home or in the garden, she found time to devote an hour of prayer in the morning, and to stop at St. Eloi daily to pray before the blessed sacrament. When leaving the church she would kneel in front of the statue of Mary to ask her blessing before returning home.

Abbé Dangicourt encouraged her reading by lending her some of his favorite books to read. Besides the gospels, epistles, and psalms, Julie loved the *Imitation of Christ*, a book she would have read to her in her last hours. But she also enjoyed reading some of the contemporary books by Rodriquez, Bonhours, and Teresa of Avila.[7] Her own natural inclination to contemplation made the works of Teresa especially dear to her. Even in those early years, the idea of becoming a Carmelite nun was very attractive to Julie. By the time she was eleven, Abbé Dangicourt allowed Julie to receive holy communion in public as he felt there would be no negative reaction among the villagers. They had come to recognize in Julie a child who was so obviously touched by God in an extraordinary way, that there is no indication that anyone objected to her receiving such a privilege.

It was then she began to visit the villagers who were sick. Her gentle manner and the warmth of her personality did much to cheer those who were suffering. As she got older, her parents allowed their daughter to stay all night with those who were critically ill or dying. Gradually, the people of the village began to call Julie the "saint of Cuvilly". Her good-hearted love for the people of the village won her that title, at first given facetiously, and later applied with genuine sincerity.

About that time the Confraternity of the Sacred Heart of Jesus had begun to enlist members throughout France after it had been established in the 1730s. In the sacristy of St. Eloi, there was a list of names of those enrolled in the confraternity in Cuvilly. The tenth name on the list was Marie Rose Julie

Billiart, and farther down were the names of Marie Madeleine Henriette and Louis François. Each member promised to spend one hour of prayer before the blessed sacrament each year. Julie's hour was the privileged one of two to three on Good Friday, the time traditionally represented as Christ's last hour on the cross. Even in her early years Julie and "cross" were mysteriously related. It was manifested in one of her first sorrows, the loss of her older sister, Marie Louise Angelique, who died January 21, 1764, shortly after her marriage and just ten days before her twenty-second birthday. Julie sensed an even greater need now to help the family.

On June 4 of that same year, the Cardinal Bishop of Beauvais came to Cuvilly to confirm the children there. Marie Rose Julie Billiart, age thirteen, was on the list to receive the sacrament. As Julie was leaving the church following the ceremony, a Knight of Malta who was in the village for a special blessing after the confirmation,[8] approached Julie. The gentleman presented her with a cruciform reliquary containing, he explained, a piece of the true cross which he had brought back from the Holy Land.[9] Julie was grateful and pleased; she had inscribed on the back of the reliquary "Given to Julie Billiart by a Knight of Malta."[10] She gave the precious gift to the parish church where it was exposed for veneration on the feasts relating to Christ's passion and death. The gesture of the knight, who presented the girl with something so prized by the community in those days is inexplicable, except for the obvious fact that Julie had been regarded by those who knew her as someone who was especially close to God.

After her confirmation Julie's longing for prayer and union with God increased. At her request Abbé Dangicourt allowed her to make a vow to live for God alone. At fourteen Julie had attained such a depth of understanding of the spiritual life that she felt drawn to give herself completely to God's service. It was rare that a woman would receive permission to make a vow of chastity at such a young age; Julie was an exception. Abbé Dangicourt recognized that Julie had such a grasp of the profound truths of religion that he intuitively felt that God was calling her to do some extraordinary work for the church, though he had no idea what that would be.

A year after her confirmation, sorrow came again for Julie when her sixteen-year-old brother, Jean Baptiste died on October 9, 1765. Now Julie's responsibilities in the family grew. Robust in health, Julie continued to be her parents' strongest support. She tried to make up for the loss of her brother. Times were changing, and tensions increased as a middle class emerged with the development of the textile industries. The social unrest which prefigured the French Revolution began to be felt in the towns and villages.

When Julie was sixteen, her father's store was robbed of most of its valuable goods; Jean François had just returned from Beauvais where he had purchased bolts of materials and lace to sell. He was devastated by the loss; he had not yet paid for his goods and would have to sell what property he had to make up for his debts. It could have been part of a pattern of increasing crime. "Over half of all thefts (in the mid-eighteenth century) were thefts of clothing or materials.... Before the advent of cheap cotton goods, these commodities were regarded as an investment for life."[11] But later, Julie described the theft as having been the result of "envy and calumny."[12] The family was suddenly reduced to poverty.

Immediately Julie's love for her parents impelled her to assume a major part of the responsibility for providing for the family. Harvest time was approaching and Julie found employment in the fields. When she was working with the unlettered field hands, they found that they did not curse or use vulgar language; there was something of God in her that inspired a reverence and respect which brought out the best in them. She worked as hard as any of them and they grew to be very fond of her.

Julie often brought a book to read during their afternoon meal and rest. At first, some of the curious workers asked what it was that interested her so. As she explained the subject of the book–most often one about the spiritual life or the gospels–the illiterate field hands became interested and asked Julie to read aloud to them. When they did not understand something, they asked her to explain it to them. Her explanations were so interesting and lively that they began to expect Julie to read to them each noontime. She was so successful in attracting and holding their attention that they even asked her to gather them on Sundays, saying they would rather hear her talk about God than go to church. While she appreciated their response, she told her admiring audience that Sundays were kept for prayer and her family.

Julie, the young teacher, brought the stories of the gospels alive for the people of her village. Frequently, she would end her "lessons" by teaching them her favorite hymns, which the parishioners sang at evensong. The field hands looked forward to their noon break and their sessions with Julie. Somehow she was able to make religion attractive at a time when many were beginning to abandon their faith.

When harvest time was over, Julie sensed her father's distress when he told her that some in Cuvilly would give him only a third of the value for the pieces of cloth left by the thieves. At once Julie volunteered to take the materials to Beauvais, a town about twenty miles south of Cuvilly, to try to get a better price. After she received her parents' consent for her to borrow a horse, she began her journey with a prayer in her heart that she would find an honest merchant in Beauvais. At the first shop she saw, she took the material in to the shopkeeper who, after hearing her story, gave her the full price of the material. "Full of joy and gratitude to God, Julie returned to Cuvilly bringing to her parents the money she had received. For six years she continued her labors in the fields, and the strongest and ablest workers could not accomplish more than she."[13] When she was not in the fields, she was often traveling to nearby cities to sell goods there.

Frequently Julie went to Compiègne, twenty miles south of Cuvilly, and while there, visited the Carmelite convent. The sisters befriended the young girl, and spoke to her of their love for contemplative prayer while they taught her to improve her embroidery. One of her favorite pieces was a satin banner embroidered in honor of the Virgin Mary with the inscription in Latin, "You are all beautiful, O Mary," worked into its detail.[14] She donated it to the parish church in Cuvilly, as well as a little purse she embroidered which was used to collect the modest offerings of the villagers each Sunday. Once again she thought

Julie rode more than twenty miles to Beauvais.

of becoming a Carmelite, but the needs of her family made her realize what God wanted of her for the present, and the desire had to be relegated to an aspiration for the future.

Work in the fields, her journeys on foot or horseback, her domestic chores, her lacemaking and her charitable works filled Julie's days, and sometimes her nights as she sat at the bedside of the dying. She found her strength in her daily mass, her morning meditations, and her visits to the church whenever possible. She went wherever there was a need in the village; but gradually, the hard work, the poor diet,[15] and exposure to extremes of temperature began to take their toll on Julie's health. "From her early childhood, she had known pain; (she suffered) the almost continuous and intense pain of a toothache, which lasted until she was eighteen...."[16] Then her eyes began to fail, and a doctor said she would lose her sight.

Marie Madeleine had been nearly blind for years, so their mother, Marie Louise Antoinette, planned a pilgrimage to the Cistercian monastery at Montreuil where Pope Innocent IV had sent a copy of the Holy Face of Rome[17] to pray for a cure for her daughters. The image of the Holy Face had become an object of veneration in the area, particularly in the cases of diseases of the eyes. The family made the journey to Montreuil where both Marie Madeleine and Julie experienced a return of their eyesight. Julie never forgot this double favor.[18] Returning to Cuvilly she continued her busy day and "...allowed herself little time for sleep and food."[19] Attacks of neuralgia plagued her at times but she still managed to be her family's strongest support.

In 1774, crimes of violence were increasing, and villages in particular, were the object of these attacks. Besides crimes of theft, from which the Billiart family had already suffered, there were beatings and threats that could come upon a family suddenly, and without any idea of its provocation. Whether it was a vendetta due to a slight offense,[20] or a result of calumny, one night while Julie and her father were at home working together, suddenly a rock crashed through the window, and a shot was fired, directed, Julie believed, at Jean François. Fortunately he was unhurt.

However, terrified that someone would want to kill her dear

father, Julie could not recover from the shock. The neuralgia returned; the pain was intense, and Julie's muscles gradually weakened.[21] But as long as she could, she kept up her work at home and in the village, sometimes leaning on chairs or with the aid of rough-hewn crutches. She continued to attend daily mass, visit the sick, and stay during the night with the dying, as well as help to prepare the children to receive the sacraments.

Her courage and concern for others spoke so eloquently to all those around her, that her confessor, Abbé Dangicourt, could not contain his admiration for her. He spoke with such glowing terms of the heroism of Julie to the bishop of Beauvais, that the prelate wished to see this "Saint of Cuvilly."[22] Julie was taken to visit Bishop de la Rochefoucauld, who commented to several ecclesiastics afterwards, "That young girl seems to me to be inspired by God Himself. I shall be surprised if we do not hear more of her later."[23] He was amazed that Julie was so advanced in the spiritual life.

For eight years Julie continued to live as normally as possible, although she frequently suffered from pain and weakness of her muscles. In 1782, a violent outbreak of fever attacked the village; an event reminiscent of the terrible time in 1709 when the same kind of epidemic killed as many as one-quarter of the population in villages such as Cuvilly.[24] Medicine in the mid-eighteenth century was severely limited as to the diagnosis or the treatment of such diseases. Doctors did not know how to stem the outbreak of the epidemic, nor how to treat the patients who relied on them for help. The one thing the doctors seemed to agree upon was to "...allow nature to take its course, aided by regular bleedings and purgations–among the few treatments on which contemporary medical opinion seems to have been united."[25]

Puzzled by Julie's symptoms, the village doctor diagnosed her case as a result of the epidemic, not accounting for the fact that she had had her symptoms for eight years. As a result, Julie's feet were bled profusely, draining away whatever strength she had left in her legs. At the end of six months of "treatment," Julie was paralyzed. "She lost the use of her limbs so completely that it was impossible for her to stand or to take a step, being helpless to the point that she had to be lifted from couch to chair while

Monsieur L'Abbé Dangicourt.

her bed was being made."[26] Her state was further complicated by violent convulsions, and for a long time she lay between life and death. Abbé Dangicourt was sent for five times to anoint the helpless Julie.

Marie Louise Antoinette and Jean François were heartsick at the thought of losing their devoted daughter. Julie's own suffering was compounded by her awareness that her aging parents' need of support was greater than ever; Louis was crippled, and Marie Madeleine was married. Julie had been their greatest strength, but now she was helpless. The convulsions frightened some of the villagers, who spread the rumor that Julie was possessed. The Billiarts suffered not only because they were watching Julie in such a state, but also from the biting tongues of the very ones who might have been a support to them.

The paralysis spread to the muscles of her jaw rendering her unable to speak at times. Often she would try to overcome the muscle contractions and could talk haltingly, but if she were silent for as long as fifteen minutes, she would again become inarticulate.[27] Most of the time she felt nauseated and could eat very little food, leaving her weaker still. She put off curious neighbors by letting them believe that she was mute and "...in this way, she was left alone with God."[28] For Julie, God was the source of her strength and patience. She began a more intense inward journey of faith when her body was rendered completely dependent upon others. During those years "...long and intimate prayer made her illness bearable, strengthened her love, and prepared her for what Providence had in store for her."[29]

Chapter II

CONFUSION AND FEAR
1788–1794

Dark clouds of discontent were continuing to appear all over France. The country had invested large sums of money in the American Revolution, taking a stand against its hated enemy, England. The debts incurred by that engagement, and the fact that Louis XVI managed to ignore or dismiss the best of his financial advisers, laid the groundwork for the outbreak of violence in 1789. The king believed that his power was absolute, and to some extent it was at the time, for "...there was no legislative body to restrict the royal will."[1] Louis XVI was not a bad king; he was simply an inept one. His mathematics and hunting were far more important to him than affairs of state.

The First Estate, the clergy, and the Second Estate, the nobility were, by and large, exempt from taxation. The Third Estate, made up of the majority of the population worked the hardest, paid the greatest amount of taxes, suffered the most from material deprivation and had the least say in the government. France was facing bankruptcy and it was the privileged classes whose decisions were creating financial chaos. There was no national budget, deficits were chronic, the royal court was extravagant, and the government found their solutions mainly by extending existing taxes, reviving old ones, or making up new ones for the less fortunate to pay.[2]

In the meantime, the ideas of the Age of Enlightenment were

filtering through to every town and village. Voltaire railed against corruption in the church, and people were feeling the power to change society for more "liberty, equality and fraternity." Old ideas were being challenged and new ones sent shock waves through the country. Ironically, the salons of the wealthy women in Paris were meeting places for the discussion and dissemination of the "new ideas" of Voltaire, Rousseau and Montesqieu, all of whom contributed to the principles upon which the populace based their rationale for the overthrow of the monarchy. Some of the very ones who contributed to the growth of revolutionary ideas became the first victims of them.

News of the changes taking place reached Cuvilly. Julie often had visitors come to her room seeking her counsel during these worrisome times. Her steadfast faith comforted the frightened and confused. She continued to help prepare children for their first holy communion and to sustain the faith of those who came to see her. Abbé Dangicourt began to bring her communion each day, and later she admitted, "I do not know how I can wait for the moment of Communion. I am in such pain; but the minute I possess my Jesus I find relief. I am well again."[3] Her strength seemed to come from her deep religious convictions, her prayer life and the sacraments.

Some of the wealthy women who owned chateaux around Cuvilly, pressed themselves into her small room to seek her counsel. Madame de Séchelles, who had known Julie as a child, built, at her suggestion, a hospital in a field east of the village, where there was a spring, to serve the victims of the epidemics plaguing the countryside. Madame Baudoin brought her three daughters and her father, Count Arlincourt, to see Julie. Julie's courage, loving kindness and good nature comforted the old gentleman so that he bequeathed a small annuity of six hundred francs a year to her. Madame Pont l'Abbé was one of Julie's friends who had a door built to her room so that the Billiart family would not be disturbed when her visitors arrived at the tiny cottage. Marie Madeleine's daughter, Felicité, was only seven when her Aunt Julie became paralyzed, but she came each day to help care for her and to run errands. Felicité would carry Julie's invitation to the village children to come to her room where she would prepare them for the sacraments. Years later, some of those whom she prepared said when they were dying, that they wanted to say the prayers Julie had taught them as children.

Julie seemed to be a safe refuge in a sea of political and economic turmoil. The crop failures of 1787 and 1788 left the poor people without the little that they had had. Inflation drove the price of bread so high that the cost of one loaf was equal to half a day laborer's salary. Shortages of food sparked riots in many of the cities of France, while the monarchy seemed indifferent. Stories of the wealth of the nobles, some of the bishops, and monasteries well-stocked with food, aggravated the populace and enhanced the expectation of a radical change in the government. Gradually, the growing unrest broke out into the storming of the Bastille on July 14, 1789. The Revolution had begun.

The Roman Catholic Church became a focal target for the National Assembly, the body that emerged to write a civil constitution in the first attempt to reorganize the government into a constitutional monarchy. By November 2, 1789, the church had been nationalized, monasteries and church property confiscated and put up for sale, and by July 12, 1790, on Julie's birthday, the Civil Constitution of the Clergy had been established. Every priest was asked to sign an oath of allegiance to the new government by which he would forsake his loyalty to the pope. The National Assembly sent the oath to Pope Pius VI for an approval which never arrived. On November 27, 1790, "It required all priests to take an oath to uphold the new constitution and as an essential component of this constitution, to the Civil Constitution of the Clergy."[4] The church lost its legal existence for eleven years. Clerics who refused to sign the oath by January 1, 1791, were considered to be traitors to the Revolution and were liable to imprisonment and death. Monasteries and convents were suppressed, and religious vows forbidden by the "Decree Prohibiting Monastic Vows in France, February 13, 1790."[5] Dioceses were reconfigured to fit the civil departments established by the Assembly and the appointment of priests and bishops signing the oath were to be by election only. A schismatic church was established in France; a fact that was later to prove to be a fatal flaw in the Revolution. "The Civil Constitution of the Clergy began, then, as an integral part of the revolutionary movement, but ended by causing civil war among the French people."[6]

While Julie was growing closer to God, many of her compatriots were rejecting anything that had to do with religion. The turbulent months leading to the Revolution were filled with growing resistance to religion, especially to the church. Seeing corruption in the wealthy monasteries and among some of the hierarchy who were aligned with the monarchy, many French citizens withdrew what allegiance they had to Catholicism. Separating the message from the messengers became an insurmountable task. By 1792, the National Assembly suppressed all teaching and charitable congregations which in effect, abolished all "public" schools in France; literally the only schools available to the majority of the population.

In Cuvilly, Julie was being grounded in faith. Spending four and five hours a day in prayer, she grew to an even more profound contemplative state. Père Sellier, in giving testimony regarding Julie's prayer life at this time, explained "...I believe she was raised to a very high degree of contemplation...at such (prayer) times she was to be seen perfectly rapt in God, motionless, all use of her senses suspended, and her countenance glowing with heavenly peace and sweetness."[7] Only when someone gently touched her or shook her arm would she be able to come out of her contemplative state. During the first eight years of her paralysis, Julie was filled with consolation in prayer. She was learning to wait upon God's time in her life. Forced into helplessness, Julie simply had to be patient, and let events unfold for her. Her life spoke to those who came to her for help more than her words. The formerly busy girl of Cuvilly who traveled, bought and sold, comforted the sick, and assumed leadership in the parish, was now waiting while the world around her was seething with potential violence.

Picardy was one of "...the most intense centers of revolutionary activity outside of Paris itself."[8] Being one of the most heavily taxed regions in France, its textile industries had suffered a long-term depression during the recession of the 1780s which affected thousands of workers in the mills as well as the part-time workers in the countryside. When the Revolution began, uprisings occurred all over Picardy breaking out spontaneously. Persons who visited Julie found someone with compassion and hope when all seemed lost. "For to see Julie was to love her—all were won by the clear, frank eyes, the simple, kindly manner, and that good smile of hers, which love had already sealed upon her lips and to which suffering gave a pathetic charm."[9] At a time when the world outside of Cuvilly seemed to be falling apart, Julie's faith and encouragement helped to make real her belief that "God is Good!"

Finally the Revolution reached her door. Her beloved friend and guide, Abbé Dangicourt, was asked to sign the Oath of Allegiance to the Civil Constitution of the Clergy. He could not sign. His heart ached at the thought of having to leave his people. Even the revolutionaries who demanded his signature taunted him with the idea that he was not much of a father to his people if he would not sign the oath. But Abbé Dangicourt could not betray his conscience, whatever the consequences. He knew that many of his fellow priests, some with the sincere belief that it would reform the church in France, had signed the oath. In fact, by March 1791, "...ninety percent of the clergy in the district of Beauvais had taken the oath, while 83 percent in Compiègne had done so."[10]

The Abbé was facing enormous social pressure. "In other sections of France, major segments of the population opposed the implementation of the oath. By contrast, in Picardy those, like Julie, who opposed its implementation were hounded and persecuted."[11] Immediately, Abbé Dangicourt had to go into hiding. The hunted priest lived in a dark, damp hovel behind a chicken house protected by some of his loyal parishioners. At night, he often emerged to say mass in Julie's room for her and some of her friends. When he could do so without drawing attention to himself, he would reach some of his people in time to prepare them for their own deaths. Each time he left his hiding place, he risked his life. After six months of this, the revolutionaries were getting too close and he fled to Mt. Valerian outside of Paris where the monks were hiding non-juring priests. A few months later, he died.

Her friend and spiritual father gone, Julie's sufferings were intensified by the fact that she was bereft of spiritual help. God seemed to have abandoned her. "There were periods that ran into months during the Revolution, when she was deprived of all spiritual help, for besides her physical suffering she was prey to the dark night of the soul that God sometimes requires of his chosen ones."[12] It was the beginning, too, of her own particular experience of the "reign of terror" for when a schismatic priest was sent to the village as pastor, Julie would not receive him. She could not support the schism that was tearing her country apart. "We must pray for him," she would say, with charity so characteristic of her, "that God may open his eyes."[13] But she encouraged others to resist the schism and even managed to arrange for hiding places for some non-juring priests and for them to meet their distressed parishioners. When the villagers did not know what to do, Julie would encourage them to remain steadfast in their faith. Better no mass, she would say, than one with a schismatic priest.[14] So effective was her resistance to the schism, that it is recorded in the archives in Compiègne:

> The only commune in the district where there were serious incidents concerning oaths of allegiance was at Cuvilly, situated in the north of the district on the Flanders road. This little village seems to have a particular character, because of the presence of a young and very pious paralytic by the name of Julie Billiart whose "fanatical" influence was very great in Cuvilly even before the Revolution.[15]

It was not long before Julie became aware of her own danger from the revolutionaries. Madame Pont l'Abbé, fearing for her life, convinced Julie that she must leave Cuvilly at once. She came in her carriage herself for her friend. Felicité could not bear to leave her aunt and begged her parents for permission to accompany her. Since Felicité was sixteen years old by now, her family, realizing that someone had to care for the paralytic, gave her their blessing even though they recognized the danger she was facing. So Marie Louise Antoinette, now aged seventy-six, and Jean François at seventy-four, were forced to say goodbye to their beloved Julie not knowing what would happen to her, fearing for her safety, and worse still, knowing that she was completely helpless. No doubt they prayed with all their hearts as they watched the carriage take their daughter to Gournay-sur-Aronde where, they hoped, she would be safe. But no one knew the extent of the Revolution. Few, if any could consider themselves "safe."

Not long after Madame Pont l'Abbé settled Julie and Felicité into her chateau, she herself became aware of her own danger. She escaped to England along with other aristocratic émigrés where she found safety, but soon afterwards, her health failed and she died. After the owners fled, the chateau was managed by a revolutionary. Fortunately his son-in-law, Camus, had a respectful attachment to Julie, and both kept her presence a secret as far as possible. But within a year, after searching for Julie all over the region, a radical group of revolutionaries became suspicious about the presence of Julie in the chateau.

Having torn down the Calvary shrine so characteristic of the villages in that area, the radicals made a bonfire of the wood and threw on it the tabernacle from the church, statues and sacred books, to build it into a huge pyre in preparation for burning "la dévote" alive. In a rage, they turned to the castle in Gournay. Hearing of their approach, the caretaker hid Julie and Felicité in the bottom of a hay cart outside the barn. Having covered both of them with hay, he rushed back to the chateau to meet the mob which stormed into the building demanding that he turn Julie over to them. He tried to persuade them that Julie was not in the chateau, but they ransacked the building swearing in drunken voices that they would "...drag the invalid from her bed and toss her in a blanket shouting that they would 'watch her dance'"[16] before throwing her onto the fire. The caretaker was able to harangue the mob so that they gave up the idea of continuing to search the house or act on their threat to burn it down. Finally, they withdrew, vowing to return. One of them carved on the wall of the chateau, "Stuff the aristocrats with bullets."

The caretaker rushed outside declaring that Julie and Felicité

Chateau at Gournay.

had to leave at once before the mob returned. He and Camus quickly hitched the horse to the wagon and drove right through the mob, still shouting blasphemies and obscenities about "la dévote" and swearing to find her. Scarcely able to breathe, and suffering intensely from pain, Julie was jostled out onto the road to Compiègne praying that God would guide her and Felicité to safety. "In this way, they passed through the mob who let their prey escape without knowing it; for those whom God protects are well protected."[17] Julie commented years later that her physical pain was not as great as the pain she felt at hearing what was being shouted all around her, and that if she could have stopped the blasphemy, she would have gladly surrendered her life.

The driver knew that he could reach Compiègne twenty miles away, and get back before the morning when he expected the mob would return to the chateau. Julie and Felicité almost suffocated under the hay but no one dared to expose her for fear of her pursuers. They arrived in Compiègne in the early hours of the morning when it was still dark and very cold. The two men lifted the paralytic off the cart and onto a bench in the courtyard of an inn. Felicité begged them not to leave Julie exposed to the cold night but both men, fearing for their own lives if they were caught, fled back to Gournay.

Felicité tried to get some wine into Julie and rubbed her hands in an attempt to warm her. In her heart Felicité thought that Julie might not make it through the night, and prayed for help. The next morning, two sisters by the name of Chambon found the young girl and her paralyzed aunt shivering on a bench, and offered them a room in their home. Julie and Felicité were able to stay with the kind women for about two months, but as soon as the sisters realized that Julie was loyal to the church, they feared for their own safety and asked her to leave. In three and a half years Julie, still hunted by the revolutionaries, had to move five times. Her favorite aspiration was..."Lord, wilt Thou not lodge me in Thy Paradise, since I can no longer find a shelter on earth?"[18] No one seems to know where Julie and Felicité lived during their time in Compiègne, so well hidden were their lodgings.

During these years, Julie's health became even more fragile. Suffering under the constant fear of being caught, living at a

mere subsistence level while Felicité tried to provide for them by
making lace, and enduring the continual shocks of the Reign of
Terror, brought Julie to such a physical state that she became
incapable of uttering a single word without great effort. She
tried to communicate by signs when she could not speak. News
reached her of the horrors being perpetrated by the radical revolutionaries. Each new atrocity filled her heart with anguish.

Without the spiritual support she had in Cuvilly, knowing that
her parents' lives could be in danger, yet being completely helpless and unable to console or support them, Julie suffered physically and mentally during the endless months of hiding in
Compiègne. Her faith was being tested like "gold in the furnace"
and her own words sustained her: "How good is the good God
who tries us! Let us live for Him, let us die for Him! If we live by
crosses, we shall die of love."[19]

In June of 1792, Julie received word that her father had died.
The grief she felt at the loss of her beloved father was compounded by the fact that she could not comfort nor help her
mother who was left alone with a crippled son, Louis. Julie had
to surrender her natural desire to be with her mother, and beg
God to provide for her, trusting that she would be cared for. At
moments such as these, her loving heart undoubtedly filled with
anguish and she was left with the only resource she could
depend on, her faith. How often she repeated to herself the sen-
timent that she used frequently throughout her life, "God will
provide, by myself I can do nothing."

In 1793, a non-juring priest, Abbé de LaMarche, heard of
Julie. This remarkable cleric was living in disguise in Compiègne
while he tried to minister to the spiritual needs of some of the
faithful there, especially the Carmelite nuns who had befriended Julie in her youth. Finally, Julie received some of the spiritual help she so desired, and Abbé de LaMarche, who had "...that
knowledge of spiritual things which may be called the genius of
sanctity,"[20] recognized in her an extraordinary holiness. He
described his meeting with Julie himself.

> It was not until 1793 that I made the acquaintance of...Julie. She
> had left Cuvilly, her native place, and been taken to Compiègne

for greater safety in the troubles which at that time agitated France. I was ministering to the spiritual needs of some faithful souls who dwelt there, notably the Carmelite nuns....Julie was living in retirement in a small room with one of her nieces who took care of her. I went to visit her; she did not speak or rather, she only spoke by signs. When she went to confession, I had to give her an hour's notice. She then prepared herself with intense fervour, and obtained as she owned to me, the grace of articulating distinctly. It was only after absolution that she fell back into speechlessness. It seemed clear to me that it was by no effort of nature that she was able to express herself in confession, but that she obtained this favour by her lively faith. I saw her from time to time for about a year. I was more and more astonished at her progress in perfection. She offered herself continually to God as a victim to appease His anger. Her resignation was perfect; always calm, always united to God. Her prayer was, so to speak, unceasing.[21]

On January 21 of that same year, King Louis XVI was guillotined; the monarchy had fallen after the National Convention had declared France a Republic. Hatred for anyone associated with the aristocracy or the Roman Catholic Church, unleashed a furor that seemed to grow more intense as each victim was led to the guillotine. By February, war was declared on Great Britain, and in March, on Spain. A Revolutionary Tribunal was established and more than one hundred thousand émigrés were declared legally dead, their properties confiscated by the government. By October, the queen, Marie Antoinette, was led to the guillotine accused of a crime in writing by her eight-year-old son, the Dauphin, Louis Charles. He had been literally taken from her arms, beaten and fed brandy until his torturers held his hand and forced him to sign the document which was to be his mother's death warrant. Marie Antoinette was thirty years of age.

Abbé de LaMarche kept Julie informed of the events taking place during the Reign of Terror. Perhaps one of the most painful for her was the story of the deaths of her good friends, the Carmelites of Compiègne. They had been forced out of their monastery finding refuge wherever some of their devoted friends could house them. Abbé de LaMarche attempted to keep in touch with them, gathering the nineteen of them together whenever he could to celebrate mass for them or give them his support. But within a few weeks, while three of the nuns were out in the country searching for a house for the community, the Republican guards gathered those in the city back in the monastery, put them all in an open cart and took them to the Concierge in Paris to await their fate.

In July, 1794, the Carmelites were led to the guillotine, singing the "Salve Regina" as they mounted the scaffold. The prioress was the last to be executed, having watched fifteen of her sisters beheaded before her eyes. Abbé de LaMarche, disguised as a workman, stood at the bottom of the steps blessing each Carmelite as she walked to the scaffold. Their heroic deaths made a profound impression on Julie; she often referred to them years later.[22] She felt the loss of her friends for they had been a prayerful support for her since she was a child.

Sometime during this period, when she was totally helpless and hunted by the revolutionaries, Julie had a profound spiritual experience, which proved to be the beginning of a conviction that eventually changed the course of her life. She reported years later that while in Compiègne, she had a vision of a group of sisters, in a habit she had never seen before, standing around a cross. The features of the sisters were so clear to her that later she was able to identify actual persons she had seen in the vision. At the close of the experience, she heard a voice say, "Behold the spiritual daughters whom I give to you in the Institute which will be marked by my Cross."[23] Following these words, she was shown some of the trials she was to undergo during her lifetime. All she could do at the time was to wait for the purposes of God to unfold in her life and, as another woman did before her, ponder these words in her heart.

The next sorrowful news to reach Julie was that her friend and benefactor, Count d'Arlincourt, who had been so good to the poor, was led to the guillotine along with his son-in-law, Count Baudoin. She was surprised to receive a message shortly afterwards that Madame Baudoin and her three daughters were escaping Paris and moving to Amiens. The grieving widow, having lost her father as well as her husband, begged Julie to come

*"Behold the spiritual daughters whom I give you in the institute
which I promise to mark with my cross."*

to Amiens as she needed the comfort and support of her good friend. She had arranged to hire a set of rooms for Julie and Felicité in the house of Count Blin de Bourdon on the Rue des Augustins. Julie's heart went out to the sorrowing widow, but instinctively she hesitated to make the move to Amiens. Her strong intuition told her that there was to be more suffering for her in that city; but finally, her loving heart and her compassion for a friend who continued to beg her to come, led her to agree to the long and painful journey.

On the way to Amiens that October in 1794, Julie stopped in Cuvilly to see her mother. Marie Louise Antoinette was nearly eighty now; she had been a widow for two years. She, too, had heard the stories of the Carmelites and the friends of Julie who had been guillotined. Her daughter was in the worst physical state she had ever been, and was on the way to live with people of nobility. There is no way to know what fears gripped her heart as she beheld her paralyzed daughter who had once been her source of strength. Julie seemed to know she would never see her mother again. The two embraced for the last time, and felt yet another kind of death within. Of all the people in the world Julie would have loved to care for and comfort, it would have been her mother; but she, too, had to be left in God's hands as the carriage took her away from Cuvilly for the last time.

St. Eloi (Parish Church of Cuvilly).

Chapter III

AMIENS
1794–1803

The chill winds of October that whipped around the carriage as it approached Amiens were prophetic of Julie's stay there. In 1794 the city, once thriving because of the textile industry, was in the midst of an economic disaster that was plaguing the whole of France. While the Revolution promised civil rights to all French citizens, and the end of clerical and aristocratic oppression, in fact, the National Assembly produced few concrete improvements to alleviate the sufferings of the poor. "Epidemics, starvation, unemployment and inflation stalked France like the four horsemen of the Apocalypse."[1] Faced with wars with Great Britain, Spain, Belgium, Austria and Prussia, the revolutionary government was overwhelmed with financial burdens, and a counterrevolutionary movement began in Vendée in 1793.

> Like all governments, that of the 1790's was a question of competing priorities, and the old, the sick and the feeble-minded lost out to more pressing demands—to trade controls and the maximum to the purging of suspects, and the implementation of the Revolutionary Government, to dechristianization and requisition—above all to winning the war.[2]

All these causes competed for money that the government did not have and consequently the old and the poor, especially those who were ill, had very little political power to demand attention.

"They lost out not because of any failure of will, at least during the Jacobin period, but because they ceased to be one of the most urgent problems facing a severely-harassed government."[3]

The "Great Terror" which had erupted in Paris in June of 1792, resulted in the condemnation of 1,400 persons in that city alone. Finally, Robespierre, having attempted to "purge" France of anyone accused of counterrevolutionary sentiments, was himself condemned to the guillotine; the French people had become weary of bloodshed. His unsuccessful attempt at suicide made his execution even more grotesque.

For a long period following the death of Robespierre, the confusion in the government and a lack of any infrastructure to establish justice, left the ordinary citizens vulnerable to the whims of arbitrary men. "Tribunals, composed of politically reliable citizens were no substitute for an established system of courts, handing down justice on the basis of a widely respected legal tradition."[4] There was no regular police force in France until 1795. In Amiens, the atmosphere was charged with uncertainty and fear. Inflation continued to force those who were once able to provide for themselves into the ranks of the poor. "By June, 1795, almost 12,000, or a third of Amiens' population had become indigent."[5]

Such was the city of Amiens in October, 1794, when Julie was taken to the Hôtel Blin on the Rue St. Augustins where Madame Baudoin and her seventeen-year-old daughter, Lise, had taken apartments for her. Felicité carried her aunt in her arms up the flight of stairs to her bed. Exhausted, Julie was grateful to have come to the end of an agonizing journey. She could not know that another kind of journey was just beginning for her.

The owners of the Hôtel Blin were members of the Blin de Bourdon family who boasted a long line of counts and viscounts, extending back past the Ancien Régime in the eleventh century. During the Reign of Terror, Françoise Blin de Bourdon, sister of the count, was at her grandmother's home, Gezaincourt, where she had been raised since her birth on March 9, 1756.

Daughter of Pierre-Louis de Blin, Viscount de Domart-en-Pontieu and Marie Louise Claudine, daughter of the Baron of Fouquesolles, Viscount of Doullens, Françoise was presented at

the court of Louis XVI in 1775 at the age of eighteen. She then
returned to Gezaincourt to care for her beloved grandmother
following her grandfather's death. It was there that the revolutionaries came in the middle of the night to arrest Madame
Fouquesolles in February, 1794. Françoise begged the mob to
spare her grandmother who was in her eighties at the time. In
spite of the fact that the household servants had come out to
meet the revolutionaries, armed with pitchforks and shovels to
defend their beloved mistresses, Françoise managed to send her
faithful friends home, assuring them that she would deal with
the revolutionaries, and all would be well. As soon as the villagers left Françoise offered to go with them if they would leave
her grandmother alone.

The thirty-eight year old Françoise was put into a rough farm
cart and taken to "la Providence" in Amiens in the middle of the
night. A devoted servant followed the cart at a safe distance in
order to report on her fate to the Gezaincourt household.
Baroness Fouquesolles was spared the report of her beloved
granddaughter's arrest, but she insisted that her "angel" would
be returning very soon, and refused to eat until Françoise was
there to help her. She died on March 27, without the comfort of
the child she had raised.

At "la Providence," Françoise learned that her father, brother
and nephew were imprisoned as well. After a few weeks, because
of severe overcrowding, women prisoners were offered the
choice of transferring to the Carmelite convent which had been
converted into a prison. Françoise alone eagerly accepted the
transfer; she had longed to be a Carmelite since her days of
studying, first at a Benedictine school, and then with the
Ursulines. Drawn to the contemplative life, Françoise strained to
listen through the walls of her cell when she heard the
Carmelites saying their office and singing hymns together in the
room next to hers. One day Françoise happened to see a news-
paper article that announced the names of those to be executed.
The members of the Blin de Bourdon family were to be guillotined within a few weeks. But, with the fall of Robespierre on
July 27, 1794, the aristocrats' lives were spared.

On August 3, her nephew, Alexander, came to the Carmelite

convent to tell his aunt that he, his father, mother and grandfather had been released and that she, too, was free. Françoise
chose to stay one more night in the convent; she wanted to
spend time in prayer thanking God for her family's deliverance,
and asking guidance for her future. Françoise went to her brother's home on the Rue St. Augustins on August 4, 1794.

After Julie recovered from her long and sorrowful journey,
Madame Baudoin arranged for her good friend, Françoise Blin
de Bourdon, to meet her. In Françoise's own words, she
described their first meeting. "This young woman had leisure in
abundance and was quite willing to come, though when she
found she could not understand the invalid's labored speech, the
visits seemed less attractive."[6]

The room was small and Madame Baudoin and Felicité tried
their best to make it cheerful. Julie was left alone much of the
time, as her niece had to find provisions for them in a city suffering from many deprivations. Julie, completely helpless, simply
had to wait until someone could relieve her of her discomfort and
care for her needs. Françoise admitted later that she was repulsed
by the sickroom. Being "of the manner born," Françoise was
accustomed to the services of servants who provided immediate
relief for any of their mistress's wishes. But a strange and wonderful attraction led Françoise to return to Julie's room again
and again. Gradually she found that she wanted to help care for
the invalid by bringing her some broth or reading to her during
the long hours of Felicité's absence. "Finally, in spite of the natural repugnance which she had at first experienced, a friendship
grew between them, as events will show."[7]

Julie had times when her speech seemed easier and she could
converse quite naturally. Madame Baudoin's daughter, Lise,
though typical of a young aristocratic woman of the times, interested in pleasure and material possessions, still seemed to be
attracted to the things of God. Lise was drawn to Julie who
would share with her thoughts about the Lord and the spiritual
life. She invited her young friends, the two Doria sisters and the
de Mery sisters, to meet Julie; they found in the invalid a spiritual mother. "The five, and Mademoiselle Blin (who was older
than they) frequently came to visit Julie, and soon they grew to

love her."[8] Once again, Julie attracted a small group around her sick bed and taught them about the gospels and the spiritual life, sustaining their faith and courage during some of the darkest hours of French history.

Before moving to Amiens, Madame Baudoin had befriended a non-juring priest while still in Paris. Later, Père Antoine Thomas, Doctor of the Sorbonne, had been imprisoned for refusing to sign the oath required by the Civil Constitution, and was condemned to the guillotine. Providentially, grave illness postponed his execution, and with the fall of Robespierre he, too, was released from prison. He was, however, still in danger from those who despised non-juring priests. In disguise, he made his way to Amiens, where some good women from Brittany afforded him shelter. Eventually, his hostesses returned to their home, and when Madame Baudoin learned of his presence in Amiens, arrangements were made to have Père Thomas join the group at the Hôtel Blin.

A small community was forming. Then Madame Baudoin, restless as usual, decided to return to Paris where, within a few months, she died, leaving Lise in the care of Julie. When the Doria and de Mery sisters all moved into the Hôtel Blin, Père Thomas became their chaplain, saying mass each day for them in Julie's room. They even began a communal life, observing a short rule that Père Thomas gave them, and often sang the Office of the Blessed Virgin Mary together. They began to call Julie their "Mother" and afterwards referred to her as "Mère Julie." The group, however, did not last for more than a few years.

One of the Doria sisters, Josephine, left Amiens to join the Sisters of the Visitation in Paris. Years later she often referred to the excellent direction she had received from Julie in her youth, and attributed her growth in the spiritual life to the guidance she received while at the Hôtel Blin. The other sister, Gabrielle, married the Count de Cornulier; but her health having been fragile, she died within three years. Lise went to Paris to live with an older sister. Julie often spoke of her concern for the young women whom she loved and cared for in her days at the Hôtel Blin. The youngest of the de Mery sisters went to live with an older sister, and she too died young. Eventually, only Françoise remained of this first beginning of a community, but throughout the four or five years of its existence, a pattern was developing and "...the ground was being prepared for what Mère Julie would do later."[9]

After their first year at the Hôtel Blin, Françoise had to return to Bourdon to care for her father who was suffering from the effects of his imprisonment as well as his advancing age.[10] She worried about the condition of her father's relationship with God, since Viscount Blin de Bourdon was an avid disciple of Voltaire, and as a result, had little use for the church. The letters that passed between Julie and Françoise while the latter was with her father are filled with Julie's advice to be present to this good man, care for him lovingly, and leave the rest to God. She cautioned Françoise against being too impulsive:

> We must depend entirely on grace to say what is to the point or to say nothing if we do not find the persons well-disposed to whom we should like to speak. Up to now, you have done your best; it was necessary to turn over this hardened soil to get to the bottom of it. We must continue to act like a wise farmer; when he notices that the only result of his digging deeper into the ground would be to bring bad soil to the surface, he prefers to cast his seed putting it into the keeping of Providence rather than dig further.[11]

Apparently, Françoise was able to cast the seeds of conversion gently, but effectively, because when her father died on February 1, 1797, Julie could write, "You must thank the Good God for the dispositions in which your father died. You could not have wished for more consoling ones."[12]

Julie's own mother became very ill only a year after she moved into the Hôtel Blin. Felicité was sent for to care for Marie Louise Antoinette, as she was unable to care for herself, and Louis François was too crippled to be of any assistance. Julie wanted to help in any way she could. She even sent what little money she had left from the amount that Françoise had left her for necessities. Two weeks after Felicité left for Cuvilly, Julie's mother died. Julie wrote to Françoise:

...the arrival of my dear Felicité has been for me the occasion of a very great sacrifice. In short, my dear friend, I have lost my poor dear mother. You will understand what my sensitive heart has felt, though by the grace of God it submits to the orders of Providence. It is always by way of sacrifice the Lord wants to lead me to himself, himself alone. Ask then for me, my good friend, that I may be completely immolated to the good pleasure of our dear Master for all the sacrifices he may ask of me.[13]

It is through her letters to Françoise that we can glimpse the affectionate heart of Julie and the deep friendship that was growing between the two women. Shortly after Françoise left Amiens for the first time, Julie wrote "...a heart like mine feels all this (absence) intensely. No, my good and loving friend, my heart will never be able to express how dear you are to me. I can only call you friend, my heart refuses to do otherwise, for it is too attached to you in the Lord for him and in him that I love you so dearly."[14] Gradually, Françoise began to respond to her friend with the intimacies of her own difficulties and cares, especially by sharing her struggles with her relationship with God.

For years Françoise thought of being a Carmelite, and she shared that dream with Julie. At first, Julie advised Françoise to develop a strong and constant spirit of prayer. She indicated that when both were completely open to God, "She (Julie) would leave myself in the hands of the Good God so that it may turn out according to his good pleasure and lead to all that may glorify him most in you and me. If afterwards, he wants to make a holy Carmelite of you, he will know what means to take for this end."[15] But two years later, the bond between the two friends had grown so that Julie would write:

As (God) has given us the same exclusive wish to seek to glorify him in all things, you must unite yourself with me, my dear child, as far as you can, so that we may fall in with the places Providence has for us. I have no doubt that the Good God has some special plan for you.... As soon as I heard of your father's death, I saw you throwing yourself into my arms. This sight struck my heart with great feeling. It seemed to me that this was to be the moment when the Good God would give you to me, and me to you, in such a strong tie that death alone would separate us.[16]

In the meantime, Julie was suffering even more in body, and oftentimes in spirit as well. Père Thomas was a great comfort to her, and though there were two years difference in their ages, Père Thomas being the younger, Julie turned to him with the simplicity of a child. She often referred to him as "Our Father" when writing to Françoise, and deferred to his opinion whenever spiritual matters arose.

The food riots in Amiens during the summer of 1795 highlighted the scarcity of food. In October of that year, Julie wrote, "Bread becomes dearer every day...."[17] She worried about Felicité who found it difficult not only to buy bread, but also to buy the materials she needed to make the lace that was the source of their livelihood. At one point Felicité thought of making the journey to Compiègne where she heard things were a little better. Julie commented that if her niece had to go, she would be "very isolated again."[18] Yet, she admitted, "How Good is God, my dear friend, to have given my poor Felicité her talent for sewing! We never tire of thanking God for it, this poor child and I."[19]

When enteric fever and malaria epidemics swept through some of the sections of Amiens in the summer of 1795, Julie was affected. It was not just the meager diet, the unsanitary conditions and the cold that caused such outbreaks, but the constitutions of the people had become so weakened that they were vulnerable to every disease and epidemic in the region. In October, Julie described her fever in her letters to Françoise. She had a "bout of fever" every other day for about five or six hours; the following day she was very weak.[20] By November, she suffered from the fever every day. Françoise had invited Julie to ask for anything she needed; Julie responded:

...I have such frequent and heavy perspiration that if I were to change as often as I ought, I should require a great deal of linens. What I do want to ask you quite simply is whether you could send me some old towels, that I could wrap around me and change for myself as needful at night. I cannot tell you how ill I feel when all my linen, soaked in perspiration, clings to me, and makes my

body clammy and cold. I think that was what gave me the cold I
have had for the past fortnight. You see, I am making full use of
the right you gave me to tell you quite frankly all my needs.[21]

Julie used the term "tertian ague," when referring to her condition, one that was used to describe malaria in her day. When the
outbreak of malaria started, she admitted she could neither
write nor sew. She wrote "...during the bouts of fever, you know
I cannot keep still."[22] Without a fire in her room, Julie shook violently with the fever and the cold. When the weather was better,
her linens could be dried in the attic, but when winter came she
never had enough towels to keep her dry. By December she had
"...got rid of the tertian ague but not of the nerve fever."[23] Left
with almost continual nausea and "fainting fits," Julie had a
philosophical, as well as humorous attitude toward her body. As
she expressed it, "You want me to tell you about my wretched
body; it is not worth it. But since you wish it, I shall say it is no
good at all."[24]

Often she thought of death; in fact, sometimes it seemed as if
the idea had a positive attraction for her. "You know that by
God's grace I look upon myself in this world as a poor exile banished from her home country, and that I desire nothing so much
as to go there when God wills."[25] Julie was one more victim of
the epidemics of malaria which were prevalent throughout the
eighteenth century since "...throughout France, infested lakes,
swampy marshes and rivers in spate helped spread various forms
of enteric fever."[26]

In 1795, Françoise renounced the property she had inherited
from her grandparents at Gezaincourt in favor of her brother
and gave the equivalent in other property to her sister.
Detaching herself from her obligations to the household at
Gezaincourt, it was becoming clearer to Françoise that she
would be devoting her life and her means to the service of God,
and in some way she knew that she would do it with her good
friend, Julie. Père Thomas encouraged both Françoise and Julie
in their desire to help restore the faith in France during a period when the troubles of the Church seemed to be lessening for
a brief period.

The little community surrounding Julie at that time reached out to some of the children in Amiens. Although they had a small group, their work was known enough so that when the churches were opened for a while in August, 1797, the bishop of Saint-Papoul was able to administer the sacrament of confirmation in the church at Saint Rême. After the ceremony, the bishop paid a visit to the residents of Hôtel Blin, and confirmed some of the children Julie's community had prepared.

Unfortunately, the law of September 5, 1797 brought a new wave of persecution to the church. This time, all the priests were asked to sign yet another oath, expressing their hatred for royalty. The period, known as the "Little Terror," began September 4, 1797. Priests refusing to sign the oath were hunted down. Père Thomas would not sign it. Three times the Republican Guards ransacked the Hôtel Blin looking for the priest. During the last attempt, the night of June 16, 1799, Père Thomas hid in the hayloft of the stables. One of the guards, candle in hand, pursued him and arrived in time to prevent the priest from pulling up the ladder. The guard shouted out to the others that he had "caught (his) bird."[27] At that moment his candle blew out, and as he bent to pick it up, Père Thomas leapt over the guard and made it safely to his hiding place. It was clear, however, that he had to leave the Hôtel Blin that night.

Josephine Doria, still with Julie at the time, possessed a small estate outside of Amiens. Recognizing the danger for all of them, she offered Bettencourt to Julie, Françoise, Père Thomas and Felicité. Gratefully, the small band hurriedly made ready to leave. At nine o'clock in the evening on June 16, 1799, the four huddled in a carriage hoping to travel the twenty miles to Bettencourt under cover of darkness so as to escape the notice of the guards. While they prayed for their deliverance from detection, the carriage made its way to the lonely chateau where the community was to spend the next four years in relative freedom. Later, Julie and Françoise reflected on these years in Bettencourt as some of the happiest of their lives.

Not surprisingly, as soon as they arrived in their new home, Julie's condition grew worse and she became critically ill. Then Françoise suffered an attack of smallpox. Once again it seemed that the cross was the sign of a new beginning. Françoise recovered quickly; her constitution being stronger. Strangely, Julie's recovery, though much slower, brought about an improvement in her ability to speak. Père Thomas forced her to respond to questions he would put to her and Julie, making every effort to get well, began to converse clearly with those who came to visit her.

Meanwhile, the Directory, a reactionary government formed in 1795, was overthrown in a coup d'état by General Napoleon Bonaparte, who freed the French people from what was, in effect, a dictatorship. He established a new system of government for the Republic, a Consulate, designating himself the first Consul, on November 9, 1799. He quickly restored peace within the country, as well as concluding treaties with their warring neighbors, Austria and Great Britain. Finally, Napoleon worked out a Concordat with the Vatican in 1801 by recognizing the Roman Catholic Church as the religion of the majority of the French citizens, in return for the Vatican's recognition of France as a Republic and acceptance of the French principle of religious tolerance. Finally, French Catholics could openly practice their faith, and the sacraments could be administered publicly.

It had been nearly seven years since the Catholic Church could freely serve its people. Churches and schools had been closed and millions of French citizens had lost touch with their religion. Père Thomas began at once filling in for Père Trinqui, former curé of Bettencourt, who had been forced to flee his parish when he was pursued by the Republican Guards since he, too, would not sign the oath.

Each morning Père Thomas, leaning out of a window of the chateau, called to the villagers through a speaker-horn, inviting them to catechism. Then he would celebrate mass for those who came in the small oratory of the chateau. At first the answer to the call was discouraging, but as more and more people met Père Thomas, Julie and Françoise, they began to respond with enthusiasm to the love and concern of the three.

In good French tradition Père Thomas taught the men and boys and Julie and Françoise taught the women and girls who came to them. Julie's speech improved to the point that she could teach effectively. When Père Thomas, no longer a hunted

Blin de Bourdon Home
House at Amiens.

man, left for a while to visit his home in Normandy, Julie and Françoise continued to instruct the women in religion, reading and writing, some arithmetic, and needlework.

Her good friend, Abbé de LaMarche, came to visit Julie at Bettencourt. Together they rejoiced at the religious freedom that had been restored, and both spoke of the great need for religious education in their beloved country. Many people had lost their faith and their confidence in the church. Julie would say, "I could weep when I think how little God is known, God is loved." As the years passed, Julie's desire to reach out to as many as she could to tell them about the "Good God" increased, and her success in teaching became more and more evident. Once more as at Cuvilly, Julie drew a group of people around her, who found in her deep and lively faith a reason to find hope again after so many years of suffering.

It was then that Père Varin, who had walked twenty miles from Amiens to see Père Thomas, came to Bettencourt. Père Joseph Varin was thirty-two when he met Julie. He had been ordained for five years, after having had his seminary training interrupted by the Revolution. For a while it seemed this royalist soldier would forsake the priesthood, but the day before his mother was led to the guillotine in 1794, he accepted the invitation of four of his former fellow-seminarians to rejoin them in secretly studying for the priesthood. Within a year of his ordination, he was elected by his fellow priests to succeed Père de Tournely who had led a small band of priests, called the Fathers of the Sacred Heart. This was an apostolic group dedicated to restoring religious life and worship in France, and keeping alive the work of the Society of Jesus which had been suppressed before the Revolution.

During the year of Père Varin's election, another group, the Fathers of the Faith—the name used by members of the Society of Jesus—approached him and the Fathers of the Sacred Heart to invite them to join forces with them. When the two groups were united for a few years, Père Varin was sent to Paris in disguise to begin his apostolic work.

In 1801, he was elected the Father General of this band of Fathers of the Faith, and came to Bettencourt to consult Père

Thomas regarding a friend of his, M. Louis Sellier, who was requesting admission into the community. This contact with Père Varin proved to be the spark that ignited in Père Thomas' heart a desire to join the Fathers of the Faith as well. The attraction of uniting with a group of priests dedicated to bringing to life the faith once again in France, was contagious. It was in this frame of mind that Père Varin came to Bettencourt and observed the work of Julie and Françoise.

Julie had attracted many of the villagers to the lessons of the catechism, and was so successful in encouraging them to rediscover their faith, that Père Varin instinctively saw in the invalid the potential for her to begin her own community of women who would work to establish the faith once again in France. At the time, he was assisting Mme. Sophie Barat in Amiens to begin another religious congregation, that of the Ladies of the Sacred Heart. But realizing the great need in his country for people to help the thousands who had been deprived of the practice of religion for nearly a decade, and that a whole generation of children had been without any education, Père Varin was anxious to recruit as many people as possible to take up the work of education.

During his many visits to Julie, Père Varin along with Père Thomas, urged Julie to invite other women to join her in her apostolate. He was deeply impressed by Julie's lively faith, her wonderful humor and her ability to make religion come alive for those she taught. Julie on her part, wondered how she could ever begin a religious community. Physically, she was somewhat improved; she could sit in a lounge chair instead of having to be in bed all day. Too, she could speak clearly now, but to think of starting a new community was practically impossible. Still, if God was using these good priests to urge her to direct her life toward this way of serving her Lord, she trusted that God would show her the way. She had known at the age of fourteen that she would give her life to serving her Lord. Perhaps, she reflected, this was the way it was meant to be.

Père Thomas was accepted by the Fathers of the Faith, and after a brief period of training with them, he was assigned to continue to support Julie and Françoise in their work in

Bettencourt. In 1803, when religious freedom was again restored in Amiens, Père Thomas suggested that it was time for Julie and Françoise to take up the challenge of teaching a larger group of people in that city. The villagers wept to see them leave. They had helped to restore faith and hope to the people of Bettencourt. Afterwards, the parish priest who followed Père Thomas heard stories of the "good Julie" whom many considered to be "a saint." But their work was ended there. Julie knew that the Spirit was alive in the people, and that the seeds they had sown would bring about much fruit. With confidence born out of the success of their work in Bettencourt, Françoise and Julie, along with Père Thomas returned again to Amiens. God had given them a foretaste of what was to come. As they waved goodbye to the villagers of Bettencourt, it was fortunate they had no idea what was ahead of them.

Chapter IV

RETURN TO AMIENS
1803–1804

The apartments at the Hôtel Blin had been rented in their absence, so Julie and Françoise planned to move into a small house on the Rue Puits-a-Brindil in Amiens. However, Felicité, now thirty years old, had fallen in love with a school teacher while living in Bettencourt and felt it was time for her to pursue her own vocation. Julie was hesitant about the marriage as she had hoped that her niece would become a member of her community, but later on, she was able to procure a teaching position for Felicité's fiance, Monsieur Therasse, in Rubempre.

Once Julie was settled in Amiens, Felicité felt that she could leave her aunt, since Père Thomas' cousin, Constance Blondel, came to replace her in caring for Julie. So, sorrowfully, after twenty-two years, Felicité left her aunt, comforted by the fact that Julie had such a good friend in Françoise.

The little house, with its cramped quarters and lack of garden, aggravated Julie's condition, and she "...suffered a great deal there."[1] But, in spite of her sufferings, Julie gathered children around her to teach them religion as "...this was her food and drink."[2] When the situation became so crowded that they had to move, they found a much larger house on the Rue Nueve, which had been a former orphanage called the "Blue Children's Home" because of the blue uniforms worn by the orphan boys who had lived there. Later, it was considered by the sisters to be the "cradle of the Institute." They moved into the new abode on August 3, 1803.

Père Varin continued to encourage Julie to begin a religious congregation for the education of young girls. The need for educators was overwhelming. The condition of the majority of children in France at the beginning of the nineteenth century was appalling. War, poverty, disease and chronic shortages of goods were only some of the reasons tens of thousands of children were abandoned every year. Hospitals for abandoned babies reported that they had received no financial assistance from the government for four years. Wet nurses, who were hired to care for infants threatened to "dump them" back on the steps of the hospitals if they did not receive their wages, which in any case were woefully inadequate.

> Abandonment, in spite of the heartbreak, and the sheer risks involved—for if the child were to die the courts could still impose a death sentence—was seen by many people in strictly economic terms, as one of the few practical expedients which they could reasonably take if the rest of the family were to survive. For desperate parents, faced with the unwelcome prospect of an additional mouth to feed, the available alternatives were tragically few. Child murder was far from being uncommon.[3]

"One third of the children regularly died in the course of their first year of life"[4] and another third before they reached the age of twenty. Harvest failures, the large number of widows created by the Revolution, the absence of schools or proper medical care, led to the existence of thousands of orphans. They were supposed to become wards of the state, whose institutions were overburdened by the sheer number of children to care for. Most suffered from poor administrators who had little, if any, effect, on receiving funds to keep the institutions operating.

In such an environment, Père Varin begged Julie to invite young women to help her gather and teach the little girls who had no one to care for them. Julie and Françoise asked their good friends, the Carmelites in Amiens who survived imprisonment, to assist them in prayer to Our Lady for young women to join them in this work. As soon as they had moved into the larger house on the Rue Nueve, Père Varin brought to them eight poor little orphan girls to care for, five of whom had nothing, and three who had a very small pension.

The first young woman to ask to join Julie and Françoise was Catherine Duchatel of Rheims, who had formerly been with Mme. Sophie Barat's Ladies of the Sacred Heart, whose purpose was the education of the daughters of the wealthy. But Catherine's heart went out to the poor children, so she asked permission to enter into the company of Julie and Françoise in their work.

A year later, on February 2, 1804, during mass celebrated by Père Varin, Julie, Françoise and Catherine consecrated themselves to God and promised to devote their lives to the education of orphans and to the formation of teachers who were to go where they were needed—never fewer than two—to instruct the poor, free of charge.[5] Then they renewed their Act of Consecration to the Sacred Heart of Jesus and the Immaculate Heart of Mary. Since it was the Feast of the Purification of Mary, they decided to call themselves the "Sisters of Notre Dame."

The little ceremony took place in a room used as a chapel where Père Thomas was able to offer mass each day for the invalid, Julie. Permission had been granted for this privilege by the bishop of Amiens, Mgr. de Villaret, even after the churches had been opened again and private chapels were closed. He had come to Bettencourt while Julie was teaching there and had been deeply impressed by Julie's holiness. He, too, encouraged her to begin a religious institute for the education of young girls.

Père Varin gave them a rule that had been used by the Institute of Mary in Rome in 1797, and explained to them that it was to be an experiment that would have to be adapted to their needs. They were to use the rule for three months to see if it suited their purposes. The end and purpose of the institute was to be the education of young girls, especially the poor.

Shortly after their consecration, Catherine's health began to fail. She asked permission to return to the Ladies of the Sacred Heart who lived in the Oratory. Eighteen months later Catherine died, leaving some furniture and personal belongings to her beloved orphans.

On February 20, two young women asked to enter the community. Victoire Leleu's brother, Louis, was a priest from Chepy near Abbeville. He had just become a member of the Fathers of the Faith when his sister expressed her desire to consecrate her life to God. Père Varin advised Louis to invite his sister to speak to Julie and Françoise regarding her intention. Victoire and her good friend, Justine Garson, entered the Sisters of Notre Dame; both women were in their early twenties and had had some education. Immediately, they took up the work of teaching, and were joined a few days later by Geneviève Gosselin from Bettencourt. Thus the ministry of education and caring for the orphans progressed remarkably well.

In April, 1804, Pope Pius VII, celebrating the reopening of the churches in France, proclaimed a Jubilee Year, and asked that missions be carried out in all the churches. When the Fathers of the Faith began a mission in the Amiens parishes, they invited the sisters to help in the instruction of the women and children. It had been years since the people had heard the message of the gospels preached publicly. The mission was a great success; the churches in Amiens were full. The cathedral alone had ten thousand people fill its great nave.[6]

Julie was taken in a sedan chair to the cathedral, where each Sunday, and four or five times during the week, she would gather young girls for religious instruction, read to them, and teach them the hymns she loved. The meetings became very popular and Julie, then fifty-three years of age, won the hearts of these girls, who had been exposed to so much turmoil and confusion in their childhood. Their teacher's faith and confidence in God gave them the hope they sought.

While the community of Notre Dame was growing during this time, Mme. Sophie Barat was forming her own congregation, the Ladies of the Sacred Heart, under the direction of Père Varin. He could see the desperate need for as many religious as possible to restore education in France. On one occasion Sophie Barat reported:

> As Mother Julie Billiart's congregation...and mine were so closely united, one day Père Varin assembled us altogether and held a

Amiens Cathedral.

little festival for the opening of our works. We met in a very small room which served as a chapel, and Mother Julie who could not walk was carried into the midst of us. After Mass, we renewed our vows and (Père) Varin gave us a little exhortation. When he had raised all present to great fervor and zeal, he suddenly stopped in his discourse and looking at us, he exclaimed: "But were we not foolish in doing what we have done? What have we undertaken? What can we hope to effect with that?" and he pointed to Mother Julie and myself. (Père) Sellier who was present said afterwards that he felt his flesh creep when he heard these words. But we were by no means discouraged. We only concluded that God who loves to work with nothing, makes use of the things "that are not, that He might bring to nought the things that are."[7]

But obviously God was using both women to accomplish a great deal. During the course of the mission, hundreds of marriages were blessed sacramentally, and large numbers of parishioners returned to the church. The priests and sisters, heartened by the success of the mission at Amiens, conducted other missions in nearby villages.

One of the members of the missionary band was Père Louis Enfantin, twenty-eight years of age, who had been ordained four years. He had attended a clandestine seminary with other candidates in hiding when Monseigneur d'Aviau-du-Bois-de-Sanzay, the archbishop of Vienne, returned from exile in disguise to prepare them for the priesthood. They were ordained in the middle of the night in a barn in Dauphine. Père Enfantin was a fiery orator, full of enthusiasm and the idealism of his new role as a priest. He had delivered a sermon during a mission in Tours that was so effective that hundreds of people who had been lured to the theater by the local prefect, who hated the church, turned away from the performance to go to the cathedral. The theater had to close as there was no audience.

This young priest had an uncanny sense of the spiritual energy of people he met. When he was offered hospitality by the Sisters of Notre Dame during the mission, he immediately saw in Julie a woman of profound holiness and enormous potential for good. Even though he was imbued with the Jansenistic spirituality of his time, that regarded the natural tendencies of humanity as dangerous to spiritual growth—a heresy condemned by the church, but quite prevalent in France—the twenty-eight year old priest was assigned by Père Varin to assume the role of spiritual director for Julie who was nearly twice his age.

At the close of the mission on May 28, Père Enfantin found Julie alone in the convent garden. After exchanging some pleasantries, he stood to leave, then suddenly turned and asked Julie to join him in a novena to the Sacred Heart for someone in whom he was interested. Julie, who had loved that devotion since childhood, readily agreed to the priest's request to pray for his friend.

In the fifth day of the novena, June 1, after the Fathers of the Faith had solemnly opened the month of the Sacred Heart, at which Père Enfantin preached one of his dramatic sermons, he appeared once again in the garden. Striding purposefully across to Julie's chair, he stood in front of her, and somewhat abruptly said, "Mother, if you have any faith, take one step in honor of the Sacred Heart of Jesus."[8] Although Julie was able to drag her body on her knees to communion, she had not walked on her legs for twenty-two years. Still, she stood, trusting that somehow this priest was an instrument of God's will for her. Hesitantly releasing her hold on the chair, she took a step. The priest said, "Take another" and then, "Another."[9] When he was convinced that she could walk, he said, "That will do, you may sit down now."[10] Julie protested that she could walk more, but he was satisfied. He had to leave, but not before enjoining her not to tell the sisters until the end of the novena. The joy that filled Julie's heart made her want to run to Françoise and the others to share her good news; but Julie obeyed the priest and for the next four days pretended to be the invalid who was so familiar to the community. None had ever seen her walk.

After she spent some time in praise and thanksgiving, Julie returned to her room by the method she had been using, moving one leg of the chair forward and then the other. She had tried in every way she could before the cure to spare the sisters and the children any inconvenience. She was able to get herself to bed, and by the time she reached her room, the community had retired for the night.

The next day, she ascended the stairs to the chapel in her usual manner, using her hands to move herself from one step to next. At the top of the stairs a low chair was left for Julie who could manage to get herself on it. But this time she picked up the chair and carried it to her place in chapel. At communion, Julie took two steps to the communion rail, presumably without the sisters noticing her.

After mass and thanksgiving, when the rest of the community had gone downstairs for breakfast, Julie went to a room near the chapel and sent for Père Thomas. He had been such a faithful and close friend, Julie considered the proscription against telling her sisters did not include this kind priest. When Père Thomas saw Julie walk for the first time in his life, he wept for joy. But she continued to keep her secret from the community, as she was obliged to do. When she was certain she was not being observed, she walked, relishing the ability to do so.

Even on the Feast of Corpus Christi, when the community went to the front of the house to watch the procession of the blessed sacrament go by, she remained seated in her chair while all the others stood. She disguised her ability to walk so well, that two days after her cure, Père Thomas expressed some doubt about its permanence. He chided her, "See here, Mother, I do not understand—you are not walking. God's works are perfect, and if you are cured you should not hesitate to walk." Julie assured him that she felt stronger than ever, and to prove it she walked up the stairs so briskly that the priest was barely able to keep up with her.

At the end of the novena, June 5, Julie lingered in chapel after mass when the community had gone downstairs. Eating in silence, one of the little girls heard unfamiliar steps on the stairs. She looked up to see Julie walking upright, and the child with large eyes and high-pitched voice cried out, "Mother is walking downstairs!"[11] As Julie entered the room, everyone instinctively knelt to thank God for this miraculous favor. Then she asked them to return to chapel with her to sing the "Te Deum," the traditional prayer of thanksgiving in the church. With tears of gratitude, their voices sang out from hearts awed and excited by this wondrous sign of God's blessing among them.

Père Enfantin was almost matter-of-fact about the cure. He was convinced that God's action in Julie was precisely so that she could work more effectively in the mission of the church. He did not allow much time for rejoicing with the members of the community. There was a mixture of humor and excitement as Julie related to the sisters and the children how she had managed to maintain secrecy from them for four days. A couple of sisters had seen her walk to communion, but they thought it might be an extraordinary favor from God who allowed Julie at least that much movement. Now to realize that Julie could actually walk was like a dream come true; it took a while for the community to absorb the idea. But Père Enfantin, in his austere manner, told Julie that the best thing for her to do was to start a ten-day silent retreat that very night in order to prepare her for her future work. Julie agreed. She prayed, "Lord, if Thou dost not will to employ me to win souls to Thee, give me back my infirmities."[12]

Word soon spread among the people who had met Julie and had listened to her speak of God during the mission. Most attributed her cure to her great faith and her simple obedience; the Fathers of the Faith took it as a sign that she was to do great work for God and the church. Perhaps Père Enfantin feared that one so well loved and gifted would become proud, or perhaps he indulged his own somewhat rough and impetuous character. But whatever the case, he decided to put Julie "through the crucible."[13] During her retreat,

> ...With an unsparing hand he subjected her to every kind of mortification and humiliation, crucified nature in its every fibre, and with a view to counterbalancing the favors she had received from heaven—all of which her new director obliged her to discover to him—put her through a course of spiritual treatment which seems to us hardly credible, but which was designed by the Father to make her advance with giant strides in the path of perfection.[14]

Julie was now able to walk, but still suffered from a weak stomach. She was unable to tolerate certain kinds of food, nor could she drink cold water without experiencing abdominal pain. The young director deliberately ordered her to eat the food in question, and to drink cold water sometimes mixed with ashes. He often compelled her to take her dinner in the refectory on her knees, and would reproach her in front of her community in a loud voice, and with the most stinging contempt. Once, it was said, he dashed a glass of water in her face.[15] The extreme measures he took with Julie made the sisters tremble. Françoise admits in her *Mémoirs:*

> ...This was not the effect of any kind of attachment because the devil, who was involved in it took him in the opposite direction. The good Father confided to me on one occasion, that he experienced, in regard to Julie, violent reactions of disgust and aversion which made all that she said and did unbearable.... He knew very well that this was a temptation and did not attach any importance to it, but his tone, and the things he did may well have sprung from this.[16]

The sisters were terrified by this treatment of their dear Julie, but he attempted to assure them that he was doing all this for "the good of her soul," and informed them that he saw her making giant strides in the spiritual life, which caused him to expect extraordinary things of her.

Perhaps the cruelest of his treatment of Julie was when he ordered her to kill her pet cat, the one Père Dangicourt had given her years before. The cat was old and sick, but it had been a welcome companion to Julie during the hours of isolation she had spent when Felicité was working to provide for them. It had warmed her feet during the cold nights of Amiens. She had a horror of killing anything; she could not bear to see the cook kill a chicken for dinner. But Julie obeyed this severe command. She put her pet in her apron to carry it fondly into the garden. After a tender farewell that must have tugged at her kind and sensitive heart, she seized "...a stick (and) dispatched it with one heavy blow on the head."[17] She then dug a hole to bury it.

Sincerely trusting that the priest was an instrument of God, Julie overcame her own repugnance to carrying out the things he asked of her, and her own disposition, which would have dealt with someone else with far greater balance, became more docile. Whatever can be said about the methods of Père Enfantin, without a doubt, Julie grew in humility and faith.

The Fathers of the Faith had been so impressed with Julie's

work during the mission in Amiens, that they requested her and a companion to assist them with their new mission in St. Valéry-sur-Somme, and from there to Abbeville. The very evening Julie finished her retreat, June 14, she and Sister Victoire Leleu left for St. Valéry.

The following day Julie wrote from her first mission away from the new community. By this time her sisters, the orphans, and her students all called her "Mother"; and indeed she was a mother, especially to the children and young sisters. Françoise, too, considered herself one of Julie's daughters, and frequently Julie referred to her sisters as "dear good daughters," asking them to pray for their "poor mother." On June 15 she wrote to Françoise:

> At last we arrived at midnight in the town of St. Valéry, a little late as you can see....The heat was dreadful; I was very hot in the coach, but since the good God wills the heat and the cold, may His name be blessed.[18]

For the first time in twenty-three years Julie was able to walk to a parish church for mass. She described her experience saying, "I must tell you that I walked from the inn to the church like a woman used to being on the move, yet it was quite a distance. I must add that the good God gave me courage, for my feet were so hot in the coach that they are both like jelly."[19] She also commented that being able to go to the parish church was a great happiness for her.

Not long after the start of the mission, something occurred to mar the joy of her recent recovery. Julie described the incident to Françoise in a letter written June 23:

> I must tell you alone a little adventure that happened to me but don't say anything about it to the children—it would distress them. On passing by the grain market a week ago, we met a carriage going very fast, but Victoire did not see it. I had to run, pull my companion by her dress and say: "Quick, Victoire, out of the way!" Otherwise, we should have been run over. I do not know whether I ran a little too fast, but since that time, my foot has been very painful. I did not pay much attention to it, and contin-

ued walking; my foot was swollen, and still is. Like a good Father, the good God has preserved us from any accident. May his holy name be blessed.[20]

With the sprained ankle, Julie described the fact that she could climb the stairs "...a little less easily because of my bad foot."[21] Père Thomas and Père Varin, not knowing of the accident began to question the authenticity of Julie's cure, as they saw her dragging herself along to teach catechism. She went into the church one day when it was quiet, and spent a few hours in prayer before the blessed sacrament. When she left the church her ankle was perfectly normal again.

Julie and Victoire taught catechism to both young and old. The former told of a ninety-year-old gentleman whom she prepared for his first holy communion, and of persons who had not been to confession for thirty or forty years, who publicly returned to God. She was gravely disturbed when a boating party—which had been organized by a group of young men in an effort to thwart the success of the mission—ran into a squall and suddenly capsized. One hundred persons were drowned within minutes. The townspeople took the accident as an ominous sign, and it drew tears to the eyes of Julie, whose heart went out to them in anguished concern.

In the parish register during the time of the mission, forty marriages were regularized.[22] When the mission was over, July 18, 1804, Julie wrote, "We left St. Valéry at 10:00 a.m. in the midst of the tears of the whole town. All regretted the departure of our good Fathers. It was really touching to see this huge crowd; everybody was sorrowful. How many souls would have remained in this state of death without this help."[23]

The mission at Abbeville followed immediately. Père Varin, Père Thomas, Julie and Victoire worked again as a team. While she was there, Julie wrote to Françoise, asking her to have her green dress taken apart, to buy enough material for a new bodice, and to have all the material dyed dark brown. Françoise was to "Do this as soon as possible, (since) I am being scolded about my attire."[24] After inquiring about the sisters and sending them her love, Julie remarked that the people of Abbeville "...do not give me time to be bored. I do not know to whom to listen next for all kinds of things."[25] By August 5, she said she hoped to be able to embrace all the sisters "this week."

When the Fathers of the Faith returned to Amiens, the civil authorities, jealous and fearful of the power of the priests' success, ordered them to leave the Départment of Somme within twenty-four hours, or to face arrest. Most of them withdrew, but Père Thomas and Père Enfantin refused to go; again, they were forced to live in hiding and in disguise. The work of conducting missions, consequently, had to be suspended. Julie was free to concentrate on developing her new community. She had written from Abbeville, "I can tell you that, with His holy grace, I am ready for everything, everything that can be for His greater glory."[26]

Look! Our Mother comes and she is walking.

Chapter V

TO GO OUT TO ALL THE WORLD
1804–1806

Napoleon was anointed as First Emperor of the French by Pope Pius VII at Notre Dame Cathedral in Paris on December 2, 1804. His civil marriage to Josephine had been sacramentally blessed by his uncle, Cardinal Fesch,[1] in a secret ceremony the day before, making it possible for her to be crowned as empress. When Napoleon took the crown from the hands of the pope, who had blessed it, and placed it on his own head and then one on Josephine's—a gesture not lost to the crowd attending the ceremony—he signalled sweeping changes in the government that were eventually to affect the whole of Europe.

Shortly afterwards the leadership of the French church went through some changes which had to be approved by the government. Bishop de Vallaret, who admired and supported the work of Julie and Françoise, was sent from Amiens to Casale. Charles François Joseph Pisani, Baron de la Gaude, was transferred from Vence to Namur, and Jean François Demandolx was sent from Rochelle to be the bishop of Amiens.

When Bishop Demandolx arrived in his new diocese on December 17, 1804, he found the Fathers of the Faith willing and ready to proceed in the ministry of rebuilding the faith of the people. But when the missions proved to be so successful, suddenly the civic leaders banished them from the city.

The bishop was faced with the task of reuniting the secular

61

clergy, who had been divided by the oath to the Civil Constitution of the Clergy into the groups of the juring and non-juring priests. During the years of dechristianization campaigns, the two groups found themselves at best, in serious disagreement, and at worst, openly distrustful or contemptuous of each other. Bishop Demandolx earnestly tried to bring about some unity among the clergy; after all, they needed to unify as they were facing the formidable task of revitalizing the church in his diocese. Some of the priests had been hurriedly educated and secretly ordained during the Revolution, and were much in need of further formation and education. The seminaries had been ransacked, pillaged, and, in some instances, burned to the ground during the years of the Reign of Terror. Now the bishop had to rebuild the seminary in Amiens.

All these difficult demands rested upon the head of a man who did not know, nor did anyone else, that he was suffering from an incipient brain tumor, which led to his death twelve and a half years later.[2] Following Julie and Françoise's meeting with Bishop Demandolx, the former described him as a good and saintly prelate who had an affectionate heart. He in turn was impressed by the work of the sisters and trusted Père Varin's assessment of Julie as a woman of profound holiness, and one who could accomplish great good in helping to reestablish the faith in France.

While Père Thomas and Père Enfantin were unofficially living in Amiens, they volunteered their leisure time to educating the members of the new community. Père Thomas, Doctor of the Sorbonne, and Père Enfantin taught the sisters Christian doctrine, history, grammar, and arithmetic. Their poverty was so great, that often the lessons would be drawn on the floor with chalk since there were no slates or blackboards available.

The life of the community began to grow in depth as they took on the rhythm of prayer and work. The morning was begun with mass and an hour of meditation. At midday the sisters made a short period of examination of conscience, and in the late afternoon another meditation for half an hour. During each day they took time for a visit to the chapel to recite the rosary, and in the evening they made an act of reparation to the Sacred Heart of Jesus as a community.

During the year 1805, Josephine Evrard, Angelique Bicheron, Elisabeth Michel, Catherine Daullee, Thérèse Boutrainghan and several others[3] entered the community. By July 2, Père Varin presented another rule to Julie and her community which seemed practical, and fit their needs. There were three main points that differed significantly from religious congregations familiar in France prior to the Revolution. The purpose of the institute was to be the education of young girls, in particular, the poor. There was to be no distinction between the sisters, that is, no choir or lay sisters, as was the custom in many other communities. Lastly, the congregation was to be unified by a Mother General to whom every sister would have access, and who would visit all the secondary houses established from the motherhouse. The rule was presented to Bishop Demandolx, who approved of it, signing it with his seal.

Therefore, October 15, 1805, on the Feast of St. Teresa, in the chapel of the Rue Nueve,[4] Julie Billiart, Françoise Blin, Victoire Leleu, and Justine Garson pronounced their vows according to the new rule, in the presence of their devoted friends, Père Thomas and Père Enfantin. To designate their desire to give their lives completely to God, the sisters took on new names as a sign of their "new life."

Julie took that of Sister St. Ignace, but because of the suppression of the Society of Jesus, it was deemed prudent for her to be called by her baptismal name which was, in fact, the one used virtually all of her religious life.[5] Françoise became Sister St. Joseph from then on; Victoire Leleu, Sister Anastasia, and Justine Garson, Sister St. John. It is not surprising that the next day, October 16, they elected Julie as their Mother General.

While Père Varin and Père Thomas were available to counsel Julie and Françoise, the community grew, not only in numbers, but in spirit as well. Julie often referred to the two priests as the "founders" of the institute. Soon after the vow ceremony, however, Père Varin was required to return to Paris, and Père Thomas left Amiens on September 10 to join a group of his fellow priests who constituted a missionary band in the diocese of Bordeaux.[6]

However, before leaving them, Père Varin, "in virtue of the powers conferred on him by the bishop of the diocese, laid on (Père) LeBlanc, Superior of the Fathers of the Faith at Amiens, the care of directing the affairs of the new congregation."[7] He also appointed the young priest, Père Louis-Etienne de Sambucy de Saint Esteve as the new confessor for the community. The latter was a professor at the College of the Faubourg-Noyon and served as the confessor for the Ladies of the Sacred Heart as well. One of Mother Barat's sisters described him, as a "...lover of the acrobatic, an unquiet genius in constant motion."[8] It was an unfortunate choice, which later Père Varin recognized. He had thought that Père LeBlanc would keep the young priest's impetuous character within bounds.

In his life of Sophie Barat, Mgr. Baunard described Père de Sambucy as "...still young, enterprising, and absolute in his notions, a man of letters, gifted with a brilliant imagination, but one whose character was restless and changeable."[9] With the appointment of de Sambucy, a new phase of suffering began for Julie.

However, initially things seemed to progress well and more women were attracted to the community. Julie saw to it that the sisters were well trained for their work of education, but her favorite task was that of giving them religious instruction. She would teach the children whenever she could, and even the other religious institutions in Amiens would send their pupils to her lessons. When Julie taught, she spoke not only to the minds of her students, but with the power of her great holiness, to their hearts as well. "Of her catechism lessons might be said what one of her daughters says of her conferences. Her words not only enlightened, but transformed; one could not hear her without wishing to conform one's conduct to them."[10]

One of her pupils testified, "What we chiefly loved was to have a catechism lesson from Mère Julie. After that lesson, we were carried quite out of ourselves; we loved the Good God so much; with naive hearts we spoke of Him, and did all to please Him."[11] While she asked the sisters and pupils to allow themselves to be transformed by the love of Christ, she would not ask of others what she had not done herself.

Although she often prepared the children for the sacraments or for some of the special feast days, it was to the young women who came to the congregation with a willingness to take up the vocation of religious life that Julie devoted most of her time. It was in her exhortations to the sisters that we learn of her very practical sense, and her natural understanding of the psychology of education. Julie took the time to advise the new teachers to take care of the personal needs of the children before they attempted to teach them the important lessons of the spirit. When she said the most basic need of the children was to know of God's love for them, Julie would tell her sisters that they must not merely talk about such love, they must *show* them how God loves them. Feeding and clothing the children was the first step. She would not have them dressed as "little nuns." They were to have becoming clothes which would represent the kind of dress they would wear as adults—simple, but attractive.

On the other hand, the sisters lived in extreme poverty. Their food was meager at best, consisting of dry bread and water in the morning, soup and vegetables for dinner, and meat on Sundays and feast days. Their beds were straw mattresses on the floor, lined up together in a dormitory. What dresses they brought with them were all dyed violet and interchanged with each other, often to the detriment of any semblance of style.

Françoise, who had been raised with the advantages of the aristocracy and who had never had to go shopping to the vegetable market, much less walk to one, trudged willingly through the streets of Amiens in a dress often too short for her, to purchase the day's meal. Humiliated by their relative's appearance, her brother, Viscount Louis Cesar, and Elizabeth, her sister-in-law, pleaded with her—for the honor of her family, if nothing else—to appear with much more dignity than *that*. But in time, the radiance of Françoise's countenance convinced them that, whatever they thought, she had found her place with God. In the end, the tears of her family were turned into a peaceful submission to the fact that Françoise had attained true happiness.

After her cure, Julie had many occasions to practice mortification and penance by the very nature of her work. Every day offered its share of opportunities to all the sisters to sacrifice themselves for the sake of the children. The little orphans were often sick, malnourished, and always dirty. Infestations of lice were constant problems. In August, 1805, a twelve-year-old girl was brought to the convent in the last stages of consumption. "She had little education and was wanting in manners, but she was simple and innocent; she loved catechism and religion and was very attentive to the Sister instructing her. Each day her condition grew worse...."[12] She died seven months later, having received her first holy communion in the convent chapel. The sisters grieved her loss, and considered her a "little protectress" for them.

Once Julie began the community in earnest, "God withdrew the exterior signs of His grace, which would have been incompatible with the life of activity she was now called upon to lead."[13] There was one exception reported by Françoise and witnessed by the sisters. On the Feast of the Purification, February 2, 1806, Julie and her sisters were together in the workroom at the convent in Amiens for the evening's instruction. While she was speaking of the feast, Julie suddenly intoned the canticle, *Nunc Dimittis*, and

> ...as she was singing the words "lumen ad revelationem gentium"[14] her gaze was lifted to the crucifix, she stopped singing and her eyes became fixed on the image of our Lord, who seemed to draw her to himself from the depths of her soul. Light radiated from her countenance and for some time she remained motionless. She would have remained so longer, but just then Madame de Franssu came in. Someone blew out the candle and made a good deal of noise, and an impulsive young Sister threw her arms around our mother, who quietly came to herself and went to her room.[15]

It is a tradition in the congregation that during this ecstasy, Julie saw clearly that the sisters were to "carry the light of the gospels to the nations" and were not meant to remain in any one diocese.

Shortly after this incident, Père LeBlanc, who had lived in Flanders, had an occasion to return to his home region and asked Julie to accompany him. He wished to introduce her to his friend Msgr. Fallot de Beaumont, bishop of Ghent. Père LeBlanc felt that Flanders, too, needed the work of the Sisters of Notre Dame, and saw the good that could be done there. "But (Père) de Sambucy, our confessor," wrote Françoise, "disapproved of this trip, though he really had no right to interfere; and that he did so was probably the work of Satan."[16]

Once Bishop de Beaumont met Julie, he wanted to have convents in Flanders as they had in Amiens. Naturally there was a need for subjects who could speak Flemish, and Julie, who could only speak French, made it clear that if she were to open any secondary houses in Flanders, that she would need sisters from that region. Undaunted, the bishop promised to find women who would be willing to go to Amiens to be formed in religious life and the spirit of Notre Dame. Even on this first trip, Julie found Theresia Louvers who expressed a desire to go with Julie into a strange city where she could not speak the language. It is remarkable that in so short a time, merely two weeks, a woman who did not know the language Julie was speaking, nor much about the institute, found such an attraction for the foundress that she was willing to go with her. They reached Amiens on June 29.

Julie returned to Flanders the following August. When she reached Ghent, Bishop de Beaumont introduced Julie to Marie Steenhaut, then twenty-four years old. After conversing a while Marie enthusiastically agreed to return to Amiens with Julie, and asked her to accompany her home to meet her mother. On the way to the Steenhaut's home, the two entered the parish church for a short visit. There was another young woman kneeling in one of the front benches and Julie knelt right behind her. While she was praying, Julie had a strong feeling that this fifteen-year-old would be a Sister of Notre Dame. On leaving the church, Marie introduced her sister, Franciska, to Julie who told her that one day she would be her daughter, too. When Madame Steenhaut met Julie, she was so impressed that she exclaimed, "I have so much confidence in you, my dear Mother, that I give you not merely my eldest, but also the three younger ones, if God be pleased to call them to religious life."[17]

On the return trip from Ghent to Amiens, Julie stopped at Courtrai to visit the Vercruysse and Goethals families, who were devout Christians. While Julie departed to call on one of the families, she asked Marie to sit down next to a fruit vendor's stand where she had bought some pears, and told her to eat them and the bread she produced from her bag. Marie reported:

> To eat thus in the street was my first humiliation. I kept fancying that among the passers-by were persons come from Ghent to the fair, then going on at Courtrai. Next our Mother took me to High Mass, and on the way she was more than once insulted by the boys on account of her somewhat singular travelling costume; they greeted her as "witch," "black sorceress," etc. She made me translate these titles into French for her and laughed heartily over them. Not so I; indeed so humbled did I feel, that when we entered the church I let her go on in front, and knelt at a distance from her. She did not notice this till we were leaving the church, when she asked me the reason. I confessed my pride, and she was pleased with my sincerity; but she spoke to me about humility in a way which deepened my esteem for her, and I was stronger in the subsequent tests to which she put me.[18]

At times, the initial enthusiasm for becoming a religious waned rather quickly. When Julie went again to Flanders in November to discuss opening a house in St. Nicolas with Bishop de Beaumont, she took Theresia Louvers with her. Françoise stated it simply, "We did not suit her; nor she, us."[19]

Between the trips to Flanders, the community moved into a larger house in the Faubourg Noyon. It was not exactly what they wanted, but the community had increased to eighteen sisters and there were four orphans living with them. The house was owned by the bishop of Amiens, and the rent was considerable for the time. Françoise wrote, "We paid one thousand francs rent and had to spend over four thousand more on necessary repairs. The bishop, in view of these improvements, gave us six hundred francs and leased the house to us for nine consecutive years. At that time he was kind to us."[20]

Fortunately for the community, a school friend of Françoise, Madame Jeanne de Franssu, who had been widowed, wished to live with Julie and Françoise as a guest, and promised to assist with the house expenses. The only other income was that of the

estate of Françoise who was convinced that God had provided
her with the means of supporting the work of the community.
Now that they had a larger house, Julie felt that they could
accommodate free classes for the poor children. She sent a
novice and a postulant, Adelaide Pelletier, out into the streets
each ringing a little bell, and proclaiming, "We let you know that
the Sisters of Notre Dame have just opened free schools for little girls. Go and tell your parents the news."[21] The message was
heeded; the first day more than sixty children presented themselves. The number expanded rapidly. Shortly after they had
moved into the house, there were thirty in community and eight
boarders.

> Mother Blin's income was only 400 francs. You can imagine that
> good management was needed to make this sum provide food,
> travelling expenses and furniture. The whole time we were at the
> Faubourg Noyon, Madame de Franssu gave us one hundred fifty
> francs a month. God gave Mère Julie a gift for management so
> that we were never in debt; debt is something religious houses
> should carefully avoid; not only from conscientious motives, but
> because of the miseries that result. And besides, God is honored
> by good management.[22]

On Julie's third trip to Flanders, she wrote that she missed
Françoise and the sisters very much. She was beginning the
phase of her life marked by many journeys—one hundred and
twenty in twelve years. Having been somewhat isolated from the
general public for twenty-three years, these new experiences provided her with a deeper understanding of the devastating effects
of the dechristianization campaigns.

In one of her letters from Ghent dated September 1, 1806, she
wrote, "I cannot help weeping, even in writing to you, when I see
my God so little known, so little loved."[23] Although she was meeting good Christian families, she could "...not forget all that I
hear on the road...."[24] There were times when she felt overwhelmed by the task of bringing the faith back to the people.
She begged her sisters to pray earnestly for her, and wrote. "It
seems to me that I need the charity of all of you so much, that
you may bear with me, with the many faults you must notice in

me."[25] And yet, her faith and hope shone through her writings, for however inadequate she may have felt in the face of so much to do, she wrote, "The Good God wants me to walk everywhere like a little blind woman. It gives him great pleasure, so it must give me pleasure, too."[26]

In the letters from Ghent she nearly always included some greeting of respect for "our good Père de Sambucy,"[27] and affection for her "little girls." Once when writing from Ghent, she neglected to mention them, and in subsequent letters wrote, "My dear little girls whom I forgot by mistake in one of my last letters: I kiss them so heartily that they must hear it a hundred miles away."[28]

The bishop of Ghent was very anxious to have sisters begin to teach in his diocese and suggested they begin at St. Nicolas in the School of St. Joseph, popularly called, *des Berkenboom*. Two elderly religious of the Congregation of St. Philip Neri still cared for a couple of boarders there and taught about fifty day pupils. But the task was too much for their failing health, and rather than have the school close, the bishop wished the Sisters of Notre Dame to staff it. The building was in dire need of repair; its walls were crumbling and it was very damp. Promises to make the needed repairs were made to Julie's satisfaction, and she agreed to send some sisters to take over the ministry.

When it was time to leave Ghent, Julie wrote, "I must tell you that many Flemish girls want to enter with us. But I think I shall bring only one back with me, whom my good little Soeur Marie will be very astonished to see, for it is her good sister Franciska."[29] Indeed, Marie must have been surprised that her younger sister had decided so soon to follow her into the community, as "Ciska" was only fifteen years old; but Julie commented that "Her mother, her aunt, her confessor, everyone is willing for her to follow this vocation. She herself desires it with all her heart."[30]

Preparations for the first secondary house of the community occupied a great deal of the time in Amiens after Julie returned. Just fourteen months after making her first vows, Sister St. John (Justine Garson) was named the new superior of St. Nicolas; she was twenty-four years old. Sister Xavier (Josephine Evrard), at the age of twenty-one, and Sister Marie Steenhaut, who had entered the community in June, were being sent to St. Nicolas in December to have special charge of the Flemish class.

Religious were not permitted to wear distinctive dress in France at the time, but since there was no prohibition in Flanders against it, Julie decided that the three sisters who were to be the first to establish a house away from the Motherhouse in Amiens, should wear a habit. Julie knew what she wanted. She never forgot the appearance of the sisters she saw in the vision of Compiègne "...a black habit of common woolen stuff, a coif composed of white linen under a stiff black bonnet, and a white linen wimple. The black veil, which completes the dress, was at first only worn in chapel; out-of-doors was added a long black hooded mantle almost touching the ground."[31] Julie had brought a pattern for the bonnet back to Amiens from Ghent. It was the style of the Flemish women at the time.

The foundress accompanied the sisters to St. Nicolas to help them get settled with the opening of school. First they went to Ghent to receive the blessing of Bishop de Beaumont. It was in his episcopal palace that they put on the habits for the first time. When they made the journey from Ghent to St. Nicolas, the carriage broke down twice; once when the axle broke, and another time when the brace "broke like glass."[32] Despite the setbacks they arrived safely at noon on Saturday, and three days later Julie wrote to Amiens, "My good daughters, we all look charming in our little outfit. We have become as used to it as though we had never worn anything else."[33]

The sisters were warmly welcomed, and three days following their arrival they began teaching school. Commencing with the mass of the Holy Spirit, the children gathered for a feast day celebration; ninety of them sat down at table for tea with milk and small penny cakes. The local authorities had promised to repair the school and the place where the sisters and two little boarders would live. Julie stayed at St. Nicolas for two months to give the foundation a good beginning.

While she was still in St. Nicolas, Bishop de Beaumont asked Julie to consider taking over another school in Bordeaux where there was a community of sisters desiring to join the Sisters of

Notre Dame. Julie was quite open to the possibility of merger, writing, "I had scarcely arrived at St. Nicolas when I received a letter from Ghent, from the bishop, informing me that I must go to yet another place to bring about a union between some other Sisters and ourselves. How grateful our hearts should be to such a good God!"[34]

She was also sent an invitation from the bishop of the Namur diocese, Mgr. Charles Francis Joseph Pisani de la Gaude, who had heard of her successful endeavors from the Fathers of the Faith, to open a school in Namur. In the middle of winter she made the trip to Namur to discuss a new foundation with Bishop Pisani, who was deeply impressed with Julie, and wanted sisters as soon as possible. When she returned to Amiens in February, she learned that a priest had come to Amiens to make a request for sisters to start a school in Montdidier, a town twenty miles from Amiens. Having returned on February 4, she set out again on February 21 with Sisters Catherine Daullee and Angelique Bicheron to open a school in Mondidier where "...these two Sisters were held in high esteem...for, thanks be to God, they did their work well."[35]

In March, Julie had to take one of the Flemish postulants home to Flanders. The girl "...was so scrupulous it was feared she was on the verge of a nervous breakdown."[36] The journeys began to annoy Père de Sambucy and her ecclesiastical superiors, who made her feel their displeasure. "Julie bore all this without complaint or attempt to justify herself. God, who can draw glory from humiliation, permitted her to omit certain formalities, and these omissions were looked upon as grave faults."[37] With the absence of Julie from the community, Père de Sambucy began to assume more authority in directing the fledgling institute than was officially his.

Chapter VI

CONGREGATION MARKED
BY THE CROSS
1806–1807

The Concordat of 1801 which Napoleon had enacted with the Vatican, gave a certain amount of freedom to the Catholic Church in France. But the appointment of bishops and the establishment of any religious community had to be approved by the government. On June 19, 1806, the statutes of the Sisters of Notre Dame received its approval; a confirmation of them was given by the Emperor Napoleon on March 10, 1807, while he was in the camp at Osterode.[1] This approbation facilitated the opening of houses, and the bishops turned to Julie to ask for her help. She wished to go wherever her Sisters were needed, and had not forgotten her promise to the Bishop of Namur who wanted to start a school as soon as possible in his city.

Meanwhile, Père de Sambucy became more aggressive in his criticism of Julie. He did not approve of her opening any houses outside of Amiens, and obviously did not trust her judgment regarding the freedom with which she dealt with the community in those early days. She did not follow exactly the experimental rule that Père Varin had given to the community as she felt that the young sisters who joined them needed flexibility and formation in the spiritual life. She believed she had the freedom to change the order of the day if it were necessary for the good of the children or the sisters.

In the beginning, she asked the sisters to observe only three or four hours of silence instead of imposing a rule of silence throughout the day outside of recreation. However, she required of them great discipline in their studies since many of the postulants, although full of good will, had very little by way of education. Products of the turbulent times of the Revolution, few of the early sisters came to the Institute with anything like the education that Françoise had received. She, in turn, became one of their most valuable teachers. While Julie taught catechism and spirituality, Françoise taught them grammar, spelling, arithmetic, but "...even these simple requirements were at times remarkable rather for originality than for conformity to the recognized standards, and whenever the Sisters were free from their class studies, they became pupils in their turn."[2]

The type of community life that Père de Sambucy envisioned was quite different from the one he saw in the Sisters of Notre Dame. His sister had been an Ursuline nun before the Revolution and when the Ursuline order was suppressed along with all the other congregations, Mlle. de Sambucy waited until she could find another community. When she was able, she joined the Ladies of the Sacred Heart, Sophie Barat's community in Amiens. Père de Sambucy gleaned his understanding of religious life from the experience of his sister whose former community was basically cloistered, and embodied a monastic type of life while teaching a few students in their convent.[3] He also imagined himself as a founder rather than a confessor, and often took offense if something happened in Julie's community if he had not been consulted or had not approved.

Julie and Françoise treated the young priest respectfully, but did not deem it necessary nor appropriate to seek his advice about the governance of the community. In fact, Père Varin, who had appointed de Sambucy to be the confessor for the sisters, said to Julie, "Mother, since God has put you here, you have the grace to act. Do not feel that you are bound to ask so many small permissions of (Père) de Sambucy, let him be simply your adviser, consult him only as a friend."[4] But de Sambucy was discontented. He did not approve of the fact that the young sisters confided in Julie, and accused her of "meddling with (their) conscience, which was...something he considered...definitely not the business of a woman."[5]

While Julie did not require any sister to reveal conscience matter to her, by her very personality she did inspire the confidence of the sisters who turned to her for guidance and advice. "And who can do better than the mother whose heart is always watchful over the Sisters whom the Lord has put under her care?"[6] Julie's love for her sisters made her anxious for their growth in the spiritual life. It was quite natural that they would open their hearts to her whenever, and as often as they needed to. Françoise commented that until they had grown into spiritual maturity, the young sisters "...need a guidance that is formative, vigilant, and near at hand. But when it is a priest who performs this office with young sisters or novices, the necessity can be a trying one, especially if he is still young."[7]

Well aware of the risks involved, Julie did not believe in encouraging long conversations with the confessor outside of the sacrament of penance. She advised her sisters, saying, "Short confessions and long meditations." However, Père de Sambucy felt that Julie was not educated enough to do the work she proposed to do and besides, she was from the poor class, a fact that entered into his assessment of her. He was impressed with Françoise, being of the nobility of Amiens, and treated her with a little more deference. But he strongly believed that because he was a priest he had every right to tell the two foundresses what they should or should not do.

Bishop Demandolx began to receive messages which questioned Julie's competence and judgment. De Sambucy presented to him the picture of a woman who was proud and ambitious, and a "gadabout." Unfortunately, the bishop tended to rely completely on his priests and came under the influence of de Sambucy in regard to his assessment of the Sisters of Notre Dame and their foundress.

When Julie had initiated the process by which she would establish a new house in Namur, the bishop had agreed to her proposal. She had submitted the names of the sisters she intended to send to the new foundation, and they had been approved. But two days before they were to leave, de Sambucy, having spo-

ken to Bishop Demandolx, brought word to Julie that instead of
the sisters named to go, the Bishop had appointed Françoise as
the new superior of Namur. He had succeeded in getting rid of
the two foundresses. After all, Françoise was devoted to Julie
and any "reform" that de Sambucy envisioned would have been
opposed by Julie's friend. The young priest used to say, "As long
as Mère Blin is in the house, I can do nothing."[8]

Julie was stunned by the change as it would deprive her of her
best friend and counsel; but both sisters took the order as another sacrifice asked of them, and submitted to the decision.
Françoise did not even allow herself time to say goodbye to her
family. In fact, the command ignored the right of the Superior
General to assign her sisters in accordance to the need of the
foundations. Julie had intended to accompany the sisters sent to
Namur; now she was ordered to accompany Françoise and
another sister to Flanders.

Before they departed, Père de Sambucy made certain that the
money Françoise provided for the community would remain in
Amiens. Still believing in his good will, Françoise agreed to give
de Sambucy power of attorney over her fortune, and thus he
secured it for the house in Amiens. At the time, Madame de
Franssu had given a sum to Julie for the works of the community, and a small piece of property belonging to Françoise had
been sold. The little capital was intended for the purchase of a
larger house, as the community was growing. However, de
Sambucy asked Julie to lend the money to Mme. Sophie Barat
who wished to purchase the "Maison de l'Oratoire" which she
had only rented, being unable to buy for want of funds. With
only a written receipt and without any stipulation as to the pay-
ment of interest, Julie released the money to the Ladies of the
Sacred Heart so they could purchase their house in exchange for
their paying the rent on the house of the Faubourg-Noyon. In
addition, de Sambucy persuaded Françoise to empower him to
act for her in gathering rents and apportioning her revenues,
which he decided should be settled on the house of Faubourg-
Noyon alone. When they left for Namur, Julie and Françoise had
no money for the establishment of the new house in Namur.

The subject of appointing a superior to replace Françoise was discussed with Julie before her departure. Père Varin and Père de Sambucy considered twenty-three year old Thérèse Boutrainghan a candidate for the position. She had been in religious life but eighteen months, after having spent some years as a cook and a nursemaid in one of the wealthier houses in Amiens. Françoise described her disposition as, "She had great physical vitality and a certain vigor of soul which could have been used to counterbalance her excess of vivacity and effusiveness—in a word, the impetuosity of youth. She was good-hearted and well-mannered, not lacking in thoughtfulness, good taste, or desire for improvement, but she was still wanting in humility."[9] Julie sensed the danger of putting Thérèse in office too soon, and suggested that she be tried out as mistress of novices to see how she would handle authority. When Julie left Amiens, she thought that there had been an agreement to have Victoire Leleu, who was now called Sister Anastasia, and Sister Thérèse together be in charge of governing the house, as Julie intended to return as soon as her business in Namur and Bordeaux was completed.

On June 30, 1807, Julie, Françoise and Sister Geneviève Gosselin, who was destined to replace Sister Xavier at St. Nicolas while the latter was to go to Namur with Françoise, left Amiens in the midst of the tears of the sisters. Père de Sambucy accompanied them for a while, but before he left the group he turned to Julie and said, "Mère Julie, you have finished your business here, you may now go and do it elsewhere." Julie's heart warned her that this dismissal was a serious threat, and that she was being separated from her sisters. As events began to show, it became clear that that was precisely what the priest intended to do.

As soon as Julie and companions were out of the town, Père de Sambucy went to the convent, had the community bell rung to gather the sisters, and then presented himself to the community as the one invested with full powers by the bishop to reorganize the community. One of the first changes he made was to announce that henceforth Sister Thérèse Boutrainghan would be the superior of the community, and (with a hint of triumphalism) changed her name to "Mère Victoire." In fact, he managed to change the names of nearly all the sisters. They were to report to him regarding everything that went on in the community, and he would be given a detailed report by Mère Victoire. He told the sisters that the absence of the foundresses would be indefinite, and began immediately to intercept any mail sent by them to the community.

For a while the community seemed to blossom. Mère Victoire won favor with the sisters, priests, and citizens of Amiens. Françoise wrote: "I do not know what came over everyone, but ecclesiastics, people in the city, and almost all the Sisters were excessive in their admiration and praise of the young superior. (Père) de Sambucy consulted her and sent people to her for direction. Many young Sisters, finding her responsive to their show of affection were drawn to her with all the emotional intensity of youth. They cut off locks of her hair, kissed her clothing, and at recreation—which became loud and noisy—crowded around her, unhappy unless they were near her."[10]

When she did not eat sufficiently, undoubtedly due to the strain she was under, the young sisters thought that it was due to her fervent desire for mortification, and attempted to imitate her to the detriment of their health. Père de Sambucy directed Mère Victoire to spend three or four hours a day in prayer and not do any manual work. Julie had seen in her temperament a need for physical labor; the priest's advice wrought damage to Victoire's health. Kindly, Françoise comments, "He was young and it is not surprising that he sometimes made mistakes."[11] The flattery bestowed on the young sister could not but cause her harm. She grew to enjoy the prestige of the job, and became very tender about any incident that might have suggested that she was not competent. The day after Julie left Amiens, Père de Sambucy was appointed by the bishop to be the ecclesiastical superior of the community in place of Père LeBlanc.

In the meantime Julie, Françoise and Sister Xavier reached Namur on July 7, 1807, and were received with gracious hospitality by Bishop Pisani de la Gaude. The foundresses had agreed that Françoise's identity as one from an aristocratic family need not be made public. The bishop, related to two doges of Venice, and himself a baron, was unaware of the background of Françoise who from then on was called "Mère St. Joseph." The first house given to them to use was the "Junior Seminary" where everything had been prepared for them. "Not so much as a match was lacking."[12]

Julie, in her enthusiasm and gratitude for so many signs of God's blessing on this new beginning, wrote to the community in Amiens at 3:30 a.m., the morning after their arrival. She said that the sisters "...found the house very well—almost too well—fitted out. How good is the good God!"[13] There was a note of concern in her exhortation to the sisters in Amiens when she wrote, "How many things my poor heart has to say to you, my dear good daughters. I leave it to you to think it out. It says all kinds of things to you, this poor heart. How it loves its poor dear daughters, but especially when they are brave, so that no difficulty can stop them when it is a question of achieving the greater glory of our good Master!"[14] She asked the sisters to write to her as soon as they received her letter and tell her little details about everyone. In fact, she told them that she was expecting to hear from them as soon as possible. But days went by and there was no word from Amiens.

When Père LeBlanc arrived in Namur on July 23, the fears of Julie for the community in Amiens were confirmed. He told the foundresses what was happening at the motherhouse, and concluded his remarks by saying, "My good Mother, at present you have no more influence in the convent at Amiens than I have."[15] Julie and Françoise began to realize the extent to which they had been supplanted. They agreed that for the time being they should pray more earnestly for the community and God's will for them, but undoubtedly both worried about the future of their beloved sisters at the motherhouse.

When it was time to leave, and Julie had to set out alone to go to Bordeaux to discuss the plans for Mother Vincent's sisters joining with the Sisters of Notre Dame, Françoise admitted that she was depressed by the thought of their separation. Françoise was concerned about her role as Superior of a new foundation; but more importantly, she was worried about what Julie would find at Amiens knowing that she could not be there to support her. The night before Julie was to leave for Bordeaux, Françoise was praying, her eyes focused on a picture of the Holy Spirit descended on the apostles. Suddenly her spirit was filled with consolation and the conviction that Julie would return to Namur. At the time of parting for the two friends, Françoise turned to Julie and said, "Goodbye, Ma Mère. You will come back to die at Namur."[16] She later admitted in a letter to Julie that her conviction that Julie would return to Namur was such a consolation to her whether it was true or not, "...it is at least true that my weakness had need of the comfort that this hope has given me."[17]

It was the end of July when Julie set out for Bordeaux. After a "...five-day walk and three nights in the stagecoach, where the good God granted me the grace of having very fine company, three Sisters of Charity and two other good ladies,..."[18] Julie wrote to her sisters in Namur that she was greeted warmly by Mlle. Vincent and her community of eighteen or twenty sisters. There were about three hundred children in the school and Julie went from class to class "embracing them all"[19] even though it was very hot. She was struck by the quiet way of the sisters when dealing with the children, and noticed that they used wooden signals for drawing the attention of the students instead of lifting their voices; she encouraged the sisters in Namur to try to do the same with their pupils.

Seeing the large number of children in the school in Bordeaux, Julie realized even more the great need for teachers, and she wrote: "...since I have seen so many of them in Bordeaux, it seems to me that I should like to go throughout the whole universe to tear these poor little creatures out of the clutches of the demon, to teach them the value of their souls."[20] In her letters she expressed her desire to know and to fulfill the will of God for her and the sisters in Namur, and of her wish to be with them. It seemed as though she were reflecting again on the awesome task that was ahead for each sister, to bring the gospel message to the children who had known so little of the love of God for them. She shared with Françoise that not having received any word from Amiens was "...a great sacrifice...for my heart."[21] She began signing her letters, "Julie Billiart, very unworthy Sister of Notre Dame."

When Julie received a letter from Françoise she learned of one of the first things that happened after the two friends were parted. Françoise wrote, "...the day after your departure little Jeannette, to console us for your absence, seized upon a brief moment when she was out of our sight to run off to her home."[22] One can see the smile on Julie's face as she responded, "(God) has sent you some trials: that naughty little girl, Jeannette, ran away without telling you. I can understand that it must have troubled you, but we need some variety, my good friend, don't we?"[23] Françoise was sure the child would return after vacation, which she did.

But Françoise had more serious worries. Elizabeth Leroy, known as Sister Anne, was admitted to the community in Namur on July 29, 1807, and became headmistress of the lace-making school which was started because of her talent and the need to provide means of a livelihood for the older girls. However, she began almost immediately to show signs of tuberculosis. Françoise attended to her needs personally, and tried to keep the children and the young sisters separated from her for fear of contagion. So while Françoise was organizing the schools in Namur, receiving new postulants and training them, she was devotedly caring for a sister approaching death. Sister Anne died February 18, 1808, after professing her religious vows on her deathbed. Under such trying conditions, it is not surprising that Françoise wrote, "I must tell you that the devil has worked over me cruelly, buffeting and tormenting me without truce; it's been a long time since I've been so relentlessly pursued—and, to crown it all, even my prayer has become more difficult.... Pray for your poor daughter that she may come out of the combat without harm."[24]

A short time later Françoise commented on her reaction to her work, when she wrote: "Right now I have some little sacrifices to make for (God) because small children who don't reason, whose attention you can't fix on anything, and whom you can't keep quiet, are extremely contrary to my natural liking."[25] The aristocratic woman who had had exquisite manners taught to her from her earliest years, was dealing with the reality of unkempt, untaught, and often rude children. Nevertheless, the school flourished, and it soon became obvious that the building was not large enough to accommodate the number of children wanting to come to it.

Julie, in the meantime, had received nothing but kindness and support from the bishop of Bordeaux, Archbishop Charles Francis David d'Aviau du Bois de Sanzay. On September 8, 1807, he gave the habit of the Sisters of Notre Dame to eighteen sisters in Bordeaux, and a new house was opened in Chartron two miles from the town. Before Julie left, there were two schools with seven hundred children in each—a testimony to the hunger for education from families long deprived of it. She then received a letter from the bishop of Amiens requesting her to return to the city as soon as possible. Immediately she set out for Amiens, leaving Bordeaux on November 12.

Julie broke the journey by resting in Poitiers with Madame Sophie Barat, who welcomed her kindly. After a few days, during which she was invited to join the Ladies of the Sacred Heart in a retreat given by Père Lambert, Julie had a strange intuition that she should go to Amiens as soon as possible and decided to continue her journey. When she went to say goodbye to Madame Sophie Barat, with whom she had a fond relationship, Julie thought she detected a coldness in her friend that she could not explain. She left Poitiers not knowing what had caused the change.

When she reached Paris, Julie went to the home of another friend, Madame Leclercq, where she remained for a few days. During her stay, she decided to visit the motherhouse of the Sisters of Charity where she had been received warmly on her journey south, but when the Mother General whom she had known, approached her, she felt once again a coldness in her manner, and was puzzled by the change of attitude of the sister. The Mother General pulled out a letter from her pocket and handed it to Julie who hurriedly opened it only to read that the bishop of Amiens forbade her to set foot in the convent at Amiens or even so much as to enter into his diocese! Furthermore, she was told that the Jesuits had once again been suppressed on November 1.

Julie did not know what had happened to have these good people reject her so, and thought of going to see Père Varin, her good friend and advisor, to comfort him and seek his advice. But once again Julie was met with disdain and rejection. Père de Sambucy had made sure that all of Julie's friends were informed of his opinion of her, and had sent letters to them accusing the foundress of jealousy, arrogance, and of being obstinate. Julie was confused by the changing attitudes of those who had been so close to her. She did not know what she had been accused of nor what she might have done to warrant such treatment. She penned to Françoise, "How much we shall have to tell each other, my good and loving friend, when it pleases his divine goodness that we meet again! Yes, many things I have placed in the sweet and adorable Heart of our good Jesus. Otherwise, I could not have borne the burden; there has been enough to kill ten poor Julies like me."[26]

It happened that Père de Sambucy was in Paris at the same time as Julie. When she went to see Père Varin, he informed her that among the accusations against her was that she spoke to the young sisters in the chapel, and that she had left orders not to allow Père de Sambucy to wear a beautiful, hand embroidered vestment. These complaints were so trivial that it is difficult to imagine the importance given to them, but apparently de Sambucy read them as signs of Julie's resistance to him. She had, in fact, given conferences to the young sisters in the chapel because that was one of the few rooms at the Faubourg that held the whole community. Père de Sambucy felt that she was attempting to supplant the priest. At another time, she told the Sister Sacristan that the aforementioned vestment which belonged to Père Thomas was not to be used on ordinary days, as it had been lent to the community, and she wanted to make sure it was cared for. Unfortunately, when Père de Sambucy requested the use of it, the sacristan imprudently responded that Julie did not wish her to give it to him to use. These small incidents were misinterpreted by someone who was only too eager to find reason to criticize Julie.

Madame Leclercq was so touched by Julie's predicament that she wrote to Père Duminy, rector of the Amiens cathedral, begging him to speak to the bishop, and ask his permission for Julie to go as far as St. Just, where she could receive hospitality from her old friend, Père de LaMarche. After eleven days, the reply came granting permission for Julie to return to the Amiens diocese. She left Paris immediately, arriving in St. Just only to find out that Père de LaMarche was out of town. By this time she was quite ill. Julie went to her friend, Madame de Rumigny in Amiens where she spent two days, and attempted to get an appointment with Bishop Demandolx to find out what the trouble was, and what was to be done. She wrote to the bishop and asked his forgiveness for whatever she had done to displease him, and then went to visit him personally. He wanted her to return to Namur immediately, but when he saw how ill she was, his attitude softened enough for him to allow her to go to her convent at the Faubourg until she was better.

Julie gratefully crept up the back stairs of the convent and went straight to her room without the sisters even knowing that she had come. She was glad to get into her own bed after so many weeks of painful experiences; she was exhausted, confused, and at a loss to understand why those whom she had trusted, now treated her with such suspicion and near contempt. Soon word began to spread among the sisters that she was home, and gradually they came in small groups to greet her. It was obvious that they were grateful and happy to have her with them again.

Bishop Demandolx had become aware of Mère Victoire's incompetence even before Julie arrived back in Amiens. In his haste to change the image of the convent, since several of his priests had commented that a former servant, who was poorly educated, and had been made the superior, did nothing to establish confidence among the parents of the students, Bishop Demandolx decided to put an Ursuline Sister in charge of the sisters. Victoire was shocked at the thought of a sister from another congregation taking over her community. She felt it timely that Julie had returned.

Mère Victoire professed great affection for Julie when she greeted her, and turned over the keys of the house to the foundress; but at the same time, when Julie was not present, she told the sisters that she had been appointed superior for three years by the government, and if they had any concerns, they were to consult her. Not surprisingly, the sisters were thrown into much confusion; and Mère Victoire, learning that the bishop did not want her to be the superior, became more self-assertive and stubborn. As Julie's health improved, Mère Victoire's declined, and eventually Victoire had to relinquish the role of the superior. The bishop then changed his mind about Julie returning to Namur, and decided that she should resume the role of superior of the Faubourg.

For a while it seemed as if peace was once again restored to the house in Amiens. Père Cottu was named the ecclesiastical superior, replacing Père de Sambucy, the bishop's attitude toward Julie changed favorably, showing his former kindness, and the sisters became more relaxed and happy, knowing that Julie was with them. The only thing that did not change was Père de Sambucy's opinion of Julie.

Chapter VII

FOGS OF THE SOMME
1807–1809

Now that Julie was settled again as the superior of the community, tensions between Mère Victoire, Père de Sambucy and Julie magnified. Victoire resented the bishop's wish that Julie resume charge of the sisters. She considered herself the superior since she had been given that office, she believed, by the imperial government. Père de Sambucy on the other hand, still considered himself the founder of the community even after he had been replaced by Père Cottu as the ecclesiastical superior. He, too, refused to accept the fact that the bishop had reinstated Julie as the superior of the house.

In addition to the friction existing in the convent, Bishop Demandolx was becoming impatient that the Sisters of Notre Dame were still without an established rule. He charged Pères Cottu and de Sambucy with the task of drawing up a rule, based on the one formerly agreed to by Julie, Françoise and Père Varin. Meanwhile, Julie was being ignored by the two priests whenever there were any major decisions regarding the community. Julie's straightforward manner of dealing with people was in contrast to that of de Sambucy's. Françoise explains for us.

No judgment is intended, but the truth is that he often accomplished his ends by roundabout ways and secret means. Even his words were ambiguous, and his remarks were full of implications. In short, his manner of speaking and acting was diametrically opposed to Mère Julie's openness and frankness. Her way was so different that it is very true she found him hard to deal with, and although she tried to see things from his point of view, she had never found in him the understanding God gives those who are working together for his glory. (Père) de Sambucy felt the same way. I can only explain this lack of sympathy as part of God's mysterious plan."[1]

Julie was confused and worried. The bishop of Jumet was expecting to have sisters come to take over the school there, and Julie assumed that she would accompany the young sisters to their first mission in order to assist them in getting started. In addition to beginning a new community, there were repairs needed on the buildings, and parents to contact. Since the elderly sisters who had staffed the school in Jumet were leaving, the bishop required sisters immediately.

Jumet was in the diocese of Tournai, so when he wrote to the bishop of Namur asking for Sisters of Notre Dame, Bishop Pisani sent for Françoise requesting her to write to Julie to inform her of the situation, and ask her to acquire permission from Bishop Demandolx to send some sisters to Jumet. Julie did as she was bidden. When the bishop of Amiens sought of Julie names of the sisters to send, she, in all simplicity, suggested Sister Victoire, hoping that in a small community Victoire would find it quieter, and have a better chance to get herself in hand.

After Julie's return to Amiens, Victoire, although seemingly happy to have the foundress home again, began to change. She told the sisters that it was Père de Sambucy who suggested that she make the gesture of turning over the keys to Julie. But she made certain that they knew she was still the superior, and that they should consult her with any of their difficulties. Julie had noticed the change and had written to Françoise.

Good Mère Thérèse (Victoire) is too uncontrolled and has not enough experience to manage to the advantage of the Sisters. In all fairness, I recognize her kind heart, but how much older she needs to be! Moreover, there is an astonishing change for the worse since my absence. She is so dogmatic and self-assertive in everything that you would be greatly surprised....What incalculable harm has been done to her by the position she has been given![2]

Françoise notes, "...from this moment...she was never completely open with Mère Julie."[3]

On the other hand, whatever Victoire did was exalted by Père de Sambucy, even to the point of his willingness to express a favorable interpretation of her daydreams with which, Françoise assures us, she was much at home. The priest had painted such a glowing picture of the young sister to the bishop that, although he personally knew nothing about her, he referred to her as an "angel," and made her the superior's assistant. In order to defend Victoire to the bishop, de Sambucy felt it equally necessary to defame Julie.

He had reported to the bishop that Julie was "jealous as a tiger, and that she was always trying to humiliate Mère Victoire, making a living martyr of her." In a note to Julie, de Sambucy had written, "The more your pride seeks to humiliate her, the more her virtue will triumph. But you are neither humble, nor charitable, nor obedient..."[4] So when Julie suggested sending Victoire to Jumet, even though at first Bishop Demandolx did not seem to mind, misunderstanding broke out again. This, he observed, was another sign of Julie's jealousy. Not only would he not send Victoire away from Amiens, but instead he selected Sister Anastasia Leleu, whom Julie called her "petit conseil" because of her confidence in the twenty-eight-year-old sister who had entered the community four years before. Furthermore, Julie was not to accompany the group to Jumet.

The sisters who were leaving begged the bishop to allow Julie to go with them, but to no avail. When the two sisters left on March 21, 1808 "quite alone," as Julie commented, they arrived in Jumet only to find that there were very few provisions for them. They were young and inexperienced and Julie, worrying about them, wrote to Françoise asking her to go to Jumet as soon as possible. Françoise was ill, but managed to get to Jumet for two days. She was so astonished when she arrived at how little they had, that she listed the meager offerings left for them, namely "...three sheets, four or five towels, a few earthenware bowls, and little else. Clearly no preparation had been made—they were in need of everything."[5] Fortunately, the parish priest was very concerned and helped to get the provisions they needed. "But the want of bare necessities, as well as the other difficulties they suffered, pointed to the value of having an experienced person to manage a new foundation, to bring order out of disorder, and get the work underway.... All these things made Mère Julie anxious for the happiness and success of our young foundations."[6]

Fearing that her letter describing the situation in Amiens would be intercepted as those in the past, Julie waited to send a letter in which she poured out her heart to Françoise with Sister Anastasia. Julie's concern can be felt in the words to her dear friend when she wrote:

> All those who observe the ways of the good God are led to believe that God wants something. When and how? That is the mystery I am willing to adore! But to keep me as though tied here, without the right of doing or saying anything to the advantage of our houses! I do not know whether the good God asks of me to remain inactive, when in his great mercy he has been good enough to give me the use of my feet. Though Monsieur de Sambucy is no longer our superior, he has not stopped mapping everything out for Monsieur Cottu. The latter has been telling us himself, "Monsieur de Sambucy says this; he says that!" I think that it is most likely he who has put it into the bishop's mind not to let me take a single step outside the house any longer. In all kinds of happenings I adore the holy will of my God.[7]

Julie could see the irony that only months before the bishop of Amiens had ordered her not to set foot in his diocese; now he ordered her not to take one step out of it. Julie heard from Sister Anastasia about a rumor that Père de Sambucy was to be the one to make visitations of the houses, but no one had mentioned anything about it to her. Plans were made for him to visit St. Nicolas, Jumet, and Namur after Easter. Julie had every reason to question just what he would say to Bishop Pisani de la Gaude, after such good relations had been established between the prelate and the Sisters of Notre Dame. Julie advised Françoise that "...if Monsieur de Sambucy goes to Namur before we manage to meet, do as you have always done. Say, 'I shall speak to *Ma Mère* about all that.' I think he will have plenty to say to you; I don't understand a thing about it. He is no longer superior, yet he does everything."[8]

As a consequence of the strained relations between Père de Sambucy, Père Cottu, and Julie, she was even fearful of going to confession, which she was accustomed to do frequently. She confided to her friend, "My greatest worry is about going to confession. I dare not say a word about what distresses me to either of them."[9] Later, one of the objections Bishop Demandolx had of Julie was that she was too particular about her confessor. And yet, while all these trials were going on, her faith shone through her letters like sparks among burning embers. She writes, "How good the good God is! Ah, how good he is! That is all my prayer: 'My Jesus, fasten me to your holy cross and hold me there, for I am nothing but misery.' The good God must have some hidden design in all this, for everything to be so disturbed without reason."[10] Yet, while pouring out her heart to Françoise and sharing her worries with her friend, she adds, "My heart and my soul are at rest in my God through all the fogs of the Somme. God alone! An eternity without end is the prize of a little moment of confusion in this wretched life."[11]

Ironically, Bishop Demandolx began to hear that things were not going well at Jumet, that the new foundation was having difficulties. He sent for Julie to ask if she had heard how things were going there, and when she replied that they were not going well, he told her that she must go to help them. Julie did not wait a minute in preparing to leave; she feared the bishop might change his mind. After leaving the bishop's palace, she reserved a place on the coach for the next day. Providentially, she met the notary who had been taking care of Françoise's property, even though she had given power of attorney to Père de Sambucy. He told Julie that there had been a bid on some of Françoise's property, and that Père de Sambucy had bade him keep the transaction secret until a certain time had elapsed. The property in question was being sold for 28,000 francs. Père de Sambucy wanted to pay off the debt of 3,000 francs to the workmen who had done some repairs on the house at the Faubourg. But Julie was puzzled by his secrecy, and considered asking Françoise to come to Amiens to put her finances in order.

When Julie reached Jumet, the sisters were overjoyed to have her with them. Bishop Demandolx had given her permission to stay only eight or nine days, which time was not sufficient to rectify all that was needed to be done. However, the sisters felt relieved to have the burdens of starting a new foundation rest on the shoulders of someone older and more experienced even for a short while. After doing what she could for them, Julie decided to go to Namur. No one had told her not to go to Namur, and because she had not heard from Françoise, she was worried about the reports of her ill-health. Julie deemed it important that she go there to find out for herself the condition of the community.

When she arrived, Julie found not only Françoise ill, but also Sister Gonzaga and especially, Sister Xavier. While she began to share with Françoise the incident of her encounter with the notary and the sale of the property, Père Minsart, their good friend, arrived. They both considered it wise to relate to him what was happening in Amiens. He, in turn, suggested that they go to Bishop Pisani and tell him everything.

Until this time the bishop was unaware of the aristocratic background of Françoise's family. In the course of making known to him what was occurring, the two sisters had to reveal Françoise's heritage, and how she was using her fortune to support the congregation. Upon learning of the situation, the bishop recommended that Françoise return to Amiens and set her financial affairs in order. They agreed that Françoise should prudently withdraw Père de Sambucy's power of attorney, and attend to the sale of her property, since the money had not yet been paid. He gave her permission to remain in Amiens for two weeks.

Reluctantly, Julie and Françoise left Namur while the sisters were still unwell. Twenty-three-year-old Sister Xavier was placed in charge of the community even though she herself was one of the sick. But no one could foresee that ten months would pass before either of the foundresses would return; it had appeared that the situation could be settled in two weeks.

On the return trip to Amiens they visited St. Nicolas. They found that the community had been well cared for, but Sister St. John, the superior was very ill. The house was damp, and the promises of the city officials to obtain another place for the sisters had not been fulfilled. Their petition for a more suitable residence had become lost on someone's desk, and no answer had been received. Julie could not rest until she found another house for her sisters; she rented it for a year. Sister St. John (Justine Garson) could neither eat nor sleep; eventually she was taken back to Amiens where all thought she might improve. Unfortunately, the twenty-six-year-old woman, having had three years in the congregation, died the following January 25, 1809. She was the second sister to die. Julie had acceded to Sister St. John's wish to go to her family's home thirty miles from Amiens, and Julie herself accompanied her. She had thought that perhaps her native air would help her recover, but it was to no avail. Sister St. John, however, was spared the ordeal that was to come to Julie and Françoise, and did not see the final dismissal of her beloved superiors.

Strangely, during her journey—after having had such a kind and friendly visit with the bishop of Amiens—Julie received a letter from him in which he chastised her severely. The incident that precipitated such an outcry took place as Julie was setting out for St. Nicolas. Some of the sisters had asked Julie what they should do if they needed any spiritual help while she was away and, without a second thought about the matter, she suggested that they go to Sister Jeanne, the mistress of novices. She knew Victoire was not competent in such matters, and understood that the sisters were referring to real spiritual difficulties. She did not intend to imply that they should not obey Victoire, who was the assistant. But Victoire lost no time in complaining about this to Père de Sambucy who, of course, went immediately to the bishop. Bishop Demandolx wrote to Julie:

> The latest thing that has happened is further proof of your high-handedness. In setting out for Jumet you took it upon yourself to

break one of the most essential articles of your rule. It is stated in the rule that if the first superior is absent, she shall be replaced by the Mother Assistant, to whom the Sisters shall render obedience. Yet you have put Mother Victoire aside and on your own authority have told the Sisters to go to the Mistress of Novices in every difficulty. What could cause you to make such a recommendation, if not your secret jealousy of a Sister whom you dislike because she is better than you are? But the more you humiliate her, the more God will shower his graces upon her. I beg to inform you that I have restored things to the order in which you should have left them. I have ordered the community to obey Mother Victoire and I have asked Père Cottu to see that my order is carried out. Moreover, since I know only too well how stubbornly you cling to your own opinion and prejudices, I forbid you under any pretext to bring Sister Anastasia back to Amiens....[12]

As soon as they reached Amiens where the sisters were overjoyed to see the co-foundress whom they thought they might never see again, Françoise wrote a note to Bishop Demandolx asking for an audience. She received the reply that he was leaving the next day and would not be back for two months. Françoise had told the sisters that she had permission to stay only two or three weeks but, "...as the weeks went by so many emergencies arose that Mère Julie kept her on as support and counsel."[13]

Undoubtedly part of the reason that both the bishop and Père de Sambucy refused to let Julie leave Amiens was the fear that if she were to go to Namur, she and Françoise might decide to leave the house at Amiens and make Namur their motherhouse. With a school established, and de Sambucy perceiving himself the founder of the Sisters of Notre Dame, both men wanted the sisters to stay in Amiens. But to do so, they needed the financial backing of Françoise Blin de Bourdon and Madame Jeanne de Franssu. No wonder there was some fear of Julie leaving the area.

When Père Cottu brought a proposed rule to Julie which he said had been approved by the bishop, and which for the most part had been written by Père de Sambucy, it was clear that what was being proposed was contrary to the original intention of both

Julie during "Nunc Dimittis."

foundresses. Françoise wrote that the bishop "...said quite clearly that he did not wish a mother general and that he wanted us to be limited to his diocese, which meant that our Mother would have to abandon the Sisters she had sent to other dioceses."

"...As for Mère Julie's visitations of the secondary houses, he thought them a mere waste of money; and many other things which were not at all in accord with the ideals our founders[14] had worked out long before we were connected with the bishops."[15]

Julie was convinced that God had inspired her with the words "a light to the nations" during her unforgettable experience on February 2, 1806, when she was lifted out of herself. So real was that moment for her that she believed the Sisters of Notre Dame were not meant to limit their ministry to any one place; they were to go wherever they were needed. Julie and Françoise requested time to consider the proposed rule, and did not think that it was the moment to establish any rule while Napoleon was pondering his "Paris plan," which meant his desire to amalgamate all active religious congregations into two groups, either a teaching or a nursing community. Although the emperor had not decreed the Paris plan, rumor had it that it would be enforced very soon.

While the bishop was away, Père Cottu, learning from the foundresses that they had reservations concerning the rule, asked them to write down what they wanted. After long hours of discussion and prayer, they both realized that whatever they presented would cause another angry storm to erupt, so they waited to see what the Lord would reveal.

In the meantime, Mother Vincent was begging Julie to come to Bordeaux. There was need for a superior there in one of the communities, as well as for a novice directress. Mother Vincent was anxious for a permanent rule as well, and wanted to discuss one with Julie. Knowing that the bishop of Amiens would not give her permission to visit Bordeaux, Julie wrote to the bishop there to explain her situation, and asked him to request the journey from Bishop Demandolx who had by this time returned to his diocese.

Archbishop Charles-Francois d'Aviau was a saintly priest who was well disposed to Julie and her dreams for the Sisters of Notre Dame. He had listened attentively to the Fathers of the Faith in his diocese who knew what Julie had hoped for the community, and he shared her vision. When Bishop Demandolx received the request from Archbishop d'Aviau, he sent for Julie and told her to go to Bordeaux, since he could not refuse the petition of a fellow bishop. Julie had great hopes for this visit as she thought that with the help of Bishop d'Aviau and Fathers Lambert and Gloriot who were there, and who knew "...our spirit perfectly, for it is their own,"[16] she and Mother Vincent could write a suitable rule. She had thought, "I should go there, for the rule can just as well come from Bordeaux as from Amiens. God will lead me because I want only his will and to seek him in all things."[17] However, the next day she received word from Bishop Demandolx not to go to Bordeaux until she was further notified. Julie turned to Père Cottu and begged him to intervene for her; the prohibition was lifted immediately, and she left on August 1.

On her way she stopped in Paris to see Père Varin, not only because she looked to him for comfort and advice, but also because she had a letter from Père de Sambucy to deliver to him. Père Varin was in some turmoil himself; the emperor had ordered the suppression of the Fathers of the Faith after

Napoleon realized how powerfully they affected the people. He was worried about a resurgence of the Jesuits in France after they had been expelled in 1764. So at best, Père Varin was not in a good disposition when he began to read the letter; when he finished, he turned on Julie with such vehemence, and spoke so harshly to her that she became ill.

Once again Père de Sambucy had written a scathing letter to his seminary friend, denouncing Julie in addition to the old complaints, for hesitating to obey the bishop who wanted her to sign her approval of the rule she had been given. Père Varin told her that the final word was that Père de Sambucy should draw up the rules for the congregation, that this should be done at Amiens, and that she was to return there immediately, and not dare set foot outside of that city again. Julie wrote to Françoise that she was returning to Amiens as she was too ill to travel, but the reality was that the shock of such a reception from her long-time friend was overwhelming her. She went to the church of the Visitation where she loved to pray, and there found a priest who was hearing confessions. The priest was so comforting to Julie that she felt strengthened enough to take the road back to Amiens, trusting that God would somehow show her what to do next.

Meanwhile, Françoise was coming under attack. When Julie made ready to leave for Bordeaux, Françoise asked her what she should do if Mère Victoire requested her to do some of the duties of the superior. Julie advised her friend to refrain from doing anything that was remotely related to that role for fear that another storm should descend on the community. However, Victoire had asked Françoise to give the instructions on Christian doctrine to the young sisters on some occasions, and since it did not belong to Victoire's duties strictly speaking, she agreed to do so. The bishop was furious, and forbade Françoise to give the instructions; if Victoire was unable to give them, they would not be given at all. Françoise's understatement, "...he (the bishop) was not exactly partial to Mother Blin..."[18] described her situation.

One other incident happened while Julie was away for a few days that caused yet more stir among the sisters even though it was quite trivial. While in the refectory, Mother Victoire said something foolish, and some of the young sisters began to giggle. Victoire, thinking they were laughing at her, was offended. She left the refectory abruptly and went straight to Pères Cottu and de Sambucy to complain of the perceived slight from the sisters. When she came back, she retired immediately to her room and did not return for supper. Françoise took the opportunity to speak to the sisters privately. She was very open with them regarding the situation as it was evolving with the bishop and the priests. In the end, she said, "...the bishop is not at all in sympathy with us.... But Mère Julie and I know where we will be welcome if we cannot remain here. Those who love us will follow us."[19] The sisters all exclaimed that they would go with the foundresses, and became very excited about the idea.

Gradually calm returned to the community. However, when the bishop heard of the incident with Victoire, he defined it as insubordination to himself, and "...now the Sisters were deprived of Holy Communion and were given to understand that the whole affair was serious conscience matter. The thing was spoken of in terms of mortal sin and hell-fire. Naturally, the Sisters were very much upset."[20]

When Julie arrived home she found the tensions in the community at high pitch. While she did not oppose the actions of the bishop openly, she did admit to Françoise that she thought he had been rather severe in imposing such a sanction on the sisters for such youthful thoughtlessness. On their part, the sisters were becoming more aware that things were not as they should be. "It was like walking on a tightrope—the slightest misstep provoked disaster. But it is certain that the bishop's severity did not win anyone's heart; it did, however, bring out the real attachment of the sisters for their two mothers, an attachment which could not be doubted from their words to Father Cottu."[21] Julie and Françoise attempted to remain open to the bishop, and asked to see him several times. Finally, Julie was told not to try to make an appointment with him unless he sent for her.

One day Bishop Demandolx did send for Julie. Françoise went as far as the bishop's palace and waited outside fearing what might be the cause of the summons; fortunately, Françoise had guessed rightly that her friend would need someone to comfort her when she came out. She described the scene as "...when the interview was over, Julie needed someone with her, for she was in tears, something which had never happened before. But this interview, as she herself said, was worse than any of the others; the prelate's tones and gestures were so harsh that, though her soul was unshaken, the effects of the shock to her nerves were with her for days afterwards; the bishop's voice kept echoing in her ears. Again the complaints had centered on Mother Victoire—Julie was making her miserable; Victoire was an angel and Julie was jealous as a tiger; and so on....These rebukes lasted a long time, the bishop stamping his foot for emphasis. Mère Julie was too deeply religious not to find a bishop's anger overwhelming."[22]

The outbursts of rage that characterized Bishop Demandolx's life at this time were undoubtedly due, at least in part, to the growth of the brain tumor which was claiming his life slowly, and which eventually caused his death. But not knowing about his condition, Julie felt very deeply the brunt of his wrath as directed toward her. The two sisters went for a long walk and at the end, they had strengthened each other. Surprisingly, Julie was basically at peace, and trusted that God would point out to her what her next step should be, but it took some time for her to recover from the experience.

Shortly after her return from Paris, Julie had gone directly to Père de Sambucy to give him the letter Père Varin had sent to him requesting him to see that a rule was written for the Sisters of Notre Dame. De Sambucy had received her cordially, and promised to work on it immediately, but he never did. Instead, Père Cottu took the old rule from the ancient order of Notre Dame de Bordeaux. It had been adapted by one of their sisters from the rules of the Jesuits who had established their community two hundred years before the Revolution. Mother Vincent had suggested to Julie that the rule could be used as a basis for a new rule, but that there would have to be many adaptations and changes. However, Père Cottu rewrote the old rule almost exactly as it had been, the objectionable parts remaining; namely, no mother general, no visits to the secondary houses, and being limited to one diocese. The proposed rule disregarded any of the houses that had already been established outside of Amiens.

Paradoxically, word came from Namur that Sister Xavier was dying, and Père Minsart wrote to Julie begging her to send Françoise "home." The sisters from Jumet communicated their dire need for another sister. There were other problems in both houses. When Julie spoke to Père Cottu about these problems, he agreed that a visit by Julie was necessary, and reasoned that he had no jurisdiction over the houses outside of the Amiens diocese. Contrary to the restrictions Père Cottu was proposing in his rule, Julie received permission to visit these houses and to take some sisters with her to help staff the schools. Once again, Françoise was left in the community with Victoire, and she was determined that this time things would go peacefully.

When Julie reached Namur she found that Sister Xavier was confined to her bed. She had been so anxious that the sisters be "perfect" that she had treated them too severely, and had made them afraid of her. The atmosphere was one of strain, and Julie sensed that there had been little spiritual progress. She also noted that two sisters who had entered at Namur, were unsuited for religious life, so she kindly sent them to their homes.

Père Minsart then found a larger and much more suitable house for the sisters, and was very anxious to move ahead with the negotiations with the owners, so the sisters could move in before someone else took it over. At first, Bishop Pisani was reluctant to have the sisters move, but eventually he agreed to the move from the small quarters. The next oldest sister who had some religious training was Sister Elizabeth, who was nineteen years old. Undoubtedly, once again Julie saw the necessity for someone who had more experience to visit the secondary houses.

When she reached St. Nicolas, Julie sent a petition to Paris for a larger house for the sisters there, because of the crowded quarters. Her visit to Ghent gave her an opportunity to speak to Bishop de Broglie about the work of the sisters there, and that prelate, having heard of some of the troubles in Amiens, advised Julie to keep her vision open to the world, and not be confined to one diocese.

When Julie returned to Amiens in November, she discovered that a typhoid epidemic had broken out among the sisters in her absence. Françoise nursed the sick until she too contracted the fever; then Victoire became infirmarian and tended the sick with kindness and efficiency. Prior to the epidemic, Victoire had asked Françoise to take over the teaching of the sisters, but again the bishop refused to have anyone but Victoire give the catechism lessons, so none had been given. Julie was grieved at what she found. Twenty-three sisters were still in bed with the fever and there were no signs that they were recovering.

Julie went immediately to the infirmary and called out, "My children, if you have faith, rise."[23] Most of the sisters got up and felt cured; four of them did not respond. After their recovery the four sisters asked to return home, and Julie personally accompanied one of them thirty miles back to her family. Françoise, who felt that the four had no vocation to religious life commented, "In short, it could be said that God was winnowing his grain, and with one sweep removed all who were unfit for our life. Indeed, there was not much time to lose."[24]

Père Cottu was becoming more insistent that Julie and Françoise accept the rule that the bishop was proposing. Strongly convinced that they could not agree to the proposed rule, the cofoundresses thought it best to seek more time. With so many uncertainties relating to the government threatening to amalgamate all religious communities and obvious tensions existing at Amiens, Julie and Françoise were hesitant to say much to Père Cottu. As a consequence Julie suggested that she and six of the "older" sisters begin a novena to the Holy Child, since it was just after the new year, to ask God to let them know what course they should take. On January 5, the small group began their novena to the Child Jesus, which included a litany to the Holy Child and other prayers, and visits to the blessed sacrament. On the fifth day of the novena Julie remarked, "I no longer have the slightest anxiety, I am in perfect peace. The Holy Child has taken us under his protection and he will deliver us."[25]

The answer to their novena came in another unexpected form. On the morning of the seventh day, Père Cottu came to Julie's office with an ultimatum. The bishop had told him that he could not establish a house on nothing, and unless Françoise settled her fortune on the house in Amiens, he would have nothing to do with the sisters. Furthermore, he would take away their chaplain and establish no rules. Once Julie composed herself, she responded that that would be Françoise's decision and suggested that he might ask her himself. When she went to get her friend, Julie could not say anything since Père Cottu could hear it, but when she got out of sight of the priest, she motioned to Françoise by waving her hand above her head that the "wind was high" in the atmosphere and forewarned her what was to come. When Père Cottu repeated the message of the bishop, Françoise felt more relief than regret as she loved Namur, and had told Père Cottu that if things got worse in Amiens, she would take Julie and the sisters there. Both sisters said they needed time to consider the request of the bishop.

Julie did not want to act in haste even though she felt at peace with what was happening. She consulted several prudent persons and received the same response from them; the bishop did not have the right to demand that Françoise give her whole fortune to one place, thereby abandoning the smaller houses. The rector of the cathedral, Père Duminy, was astonished at the bishop when he heard him say, "If Madame Blin wishes to remain at Amiens she will have to sign over her income."[26]

Even Père de Sambucy did not go as far as the bishop; he would have settled for part of Françoise's fortune. But now Julie was gaining clarity and strength regarding her decision, insisting that Françoise have complete control of her income; "All or nothing" was her reply. The co-foundresses had been assured by other clerics that they did not have any obligation to accept rules that were not of their spirit. Bishop Pisani de la Gaude had written to invite them to come to Namur with all their sisters, that he would welcome them and give them the liberty to go wherever they were needed. While the door was definitely closing in Amiens, another one was opening in Namur, and this one was adorned with a welcome sign.

Chapter VIII

REFUGEES
1809

While circumstances indicated that the sisters would have to leave Amiens, in many ways Julie and Françoise were reluctant to abandon what they had begun. In fact, Julie said to Père Cottu, "I will never leave here, Father, unless the bishop sends me away," to which he mistakenly answered, "He will never do that."[1] Françoise reasoned that she could not give her fortune to one foundation; she had no idea how it would turn out. If it did not succeed, she thought, perhaps it would be better to give her money to the seminary which was in dire need as well. Besides, even Julie was "...plunged in uncertainty and could only feel her way along, step by step."[2] Neither one wanted to change the vocation to which she felt called—that is, to bring the message of God's goodness to the poor wherever they could do so. The community itself made it difficult to discern God's will. The sisters were young, uneducated, and although blessed with boundless good will, they were sometimes misguided.

During Père Cottu's retreat to the sisters at Christmastime all of the sisters suffered from serious "...temptations, each in her own way, and all were surprised to find that after the retreat they were worse off than they had been before."[3] Julie had relieved them of their charges, taking on the cooking for the community herself, so that the sisters could have a good retreat, but peace in the house was disrupted. Françoise was convinced that "The young people who had so generously banded together to make war against them (evil spirits) could hardly expect to be spared their attacks; and they were worn down by them, especially during the last trying days at Amiens—they never had a minute's rest."[4]

Finally the sign that Julie was waiting for came on the morning of January 12, 1809. Bishop Demandolx sent a letter to Julie through Père Cottu, who had signed it as Vicar General. The bishop informed Julie that since he had rented the house at the Faubourg-Noyon to the Sisters of Notre Dame, and since the foundress was guiding the sisters in a very different spirit than the one he expected, that she might leave and go to any diocese she chose. He, on the other hand, would take back the house and form there true Sisters of Notre Dame. Julie's heart filled with a sense of gratitude; it was clear to her that God was speaking through this letter and was now pointing the way for her; she had decided to leave of her own accord. She had refused the suggestions of several priests that she go to Namur and write to Bishop Demandolx from there to say that she could no longer remain in Amiens under the circumstances. Now she accepted the dismissal in peace. Père Cottu said verbally that she could take any of the sisters who wished to accompany her. She immediately sent for Françoise, and asked him to repeat what he had said, so that she too heard the permission given for the sisters to leave.

Françoise advised Julie to leave at once; she had become accustomed by this time to a capricious change of orders from the bishop. But Julie did not want to act in haste. Rather, she wanted to make sure that this was indeed God's will for her. She wanted to give God the chance to confirm what had happened, although she knew in her heart that the bishop would not change his mind.

When Père Cottu asked which sisters would go with her, Julie named several, among them Sister Ciska Steenhaut, a seventeen year old from Ghent, who spoke French very well in addition to Flemish. Père Cottu insisted that they leave Ciska in Amiens, but Julie protested that he had just promised them that she could take all the sisters with her if they wished. Père Cottu reconsidered what he had said, and then commented that the bishop would wish some of the sisters to stay. The conversation is recorded with Julie beginning as follows:

"Father, I am sure she will not wish to remain."

"Leave her just the same."

"I promise you, Father, she will want to go."

"See how stubborn you are? That is the very thing that displeases the bishop so."[5]

Françoise observed that the conversation was getting heated and so promised to leave any of the sisters who wished to remain. Both said that they would take with them only those sisters who expressed a desire to leave. Père Cottu was worried; that very day he sent for Ciska. Julie advised the young sister that she was free to do as she wished. Ciska protested that she wanted to go with Julie and that she had already made up her mind. Wishing her well, Julie sent her to Père Cottu. The conversation between Ciska and the priest was remarkable considering the times and the attitude of the day regarding clerics, not to mention Ciska's youth. It was recorded as follows:

"You know Mère Julie is leaving," said the priest. "What do you think about that?"

"Father, I will go with her."

"But, child, you will lose your soul. You are on the wrong path; Mère Julie is deluded."

"I belong to Mère Julie. I will follow her."

"Do you know that I may refuse you Communion? You are being disobedient; the bishop does not wish you to leave."

"I will follow Mère Julie!"

Père Cottu was undone, and sent for Père de Sambucy. When the priest returned, he warned Ciska about the state of her soul and told her that even if she went to Namur, the bishop of Ghent would send her back. But Ciska held her own during all the attempts at persuasion, and insisted that she was Mère Julie's daughter and had every intention of going wherever Julie went. Finally, Père Cottu took Ciska to the bishop; once again she was told that she must stay in Amiens. Ciska knew that she did not have vows, and was not under any obligation to the bishop to go or to remain in any city. Again she clearly stated that she would go with Julie. Before leaving she knelt for the bishop's blessing, which he refused to give her.

Now Père de Sambucy was really frustrated. He wrote to Bishop de Broglie of Ghent, with whom he had studied for the priesthood, and asked him to intervene with Ciska, but it was too late. Bishop de Broglie was well aware of the case and saw the contradictions in de Sambucy. Without Julie knowing it, Père Varin, although harsh with Julie at their last meeting, had written a strong letter to Père de Sambucy, reprimanding him for injuring Julie's name with the bishops. Of all the people who should have taken up her defense, Varin stressed, he should have been one of them. De Sambucy, out of guilt, and to restore his own prestige with the bishops, wrote letters to the bishops of Ghent and Tournai in which he cited the virtues of Julie and attempted to take her part. Bishop de Broglie could hardly take him seriously. Ciska had won!

With all that was happening, Julie wanted to inform the sisters herself. After explaining the events that had just taken place she said, "Those who love us will come with us. But I wish to make it clear that no one is under any obligation. I will accept anyone who wishes to come, and I will feel no ill will toward anyone who prefers to remain."[6] All the sisters cried out that they would go with Julie; Victoire said, "If I stay, it will be because they put me in prison. I will go with Mère Julie."[7] But Victoire was subjected to threats, pleading, and the constant effort to win her over, and because "...of the complete confidence she had in (Père) de Sambucy's advice, her weakness and inconstancy of character, in the end (all) vanquished her."[8]

Now the task of moving the sisters and the material goods that Françoise and Madame de Franssu had purchased for the house in Amiens had to get underway. Bishop Demandolx sent a strong letter with Père de Sambucy in which he demanded that the boarding school and chapel be left just as they were. Julie protested that all the furnishings had been bought by Françoise, and therefore did not belong to the bishop. She explained to

Françoise that out of justice to the congregation, the things that were needed in Namur must be sent there, and whatever items were left would have to be sold to provide the means to supply the needs of the larger community.

However, in order to make sure that the sisters who were remaining would still have the blessed sacrament in the house, and out of her feelings for Madame de Franssu, who was heart-broken at the thought of losing her dear friends, she left the beautiful tabernacle that Madame de Franssu had purchased for the sisters, as well as a ciborium. She made it clear, nevertheless, that these things were being lent, and that any sisters who wished to stay in Amiens should be treated with the same charity due to any other person, but they were no longer Sisters of Notre Dame, and therefore the co-foundresses were not responsible for them.

Julie asked Françoise to write to Bishop Pisani de la Gaude in Namur to advise him of their coming, and to give him some of the details of what had been happening in Amiens. She named the six sisters who would follow in the carriage after the one she and five others would take. Julie's eleven year old nephew, Norbert, would go in the carriage with her. She had agreed to look after the boy and see that he received a good Christian education in deference to her brother, Louis, who had been so attentive to their mother.[9]

Finally the day arrived for their departure. Julie went through the school blessing and embracing all the children, and handed out little prizes to them. The students had no idea that this would be the last she would see of them. Shortly after the noon meal, the carriage arrived. Hastily it was packed with as many goods as it could accommodate, and then it was time to leave. Julie could not hold back the tears as she said goodbye to her sisters; there had been much to suffer in Amiens, but it had also been a place of many graces. It could not but tear her heart to leave the place where the congregation had begun, and which she had always assumed would be the motherhouse. She was concerned, too, about leaving Françoise to face the sufferings yet to come in settling all their affairs at the Faubourg. She embraced all the sisters who wept with her, gave them her blessing, and climbed into the carriage, waving goodbye as they began the eventful journey to Namur the afternoon of January 15, 1809.

It was the middle of winter and it was bitterly cold, not the best time for travelling, but circumstances were such that there was little choice in the time to go to Belgium. The first night of the journey, despite her fatigue, Julie wrote to Françoise, "My good and loving friend, thanks to the Lord we have arrived safely, very cold but full of courage, in great peace and union with our Lord Jesus....Tell all my dear Sisters that the little travelers are full of the spirit of the good God, that their hearts are overflowing in many thousands of acts of thanksgiving for the mercies of the Lord. How happy we are to be cold when the holy charity of our Lord Jesus is consuming our hearts!..."[10] They had reached Doullens, and were resting for the night. She commented that little Norbert was well and had been very quiet on the journey, trying no doubt, to keep warm.

The severe cold had made the roads slippery and dangerous. The fact that the driver was surly and ill-humored was not helped at all by the fact that the horses could barely keep from slipping and falling on the road. He ordered the passengers to get out and walk for more than fifteen miles through the ice and snow. Julie was anxious for the health of the sisters and Norbert, and tried to keep up their spirits by singing hymns and with words of encouragement.

One evening they reached a wretched-looking inn that seemed to be the only one available for them. It was isolated in the fields and looked more like a den of thieves than anything else. When the sisters entered the building, the proprietor's manner was anything but reassuring. He was talking to a group of sinister young men who, after looking over the young sisters, gave the owner a knowing glance, and said they would return later.

As Julie stepped outside again, a young man approached her and said quietly, "This is no fit place for you. Try to go further on; do not stay here." Julie wanted to question him more but strangely, he was nowhere to be seen. Suddenly she was full of fear for the sisters and knew they had to leave immediately. The carriage was in the courtyard and the horses had been taken to the stable; the driver was not to be found. "Besides, he was always grumbling; it was late, and the horses needed rest...."[11]

Julie was trying to think how she could persuade the driver to harness the horses again and push on; no one seemed to know how far they would have to go to reach another inn. The cold was even more intense by now, and trying to convince the driver to resume travelling at that hour would not be easy, especially when the request would hardly sound reasonable to such a man. Julie hastened back toward the inn, trying to conceal her fear from the innkeeper and the sisters, whom she did not want to frighten.

Sister Bernardine (Pelletier) had also stepped outside and she was approached by an elderly woman who had repeated the very same words as the mysterious young man. When the sister looked back at the inn for an instant, then turned to ask the woman to come with her to give Julie the same message, she too had disappeared. Excitedly Sister Bernardine related her story to her superior. Now Julie was certain she had to get the little group out of that house, and said a prayer to her good God whom she trusted would not abandon them. She was grateful that she had placed their journey under the protection of the angels.

The innkeeper served the sisters a frugal meal on plates that needed washing, and when Julie asked to see the rooms they would use for the night, she was told that there was only the room they were in, and that the family would sleep in the barn. Julie responded that she would not hear of such an arrangement, and at that point noticed through the window that the driver was approaching the house. She met him outside, and using some kind words, and a little present of money, convinced him of the danger of staying in such a place. Julie told the innkeeper that she wanted to cover another four miles that night, and that they were anxious to save the time.

"At that same instant," she later related to (Père) Sellier, "and without our being able to explain it otherwise than by the intervention of the blessed angels, my daughters with all their packages were somehow or other in their places in the coach, the horses, moreover, put to, and only waiting for the signal to start. We pursued our way rapidly in spite of loud opposition from the innkeeper, and in a short time we reached a village where we were able to pass the night without mishap. When I considered all the circumstances of this event, and above all the very rapid manner in which we had got off from that inn, I could not help seeing in it the Hand of Divine Providence, who by means of His angels had delivered us from a great danger."[12] They later learned that they had been spared from a house which had a very bad reputation. When they had so narrowly escaped the grave danger they were in the sisters praised God with grateful hearts; it was another sign of God's goodness to them.

On another day the coach got stuck in the deep mud, and once again the travelers had to get out and walk in the freezing cold ahead of the carriage. Worn out and shivering, they reached a small hamlet. This time Julie was very cautious before entering any building. Sister Bernardine remembered the incident years later when she described how Julie walked through the street counting on God to guide her, and saying as she passed some houses, "Not here!" and at another, "No! God is not there!" until at last she said of a poor house, "This is the place. Let us knock."[13] When the woman of the house opened the door, she was thrilled to see sisters; she had thought that there were none left anywhere. Joyfully the family welcomed the sisters and they slept securely that night.

As they reached the Belgian border, Sister Ciska rejoiced at seeing some signs of her homeland. She pointed out with pride the fertile fields and the characteristic belfry towers of her native land to the French sisters who had never been out of their own country. At last they began to see the outline of Namur; after five days of walking in snow or riding in a freezing carriage they rejoiced at knowing they were coming to their new home at last. The sisters in Namur were beside themselves with joy for Julie was with them again, and this time she would stay. They welcomed their new sisters warmly, and the new arrivals, on their part, were thrilled with the house to which the Namur community had moved only weeks before.

The following morning the second carriage, which had left

Amiens three days after the first, arrived with six more sisters. Julie complimented Françoise on her choice of a driver who was much better than the one they had. She wrote to her, "If you are sending Sisters by carriage, take the same man you did before. The Sisters are perfectly satisfied with him, and he is much cheaper than the one I took.... He (Julie's driver) did not overtax his horses, I can tell you; but one has to put up with all kinds of people. With the help of the good God, I walked more than five leagues on foot in ice and snow. All this happened by the permission of the good God; may his holy name be blessed!"[14]

Before Julie reached Namur, Bishop Demandolx had written a letter to Bishop Pisani de la Gaude in which he detailed all his complaints about the foundress. Père de Sambucy had done so also railing against Julie and giving him reasons why he should not accept Julie or her sisters in his diocese. With these letters so fresh in his memory, it is not surprising that Bishop Pisani was less than enthusiastic in receiving Julie when she appeared at his palace the day after her arrival in Namur. He greeted her with, "You come to Namur uninvited, Sister, taking it on yourself to uproot a community in the dead of winter? Take care, Sister Julie, even persons with visions have been lost through disobedience.... You came here without first sending me word of your plans."[15] Patiently Julie asked the bishop if he had received the letter Françoise had sent him telling of the reasons for their departure. When Bishop Pisani found the letter and read it, his disposition changed, and Julie shared with him the letter she had received from Bishop Demandolx dismissing her from his diocese. Now he understood why Julie had to leave in the dead of winter.

Describing the two-hour interview, during which Julie listened to all the accusations against her, she wrote to Françoise, "If you had heard bits of the letters written to his Lordship of Namur; there was enough in them to throw me into prison on the spot."[16] Julie responded to the complaints made against her with such patience and modesty that the bishop's words became kinder and more gentle; he asked Julie to dine with him.

In the months that followed Bishop Pisani was deluged with letters from Amiens. De Sambucy wrote so often that the bishop began to suspect his motives. He could not help but wonder why so many persons worthy of respect would have that many concerns about Julie. He was very cautious after her arrival, and suspended judgment regarding her until he had time to form his own opinions about the foundress. Even Père Minsart, who was so devoted to the sisters in Namur and who was at the convent when Julie arrived, was very reserved in his greeting to her. He had heard that one of the accusations Père de Sambucy had made against Julie was that she was very harsh in her dealings with the sisters, and the journey through the bitter cold did not reassure the kind priest. Once again Julie was met with coldness, and had to win over the very people she looked to for support.

The sisters on their part were thrilled with their new home. Julie wrote shortly after they all had arrived, "Good Sister Jeanne (Godelle) is delighted to see such a beautiful house. Everyone likes Namur enormously. As for me, I have plenty to do; I don't know where I am. All the good Sisters embrace you. They are all so pleased with the house, the garden, the solitude. It seems to me that I have never been anywhere else but in Namur." And in the same letter, she notes sadly, "Our poor Xavier is getting closer to eternity."[17]

Meanwhile, Françoise was meeting the mounting pressure from Bishop Demandolx and Père Fournier to keep the remaining sisters in Amiens. As soon as Julie's carriage had departed, Père Cottu sent for Françoise and Sister Jeanne, the novice mistress who was to go to Namur in the next carriage; they responded immediately. After cordially receiving the two sisters, the priest kept up a trivial conversation. When they returned to the convent, Françoise was surrounded by the sisters, some in tears, all trying to tell her what had happened at the same time.

She learned that, "...as soon as she and Sister Jeanne were out of sight, Père de Sambucy came in and had the bell rung to summon the community. He lectured them, mingling anger and kindness, trying to win or frighten them into submission. He came, he said, as the bishop's representative, and he drew a vivid picture of the regret they would feel if they persisted in going against their bishop. 'At the moment of death,' he declared, 'you will be filled with remorse for your disobedience.' Once again, de Sambucy repeated the old accusations against Julie; such as, she is disobedient, she is under a delusion, and besides, the bishop of Namur will be sending her back; they'll see. As his desperate attempt to dissuade the sisters from following Julie became more intense, he even said, 'The Sisters of Montdidier, too—you will see; the police will be after them!'"[18]

At this point, Victoire rose to Julie's defense saying, "But, Father, where is your charity?" De Sambucy was annoyed. "Be quiet, Victoire," he answered, and turning to the sisters, "Come now, I'd like those who intend to stay to say so." Apart from those who declared that they would follow Julie, no one else said a word. Most of the sisters were weeping by this time. Looking for a way out of the situation, Père de Sambucy told them that Père Cottu would be coming the next day to hear their confession, and they would all declare their intentions to him.

When Père Cottu came the following day, he could not persuade the sisters to stay either, and when he heard their confessions, he gave them absolution as there was nothing to warrant that he act otherwise. He was accused of being too lenient and he was replaced as confessor by Père de Sambucy. It was said that he resigned from the position as confessor to the sisters, and soon afterwards, worn out by the tensions within and without the community, he fell ill.

Père de Sambucy announced to the community that he would hear the confessions of the sisters instead of Père Cottu. Françoise told him that if he intended to refuse absolution to any sister who would not agree to stay in Amiens, that it would be quite useless for her to go to confession. "In that case," he answered, "I would rather you would not do so."[19] When she told the other sisters what he had said, none went to confession except Sisters Victoire and Clotilde, and a few of the boarders.

Father Fournier, the vicar general of the diocese, came to see Françoise. With angry words, he too tried to persuade Françoise that Julie was deluded, that the bishop of Namur would send her back, that Julie was opposed to the principles of the gospels and that her hard and imperious character laid an iron yoke on her daughters.

"Why, then, Father, do the Sisters wish to go with her?" asked Mother Blin.

"The human spirit is prone to error," the gentleman replied.

"But Mère Julie has certainly done no wrong."

Father Fournier had to agree. But he came back to the question of her so-called disobedience.

"But, Father, disobedience in what?"[20]

Whatever else Père Fournier said to Françoise she answered respectfully, and with confidence that if God blesses the work of the Sisters of Notre Dame, they would always be at the service of the bishop; to which he replied that the bishop would not want them. Following this encounter, Père Fournier wrote a lengthy letter to Françoise detailing his grievances against Julie. It reads as follows:

Madam:

It is impossible for me to keep silence when I see episcopal authority disposed and rejected by persons who make profession of piety; and I feel it my duty to enlighten you as to the path of error into which you are being led by a woman who is victim of illusion. You are evidently, Madam, since you have said as much to others and even to me, that it was from a motive of obedience that Sister Julie made her decision to withdraw from Amiens and take the Sisters of Notre Dame with her. I like to think that you really believe this was the motive, for though you would not deceive others you are being tragically deceived by Sister Julie.

If she had shown you the letter that she received from the bishop, if she had repeated exactly the message delivered to her by Father Cottu, which the bishop himself wrote down so that no changes in it might be made, you would have seen that our bishop ordered Sister Julie to withdraw from his authority only if she refused to recognize him as her superior. You have no doubt, Madam, I am sure, that the bishop had a right to express himself in these terms to a woman who was his subject according to the laws of both church and state. Such, then, was the order to which Sister Julie rendered "obedience." Such obedience is far from meriting praise; it is prompted by a will resolved not to obey. What proves her obedience false is the fact that she took Sister Ciska with her though the bishop forbade it.

If Sister Julie did not explain to you the precise terms of the bishop's order, if she hid from you the reasons why he dismissed her, she, by that very fact, demonstrated her bad faith, her woeful lack of Christian simplicity, that basic virtue recommended so strongly by our Lord, who warned us to be simple as doves, adding that if we did not become as little children we should not enter the kingdom of heaven. Sister Julie thinks of herself as one sent from heaven to form a religious congregation and to govern it according to her own will. Where are the marks of this heavenly mission? When did God ever say to a woman, "You shall found a religious order, you shall rule over it as you please, you shall listen to no one, neither bishop nor confessor unless they be reasonable enough to enter into your views. I give you absolute power over the young people who rally under your banner; whatever you do will be well done." God must have spoken to her in some such terms for in vain do her superiors point out to her the waywardness of her actions. The rigidity they observe in her, the attachment to her own opinions, no tyrant could equal. Her superiors can say nothing to soften her; she is as hard as a rock. What she sets her will on, what she chooses to think is always best, the one thing to be preferred. But, Madam, the sacred hierarchy, the bishops of the Church, are instruments of God's authority in spiritual things. It is God's will that the faithful obey their pastors; to the bishops he has declared: "He who hears you, hears me; he who despises you, despises me." Again, he warned us: "Whoever does not hear the Church, let him be to you as the heathen. Sister Julie may talk of her revelations, but these pretended revelations are nothing but the deceits of the devil to lead souls astray. When one has neither humility nor simplicity, when one is obsessed with a passion for dominating others, in spite of the warnings of superiors, one can scarcely expect to be favored by God with true, genuine revelations. Moreover, even when revelations are genuine, they must be submitted to the judgment of bishops and confessors to determine their truth.

And so, Madam, if you will consider your own real interest you will not trust Sister Julie. She is under illusion, she is deceiving you, she is leading you astray. On the other hand, you lose nothing by hearkening to your bishop, whom Jesus Christ has commanded you to obey; while you run a very grave risk in allowing yourself to be dominated by a woman to whom God has not entrusted the care of your soul's salvation. You must choose between your bishop and Sister Julie; you yourself have to make the choice. Religion, reason, your conscience, your temporal and eternal happiness—all cry out to you the course you must take. Make your choice, then; your eternal destiny, for good or for ill, depends on it. Accept, Madam, the assurance of my respect.

Fournier, Vicar General[21]

When Françoise read the letter, she reflected again that Bishop Demandolx had expressly advised Julie to leave his diocese if she would not accept the rule restricting the Sisters of Notre Dame to Amiens. Later she noted the irony that Père Fournier was one of the first to attempt to recall Julie to the Amiens diocese and to speak of her as that "saintly woman." Now Françoise had to ponder her response to this good man who had been given such a false view of her dear friend. She wrote a lengthy letter in return.

Reverend and dear Father:
The respect that is due to your character and to your intention of enlightening me make it as duty for me, before leaving the country, to answer the letter you did me the honor to write.

In reply, since I lack both learning and authority, I can only set down the facts. First, I must tell you that during the fourteen years I have lived with Mère Julie I have witnessed in her, in every form and circumstance, a virtue which has never proved false. As for the revelations she is supposed to boast about, if she has had any she has never let me suspect it. On the contrary, I have always seen her walk in the sure path of obedience.

For more than twenty years she was paralyzed, bedridden, a prey to great suffering: God seemed to be forming her in a kind of novitiate for the work he destined for her. When her illness was partially cured, she was chosen as one set apart and was urged to begin this work although she experienced the greatest repugnance, and made known how she recoiled from such a burden. Later, though she was still paralyzed, nine or ten young women gathered around her as auxiliaries. She pleaded with God to restore her power to walk, or to disband these young people, whom in her helpless condition, she would not be able to train or form. It is well known how her prayer was answered suddenly and completely. If I am not mistaken, there is in the bishop's office a document attesting to this miraculous cure. This good mother had no wealth but her virtue, and so it was necessary that someone would provide the temporal resources needed to begin the work. God gave me the good will, and I think I should always second her efforts in this way. From the very beginning our principles, views, desires, have all been for the general good of souls. To attain our end, we proposed to train young Sisters who, later on, sent here and there on mission, would feel that their needs would be cared for; it was with this understanding that they dedicated themselves to the work. So true is this that there is no one Sister today—and I include those already on mission—who would not be desolate at the thought of losing this maternal care. I speak from actual experience; it has already been necessary to reassure them and console them in their grief. What more shall I say, Reverend Father? I admit that when we came under the direction of the bishops, we hoped to find them willing to limit in some degree the exercise of episcopal power to give us freedom sufficient to carry on our work according to the primitive spirit which God accords every congregation. Such a bishop would have seemed to us the angel protector of a sacred trust; by his watchful care he would have safeguarded it from error and danger, vigorously opposing and punishing disorders, so that the primitive heritage would be maintained by his authority regardless of external change.

You may object that our first superiors set down nothing in writing which would define and describe this primitive spirit, even in the statutes they drew up for the government. To this I reply that the spirit of our congregation is well known. I would like to say also, that Mère Julie was present at several meetings when our first superiors discussed the purpose and spirit of the congregation and the formulation of a rule; and that she was aware that they hesitated to draw up a definitive rule because of the uncertainties of the political situation, deciding to postpone the work to a more favorable time. That time never came. But if the bishops had so desired, what would have prevented them from doing, as far as circumstances would permit, what the first superiors were unable to do?

The Bishop of Amiens was not willing to enter into these kindly views; his is the authority, and we respect it. He objected strongly when Mère Julie had to make her visitations; he considered them too costly. And yet, did the convent in Amiens lack anything as a result? It is certainly true that a convent lacks a great deal when it is deprived of the superior; and it is for this reason that as the houses grow more numerous some one person is needed to provide for all the houses of the congregation. It seems that at the beginning of a congregation this office belongs to the one chosen by God for the work, the foundress. She is the one upon whom the Spirit of the Lord is poured out. Such at least is my view of the matter. Bishop Demandolx sent us a set of rules which were taken from the ancient congregation of Sisters of Notre Dame at Bordeaux. It would have been easy to adapt them to the need of our congregation by making the necessary changes. We saw that there were several essential adaptations needed, but we did not dare say so. In any event, we felt it useless to make suggestions because the bishop had already made it plain that he would have nothing to do with our institute unless I first settled my entire income upon the single house of Amiens; he said I might take it into my head to go elsewhere and leave him with the burden of providing for a whole community, and he could not afford to do it.

I could see the logic of this reasoning, and I was not shocked by it. I saw in it the concern of a good father, who was looking out for the welfare of his children; nor was I troubled that so little confidence was shown in my personal integrity. Yet the difficult and critical situation of the times would not allow me to yield to the bishop's demand. In this dilemma, we asked permission to postpone our decision, hoping that time would bring its own solution. But by the permissive will of God, this action of ours was interpreted as a refusal to obey and called forth the bishop's letter of dismissal from the diocese, written in the hand of Father Cottu. To this letter was added the verbal permission to take all the Sisters. And yet a moment later it was said that the bishop might wish to keep several Sisters, and on another day three of the Sisters were specifically named to stay.

Our mother made a point of leaving all the Sisters free to come with her or to remain. She felt that since none of them had made vows, they should be considered as novices. But no authority can prevent a novice from returning to her home or following another call; Julie therefore saw nothing amiss in allowing Sister Ciska to leave Amiens with her, for Ciska, like the other Sisters, would have been inconsolable if she had not been able to accompany Mère Julie. I cannot help remarking here that it would indeed be strange for the Sisters to cherish such sentiments of love and devotedness toward a superior if her rule were in fact, as some have said, "hard and tyrannical." No, Father, this charge is not true. I refer you to Mother Victoire, should you wish to question her. There are few women whose rule possesses such a combination of strength and gentleness as does that of Mère Julie.

What else do they allege against her? "Preaching in chapel." It is true that several times at the novices' reception she said a few words in chapel. But as soon as she learned that this shocked some who were present, and rightly so, she did not do it again. What more can anyone see in this than a fault of ignorance which she repaired by her docility. I have no intention of absolving her from every defect or shortcoming. Several times she made mistakes inadvertently. But what need is there to make these mistakes look like crimes?

As for the reproaches made concerning confession, it may be that once or twice she told a Sister that some scruple or other need not be told to the confessor. This is the interpretation I give, or else I would call such charges downright calumny. The Sisters cannot understand these accusations, and I must tell you how grieved they are over this swarm of criticisms, which they know very well are not true. It is this kind of thing that has served not a little to confirm them in their decision to follow Mère Julie.

I ought also to add that insufficient attention has been paid to the fact that a great difference exists between a religious order long established, and one in process of formation where members are not yet bound by a religious rule or vows. In this case, are not founders and foundresses free to bind themselves only by such rules as they think suitable for the purpose they had in mind?

I have the honor to be, with the profound respect I owe you,

Your humble and obedient servant,

February 28, 1809   Frances Blin, S.N.D. (unworthy)[22]

After gaining some peace and strength by writing her reply, Françoise felt an uneasiness about sending the letter to Père Fournier. She consulted Père Borromée Lefevre who came each day to celebrate mass for the community, and he agreed that perhaps it was too late to write such a defense. If, he reasoned, there would have been any chance of reconciliation, he would advise her to send it, but in his opinion, there was none. She put the letter in her pocket and carried it to Namur.

Just when she thought that no more could happen, Françoise was confronted by Père Dalainville who had just returned from giving a mission. He had stopped by the bishop's house where he learned of the disruption of the community, and arrived at the Faubourg in a state of wrath. He was a tall, powerful man who spoke in a loud voice that cowed lesser persons. He used all the energy at his disposal to express his outrage to Françoise for even thinking of following Julie whom, he said, was under an illusion. He spoke with utmost sincerity, but his manner and his anger overwhelmed Françoise until she rose, and speaking in her most genteel manner, asked him to pray for her. He calmed down somewhat and promised to keep her in his prayers. When she later recounted the incident in a letter to Namur, Julie wrote, "Look on Monsieur Dalainville as the instrument of Divine Providence, used for putting the last touch to the designs of the good God. Even though he were to shout so loudly that I could hear him from here, that good priest would not frighten me. He ought to be face to face with the bishop of Namur, who would show him that where one is free, one can go to the ends of the earth for the greater glory of the good Master, whom we have the happiness of serving."[23] Julie added at the end, "...Monsieur Dalainville's voice must not scare you. The very strong expressions he has used do not surprise me in the least. He might have moderated them; truth does not make so much noise."

The one who was confused and greatly distressed by all that was going on was Madame de Franssu. She had given much to the community, in material goods as well as financially. Père de Sambucy wanted her to take back some 11,400 francs she had given to Julie that was part of the money she and Françoise had lent to the Ladies of the Sacred Heart. But Françoise, after consulting with Julie, would not surrender the note for the whole amount that she possessed. Both she and Madame de Franssu knew that the Sisters of Notre Dame were now in Namur, and both wished their resources to go to them. Fortunately, Madame de Franssu received word from her good friend, Père Enfantin, advising her not to listen to Père de Sambucy. She retreated into silence even though de Sambucy ordered her to try to convince the sisters who remained, to stay in Amiens. Trusting in the wisdom of her friend, Françoise, she refrained from saying anything, but it did not hide the fact that she was heartbroken at the thought of the coming separation.

Eventually Françoise was able to send as much as she could to Namur, and dispose of the rest. Victoire finally proclaimed that she would stay. Julie wrote to Françoise to tell Victoire that she would always remain in her heart, that she would pray for her and wished her well. Victoire was deeply disturbed; she told Françoise, "My whole trouble is that I feel myself being torn in two. I see very well that Mère Julie is right, but I am being dragged in two directions." She was told by de Sambucy that if she left Amiens, "...the police would bring her back."[24] She was further convinced that if she stayed, she could be the means of reconciliation with the bishop.

After sending six more sisters to Namur, there was only Sister Angelique Sachy left to accompany Françoise. Victoire, having made her declaration that she would stay, began to avoid contact with the other two sisters. It was obvious that there was the beginning of two communities at the Faubourg. Right to the end Père de Sambucy kept expecting the sisters in Namur to return, begging the bishop's forgiveness. He assigned one of the boarders the office of portress, and ordered her to report to him anyone who came to see Françoise. He even threatened to write to the government when his attempts to disparage the bishop of Namur for receiving the sisters, but to no avail.

In reflecting on the events of this time, Françoise wrote in her *Mémoirs*, "All that was said or done against Mère Julie at this time resulted from a long series of mistakes and misunderstandings on the part of persons who were zealous and good, but who seemed, as it were, blindfolded. In cases like this, one can only adore the permissive will of God, without attempting to pass judgment. Besides, God can make use of these errors, inconsistencies, and misjudgments, imprudent words or hasty actions, to carry out his designs. And he readily pardons such things when they do not proceed from malice—as we know these did not."[25]

On March 1, 1809, the carriage arrived to take Françoise,

Sister Angelique, and a boarder, Felicity Chary, who begged to go with them and whose parents agreed, to Namur. Victoire came to bid farewell and was bathed in tears. Madame de Franssu was so grief-stricken at the parting that Françoise broke down in tears as well. They embraced each other warmly. She was leaving not only the place where she and Julie had begun the congregation, but the place where members of her family lived. In spite of all she had been through, Amiens held many beautiful, as well as sorrowful memories for Françoise; it was not easy for her to say her final goodbye. Yet her heart told her that Namur was her place of refuge. Remembering the kindness of Bishop Pisani and the knowledge that the sisters would be together again strengthened her for the journey.

Mère Julie returned to Namur.

Chapter IX

CENTER OF THE SPIRIT
1809

When the three travelers reached Namur after an uneventful journey, they were met with great rejoicing and affection. Julie and Françoise had much to talk about and thanked God for bringing them safely to Namur where they felt so much at home. Bishop Pisani de la Gaude had interviewed all of the sisters one by one, and was convinced that the accusations against Julie were exaggerated at best, and in many cases completely false. At last Julie and the sisters enjoyed the confidence of the bishop and felt his support. She had written to Père Varin just that month, "We are very comfortable in Namur. His Lordship shows us much kindness here, in spite of being inundated with letters, almost all against me. But the good God who reads the depths of our hearts knows our departure was the effect neither of whim nor of inconstancy. It was brought about by a very special dispensation of the good God."[1] Françoise found Julie and the community in a very different atmosphere than the one she had left. It was truly a "homecoming" experience for her.

Françoise had not seen the house on the Rue de Fosses[2] which Père Minsart had been able to lease for the community. She marveled at the spaciousness of the former mansion of the Counts Quarre, and loved its garden area which was being slowly restored by the sisters. She was amazed by the amount of work the community had accomplished in the short time they had

The children of the poor were the best beloved of Julie's flock.

been there. Julie had seemingly boundless energy, and supervised every aspect of the workmen's renovations. She was aware of the smallest details of the endless tasks required for turning the large house—which had been in a state of chaotic disrepair—into a boarding school, a convent, and a chapel. She worked alongside the sisters, exhorting and teaching them, and, at the same time, showing them that whatever work had to be done, peace of soul and union with their God should sustain them. She was described as being "...one of those who have the rare gift of getting things done thoroughly, quickly, without surrounding themselves and everyone and everything with a fog of fuss."[3]

Bishop Pisani had promised that when Mère Blin came to Namur he would permit the sisters to have mass in their own chapel. They had been going out to the parish church each day, but did not have enough cloaks for all the members of the community. Some did not even have proper shoes to wear outside in the bitter cold. Julie had written to Françoise a month before, "The church is not far, but there are so many Sisters. They are all practically barefooted. I do nothing but buy shoes."[4] Often they had to take turns going to mass since some had to wait until the others came home to give them their cloaks to wear. Now that Françoise had arrived they all hoped that they could have mass in their own chapel. However, the bishop waited until April 21, 1809, when he would be free to celebrate the first mass for them.

After what seemed to be endless waiting—which Julie believed was because of her sins—permission was finally given for the blessed sacrament to be reserved in their chapel on September 21. Gradually, the community at Namur was forming the center of the Sisters of Notre Dame where young women were welcome to join them. Students were filling the classrooms, and young sisters needed to learn teaching skills; but the more important task was to help them grow in the knowledge of their religion and the fundamentals of religious life.

Julie's own holiness spoke more to the sisters than anything she could say. Hers was not a stiff, or ethereal sanctity. Her conferences to the sisters, which many of them wrote down, were filled with homey as well as sublime exhortations. The sisters were to be women of prayer, for without prayer there would be no Sister of Notre Dame. Prayer opened up the heart to God's transforming love without which nothing of good could be done. Françoise commented, "In saying without prayer there is no Sister of Notre Dame, she implied that without prayer there is no transformation of the world, no true community and no union with God in Christ by power of the Spirit. In short, no apostolate, and no religious life."[5]

Together they were facing a post-Revolutionary France, riddled with confusion, and struggling with the whims of Napoleon. It was not just a case of society's neglect or lethargy; Julie and her sisters lived through a time of a full-blown rebellion against the church she loved, and now, some of its former members were making an attempt to return, but they needed help. Julie knew that what she had begun, at God's invitation, was the most important work on earth, and her sisters had to be ready for it. She would remind them that there were very few priests to serve the people and that they were being called to do the same work as the first apostles saying, "And what are we to have been chosen by God for the noblest work that can be accomplished in this world? God alone knows the full value of this work. When I see you occupied in it, you seem to me greater than all the potentates of earth. For all we know, the Lord may have brought us together here to win for Him one single soul.... And would it not be a wonderful thing to put one soul on the road of salvation—a soul that cost the blood of a God?"[6]

But in her zeal, Julie knew that neither she nor any of the sisters could accomplish the tasks alone. She had great sensitivity, and a humility that comes from recognizing that God would have to do the work; they could only provide the channel for the graces held out for those they met. She admitted, "We should like to see more abundant fruit (from our labors) that would be very desirable, but we live in a century which is not favorable. We must be satisfied with doing our duty well, trying to give good example and then leave everything to the mercy of the good God. That is what the good God asks of us."[7] And so she would counsel her sisters to have great faith and profound confidence in God's loving-kindness.

The Sisters of Notre Dame were to embody the spirit of the congregation, which she believed to be so important that she told the new members, "Let your great concern, your one and only concern, be to acquire, to preserve, and to renew within yourselves unceasingly the spirit of your holy institute."[8] The first characteristic virtue of that spirit was simplicity, which she called the base and foundation of the order. She would pray, "My God, give me, I beg of Thee, good daughters, entirely simple, and I shall find in them treasures out of which I can make good Sisters of Notre Dame."[9] To be simple, said Julie, was to be like a sunflower which "...follows all the movements of the sun and ever turns towards it. Even so, the mind and the heart of a religious who possesses this virtue are always turned towards God alone, from whom she receives the light which beautifies and guides her, and the warmth which vivifies her."[10] She would have no false pretenses or artificial airs in her followers; no, they would be women who are entirely open to God, as a crystal is open to the rays of the sun. They were to be sincere and honest in their relationships to their superiors and their sisters.

Guided and inspired by Père Thomas and Père Varin who were formed by the teachings of their spiritual father, Ignatius of Loyola, Julie prized obedience as the second characteristic of the Notre Dame spirit. She thought of obedience as St. Ignatius envisioned it for his followers. Having been trained in the military, he asked of his followers the kind of readiness to obey that soldiers are required to give their officers. He believed that the Jesuits should be willing to give as much loyalty and allegiance to their superiors as their secular counterparts gave to those who commanded them. The obedience of the Sisters of Notre Dame was to be the same as that found in Ignatian spirituality. They were to be open to the direction of their superiors with the belief that their obedience reflected a willingness to do anything that God would ask of them. Julie placed such a high value on the readiness to obey of her sisters that she told them, "Obedience therefore, should be our principal virtue; without it, all the other virtues are unreal or imaginary."[11] Many times in her life, Julie's obedience to her superiors had cost her dearly; she never asked of her sisters what she herself had not experienced. She believed that obedience was the antidote to the self-centeredness with which all persons have to struggle. Julie told them, "The spirit of obedience is the very soul of our holy institute."[12]

But even with simplicity and obedience, it would all be for naught unless they were animated by the third characteristic, charity. It was a strong love that Julie called her sisters to practice. Not a sentimental kind of feeling toward one another, but one marked with faith and courage. She told them, "My good daughters, with the least spark of the spirit of faith, we become heroic in the practice of charity, through our conviction that it is God Himself who is manifested to us in our neighbor."[13] She took seriously Christ's words, "Whatever you do to the least of my brethren, you do unto Me." In the everyday experiences of communal life, Julie saw many occasions to practice the kind of charity she asked of her sisters. "To show kindness and good will to all; to know how to keep for oneself the most difficult tasks in order to lessen the fatigue of our Sisters; to keep back every harsh or impatient word; to bear generously all that wounds us in our contact with others—all this is what holy charity requires in every good Sister of Notre Dame."[14] For her, charity demanded a virile personality, not the helpless, fragile type often considered in the eighteenth and nineteenth centuries as the epitome of womanhood. She wanted strength in her followers; they would need it for the type of work set out for them. Her analogy of what charity would do for the congregation was a vivid one, namely, "Holy charity unites us as cement holds together the stones of a building. This explains how strong souls among us sustain those who are weak, and the entire edifice can thus resist all shocks."[15]

These three characteristics which were the foundation of the spirit of the congregation could only come about if the sisters practiced mortification, so central in the asceticism of the early nineteenth century, and by their growth in humility and in confidence in God. What she asked of the sisters was no less than their complete abandonment to the good God. Such characteristics were not easy to accomplish. "But," she wrote in a letter to Françoise, "...we know, both from our own experience and from that of other religious congregations, that in these times with their almost complete breakdown of morals, great courage, vigilance and humility are necessary in order not to grow discouraged or give way before so many difficulties."[16] Throughout her life, while she was urging her followers to relentlessly pursue the path of virtue, she kept asking them to pray for her as well, that she, too, might grow in holiness. In June, 1809, she closed a letter to Françoise with the words, "All yours, Julie Billiart, very unworthy Sister of Notre Dame—everybody says so."[17]

Her dealings with the sisters were marked by firmness tempered with love. She refused to handle sisters with velvet gloves when she saw their needs, yet hers was a sensitive heart. With her gift of the reading of hearts, Julie knew when to act and when to let God do the acting in a soul. In referring to one of the sisters, she said, "I will not say anything to her; grace will have to move her from within."[18] She had sent advice for Sister Xavier on how to treat her students, which reflected her own attitude toward discipline: "May she be full of kindness and gentleness for them and ask our Lord when she ought to use some firmness. Firmness is good but, as St. Francis de Sales says, flies are caught not with vinegar but with honey."[19]

The first sisters would set the tone for those who would follow them; Julie was most anxious that they be good models for the rest. She herself set the example by living what she was preaching. Françoise noted, "...even when she scolded, resisted or wounded you, it was impossible not to love her because she was so loving and lovable in God and for God, that she knew how to heal the wound she made."[20] Her confidence in God's love and her inner peace and calm, even in the midst of intense suffering, radiated peace to those around her. Eyewitness accounts were given years after her death of the fact that after receiving holy communion Julie was rapt in prayer, that the presence of God in her was manifested by an aura of light surrounding her head. For a long time she was unaware of the phenomenon, but once she found out she had a larger veil made in order to cover her face while making her thanksgiving after communion. To the sisters this was just another indication that God's love was shining through this woman, Julie.

All that she would have for the Sisters of Notre Dame or whatever advice she would give them came from her profound belief
in the goodness of God. She was undoubtedly influenced by the
French school of spirituality from the seventeenth century,[21]
which used the term "le Bon Dieu" often, and sometimes as a
term for God. Julie had frequently visited the cathedral in
Amiens during the missions or for mass, and passed the famous
statue of "Le Bon Dieu" which was greatly honored by the people of that city as it is even today.[22] The "good God" was a very
familiar expression, used often in everyday speech in her day, to
which Julie added, "How good is the Good God!" the phrase
which has become a motto for the Sisters of Notre Dame. In the
worst of circumstances Julie would exclaim, "How good God is!"
She saw that no matter what happened to her, God would bring
about some good in the end; she counted on it. She knew that
both she and the sisters must develop a deep interior life, as she
said, "Ours is one of the most difficult vocations because we
must live an interior life in the midst of external work. If that
interior life were lost, our congregation would not last, or if it
did live on, it would be only an outward life, by uniformity of
customs—even that would soon come to an end. It is in the motherhouse especially that this primitive spirit must shine forth."[23] It
is not surprising that Julie asked for magnanimous souls to carry
on the work of the congregation.

Françoise was home but a few weeks when word came from
St. Nicolas that the sisters needed Julie there. The house was
much too small, and unsanitary. (There was a report of fleas in
the house although only two were actually seen.) Parents were
upset and starting to remove their children from the school, and
the young sisters needed help. Julie left Namur on April 22, the
day after Bishop Pisani said the first mass for the sisters in their
chapel.

Julie wanted to consult the Bishop of Ghent about this house
but she was a bit leery, not knowing what kind of reception she
might receive from Bishop Maurice-Jean-Magdeleine de Broglie,
one who had known Père de Sambucy in his early days as a
priest. She knew that de Sambucy had written to his friend; she
did not know which version of the Amiens account he had

heard. To her great joy and relief Bishop de Broglie was very cordial to her when she arrived at Ghent. He asked Julie how things were in Amiens, and when she told him about the dismissal and its reasons, the bishop was satisfied. He assured her that he wanted Sisters of Notre Dame in his diocese, and that she could bring as many sisters as she wished.

Bishop de Broglie inquired how she stood with the bishop of Tournai, and Julie answered, "Your Excellency, my name has been well blackened with the Bishop of Tournai, and I do not know if it has turned white again." Laughing heartily, he answered, "Oh, in these parts they know well enough how to blacken a name."[24] After telling her not to worry, Bishop de Broglie told Julie that he was leaving for St. Nicolas the next day. When Julie arrived there, she found that the bishop had just gone to dine outside the village. With the help of a boarder from the school, she managed to find him. She explained the poor conditions of the house where the sisters were living. Later, the bishop visited the first house the sisters had used, which was very damp, and ultimately had caused the death of Sister Saint Jean, the first superior there. When he saw the second one, he realized how insufficient it was. He tried very hard with the authorities of the city to find a suitable house for them, but met with nothing but resistance.

Julie's frustration with the people of St. Nicolas can be heard in her words to Françoise at Namur, "St. Nicolas is not worthy to have such good Sisters. His Lordship did everything possible to have us stay for the poor, but their indifference has caused it all to fail.... I have a lot to tell you (but only for us two, heart to heart) about what I have had to go through."[25] The Flemish did not like the idea of having French teachers for their children, and furthermore they resented the fact that the sisters had left the first house which they had provided. It became clear to both Bishop de Broglie and Julie that the community was not welcome in St. Nicolas, and he decided to transfer the sisters to Ghent. When the townspeople heard that the sisters were leaving they vented their anger by shouting at the coach as they pulled away from the house. Frightened by the rage of the crowd, the sisters looked to Julie whose eyes were shining and whose face was serene. She was reflecting on how Christ allowed them, once again, to suffer what he, too, had known, rejection from the very people they wished to serve. After a while, the young sisters became calm, grateful that their ordeal was ended.

Bishop de Broglie found the travelers a place to stay at the house of the Sisters of Charity, who gave them two rooms and a small kitchen. The furniture that they had used in St. Nicolas belonged to the parish. Consequently, they had to use their ingenuity to make the best of what little they had for the time being. There were seven sisters altogether, and they had but four straw mattresses. Offering one to Julie, the rest of the sisters gathered their cloaks around them and slept on the floor, using the twigs and sticks they had for fuel, as pillows. They had assured their hosts that they had everything they wanted. Julie rejoiced at the opportunity to practice real poverty, and made the best of the situation with her sense of humor. When darkness came, they had no light. For their dinner they had only some dry bread, which they passed around to each other groping for the other's hand in the darkness. Suddenly there was a knock on the door. A kind gentleman, the director of the hospice, had brought them a lamp and a jug of beer. Now at least, they could swallow the dry bread a little easier. Eventually, the dry bread began to produce mold but, as Sister Marie Steenhaut exclaimed, "Mère Julie used to bless it and it never did us any harm."[26]

Julie was very tired, but her sense of humor never dimmed. On May 8 she wrote to Françoise, "During a single week I was three times in Ghent and back (to St. Nicolas)—coming and going that makes six journeys. I had to travel like a bullet, and in all this I wanted to see right to the end the holy will of my God .... Ah! my good friend, the good God must be my strength in all the fatigue I have experienced since I left. And in all that, poor Brother Ass always goes on through cold and heat and everything. I was very tired, for the whole little removal of our good Sisters had to be arranged, and there were a hundred worthless things. For you know that in removals you think you have nothing, and you have all kinds of nothings."[27]

The next day Julie was out early to buy some provisions for the sisters. Once she had the bread, butter, salt and potatoes she told Françoise, "We are the happiest people in the whole town of Ghent on our straw pallets."[28] Somehow, with very little money Julie was able to purchase supplies and always have a coin left in her purse, a gift, she concluded, from her good God. After a short while living with the Sisters of Charity, Baron Coppens offered the sisters the use of a large house with a garden. In June, the sisters moved into their new quarters, and began teaching. They prepared themselves for their task by making a retreat given to them by Père Bruson, whose enthusiasm for the work was contagious.

During all the negotiations of trying to get a house in St. Nicolas and again in Ghent, Julie hinted to Bishop de Broglie that she could always return with her sisters to Namur. But the bishop was determined to have the Sisters of Notre Dame in his diocese. Several times he told Julie, "Mère Julie, it is your vocation to go anywhere in the world; you are not made to stay in only one diocese. That was," Julie added, "without my saying a single word of what was in my heart. How good the good God is!"[29]

When Julie returned to Namur, she found everything going well in the community. For a few weeks she took up the task of renovating the large house and training the sisters. Now being with the sisters, she soon noticed that one of the newest members, Elizabeth Savary, a protege of Père Dalainville, showed signs of being unsuitable for religious life. Julie finally decided that she would have to accompany the girl home to her family although the thought of going to France was in no way appealing to her. The journey was anything but peaceful. Julie wrote from Plessis Saint Just on June 4, 1809:

First of all, I cannot describe to you how much that little traveler tried me. Nobody but I could ever have kept her in check. There was no single stratagem she did not use in order to return to Namur. I had to care for her as for a child who wanted to monopolize my attention. She was seized by frenzied feelings of friendship for me and wanted to bite me. There would be far too much to say about her; let us go on to the moment of separation. I had to warn her that I was going to leave her, that I would not accompany her to Amiens, but that I would write a letter at the last stopping place. Tears, cries, during—I don't know how much of the way. I had always treated her gently, but I had, at that time, to use the greatest firmness to bring her to her senses. When I was fairly near Amiens I left her in care of a driver, a very good man whom the good God had given me at considerable cost. I took another way on foot.... (Père) Dalainville...received her very ungraciously. The good God permitted me not to show up; there would have been sparks flying.[30]

It was another one of the most difficult journeys Julie had to make.

The convent at the Faubourg-Noyon in Amiens had undergone great changes as soon as Françoise had departed. Since Père de Sambucy considered himself the founder of the Ladies of Christian Teaching[31]—one of the first titles of the Religious of the Sacred Heart—and was in the process of writing a set of rules for them, he felt he had the right to appoint superiors from their community without consulting their foundress, Sophie Barat, who was in Amiens at the time. Without her knowledge, Bishop Demandolx, at the suggestion of de Sambucy, appointed one of her novices, Marie Prevost—who had entered the community only a few months before—to be the superior of the convent so recently vacated by the Sisters of Notre Dame. He also ordered the transfer of two other of her novices to the Faubourg. Mother Beaudemont, the superior of the house of Mother Barat's sisters, completely devoted to Père de Sambucy, wrote a letter of congratulations to Marie but failed to inform her own Superior General, Mother Barat of the appointment. So ignored was Sophie Barat during this period that she described it later as, "...this solitude in which I am living."[32] When she did discover what had transpired, it was too late.

Mother Victoire was not at all pleased when Marie arrived to take over the role of superior. Friction developed between the two women as Victoire refused to accept a sister of another congregation as superior. Since she had fallen from favor with Père de Sambucy, she was sent to Rubempre, seven and a half miles from Amiens. Mother Marie was directed to convince those Sisters of Notre Dame who were in the secondary houses in

France to leave Julie's group and remain with the Amiens community.

It was by strange coincidence that Mother Marie was in Montdidier the very day Julie reached a place just outside that city. Julie had asked the driver to deliver a letter to Sister Marie Caroline who had, along with three other sisters in Montdidier, made it quite clear that she had no intention of following anyone but Julie. The letter contained instructions as to where to meet, for Julie intended to take the sisters back to Namur with her.

However Mother Marie was in the convent when the driver arrived, and persuaded him to tell her where Julie was. At once she and a companion walked the two and a half miles to the place where Julie was staying. She informed Julie that Sister Marie Caroline and the other sisters had been replaced, and had left the day before to stay with Sister Marie Caroline's mother in Plessier.

Mother Marie spoke of the possibility of reunion between the Sisters of Notre Dame and the Sisters in Amiens in vague terms. She expressed sympathy for Père de Sambucy, and as she listened Julie surmised that the house in Amiens was falling apart due especially to lack of funds. Françoise later recorded about the situation, "The 23,000 francs due us was a flea in the ear of de Sambucy, who was eager to secure at least half the sum for the house at Amiens; but the bishop had his own ideas in these matters and still held to them. Julie saw nothing of the spirit of God in this and said quietly: 'If God gives the grace, you, Madam, will do good in Amiens; and we, in Namur.'"[33]

After arranging for a carriage to take Mother Marie and her companion back to Montdidier, Julie left for Plessier in search for her sisters. She called on Père Trouvelet to ask if he knew their whereabouts, but he was engaged at the time so she had to wait. Now that her sisters had been replaced at Montdidier she felt that her trip back to France was providential. She had not intended to come just for the purpose of bringing her sisters to Namur, but it seemed that the circumstances proved it right to do so.

Since Père Trouvelet's meeting was quite long, Julie decided to take a short walk. Just as she turned the corner of a high wall,

Julie came face-to-face with Sister Marie Caroline and the other sisters. Their surprise at seeing each other was only exceeded by their joy. The sisters had no idea that Julie was in France, much less in the same town as they were. They had resisted all the pressures put upon them to leave Julie, and now it was a relief to be with her again. They felt safe and happy to be reunited with their "Mère Julie," who immediately arranged for a carriage. After staying with the sisters in Ghent for two weeks, the Montdidier exiles travelled to Namur on June 23, their real "home."

Julie was not back for long before an appeal came from St. Hubert in the Ardennes for Sisters of Notre Dame to establish a school in the village. Bishop Pisani advised her to go immediately to look into the possibility of sisters going there. Workmen had begun renovations on a building for that purpose. After inspecting the buildings and making suggestions for some changes—since she had decided that she would indeed send sisters to St. Hubert—Julie took advantage of the opportunity to visit the sisters in Jumet.

On her return trip, while passing through the village of Fleurus, she attracted the attention of some children who had never seen a sister before and were curious about her. She stopped to speak to them when suddenly a policeman, who was quite intoxicated, approached her and asked to see her passport. Julie never carried a passport so she had to admit that she had none with her. The policeman, in slurred speech said, "Very well, Madam, you must go to jail."[34] Whatever protest she attempted was to no avail, so she had to follow the man to the mayor's office. The young mayor was intimidated by the drunken officer and hesitated to say anything contrary to him, though he knew passports were unnecessary for travelers unless there was someone under suspicion. Even when a servant ran for the local pastor, the priest could do nothing to help Julie.

Finally, Julie reached deep into her pocket and found a letter addressed to her from the bishop of Bordeaux which she had forgotten she had with her. She showed the letter to the group and said, "Gentlemen, you can see from this letter that I am not an adventuress."[35] This identification was enough for her accuser. The man apologized, and let her go. Julie continued on her journey with a prayer of thanksgiving in her heart for having been spared a prison sentence.

Soon after her return, she accompanied three sisters to St. Hubert to make up the new community. Sister Marie Caroline, the twenty-four-year-old sister who had recently come from Montdidier was named the superior. Julie remained there eight weeks to help them get settled. "She (Julie) put her heart, soul, and all her strength into the work of establishing a new foundation, thinking of everything, buying whatever was needed, bringing order out of disorder. Only with a special help from God could she continue to sustain such a burden of work, which meant constantly beginning all over again," wrote Françoise in awe of her friend.

But all these new foundations took time and money, not to mention that the house in Namur needed more extensive repairs. Out of justice to the congregation, Julie knew she had to retrieve the 23,000 francs owed to them by Père de Sambucy. Since Françoise had transferred the power of attorney to Julie because the latter had proven herself gifted with business skills, Julie believed that she could secure the money from the notary holding it as well as settle a lease that had to be renewed on some property from the Blin estate. Once again she set out for Amiens, beyond doubt, hoping this would be her last trip there.

Chapter X

JOURNEYS TO AMIENS
1809–1810

Julie sent notices to the notary in Amiens and to the farmer, Lempence, who had leased land from Françoise, that she would be coming to settle accounts with them. Having taken the coach to Lille, Julie decided that she did not wish to pay the extra fare to Arras as it was too expensive, so she sought other transportation, but to no avail. There was nothing to do but to walk the seventeen and a half miles to the place where she was to meet Lempence.

Finishing her business with him, she asked if he could find some means of travel for her as she had to go the rest of the way to Amiens. The next morning, the farmer arrived with a manure cart, and invited Julie to board the driver's seat next to him. Since the man was extremely large, Julie had to squeeze herself into the seat and was nearly crushed. But the hardship did not come so much from being pressed into a small space as it did from the incessant talk of the driver; he wanted to exchange a piece of land belonging to Françoise in order to build a house for himself, and obviously he felt compelled to give his passenger every detail of the crops he would plant and what he would grow. Julie confided to Françoise that "...she never made a more difficult and fatiguing journey, even apart from the discomfort of the cart and a downpour of rain."[1]

At length they arrived at the Peacock Inn in Amiens where

Bishop Demandolx, of Amiens.

Lempence usually stayed, and in spite of the fact that "...she was so tired she could scarcely talk,..."[2] she went straight to the notary to complete the business of renewing the lease. She asked Lempence to deliver a note to Madame de Franssu, whom Julie was anxious to see, since she was understandably reluctant to appear at the Faubourg.

Victoire, who was still at the Faubourg, recognized Lempence and asked him if he knew where Julie was. When she learned from the farmer that the foundress was in town, she cried out with pleasure and insisted that he tell her where she could find her. She went immediately to the inn and threw herself at the feet of Julie, "...weeping, laughing, and asking pardon, all in one breath."[3] When she was able to compose herself she told Julie that none of the sisters at the convent were content; that she herself had not made vows there, and that Sister Scholastica, who had made vows for one year, was sorry that she had done so. She spoke earnestly of Julie returning and taking over the opening of another convent in Arras which was to be sponsored by some rich farmer's daughter. Julie listened patiently, but said very little.

Suddenly, Madame de Franssu appeared, and Victoire was embarrassed at being discovered. Madame de Franssu greeted Victoire with surprise and displeasure, as she had grave reservations as to what the impulsive sister would do next. She feared that when Victoire left Amiens, that she too would have to leave the Faubourg. Since she had settled into a comfortable existence which had nourished her spiritual life, and was physically unwell, she dreaded the thought of having to find another home.[4] Victoire felt uneasy, and muttered some excuse for having to return to the convent.

After Victoire's departure, Madame de Franssu inquired of Julie whether she had received a letter from Père Varin. Since Julie had not, she was informed that Père Varin had advised Madame that the money she had given to Julie should be returned to the Sisters of Notre Dame. Madame de Franssu had been pressured by Père de Sambucy to change her mind about the money, and say that it was intended for the house in Amiens. But now the good woman was comforted by the assurance of Père Varin that she should insist that the money be returned to Julie.

She advised Julie to write a note to Père de Sambucy and request half of the money he owed her (since Madame knew the priest did not have the whole sum) and the other half as soon as he was able. Julie wrote the note exactly as it was dictated to her and sent it to Père de Sambucy by Lempence. The two women bade each other an affectionate farewell and parted company.

Once she left Julie's company, Madame de Franssu felt so weak at the thought of facing de Sambucy again, that she stopped for a little wine to fortify herself before returning to the Faubourg. She rightly guessed that he would press her to write again to Père Varin and ask him to reconsider his permission for the money to go to Julie.

When Père de Sambucy burst into the room where Julie was waiting, he was all cheer and friendliness. He greeted her with "Good Mother, I am delighted to see you! We have a great many things to talk about."[5] Julie was astounded, later writing to Françoise, "Monsieur de Sambucy arrives as if nothing had happened—no, you have never seen anything like it! There he was, calling me *good mother* any number of times, and I did not know what all this was leading up to. So much kindness for you and for me, for everybody in the convent!.... Do you know, my dear good friend, what he wanted of me? Ah, ah, would you believe it? That I should unite his houses with that of Namur!"[6]

Julie was confused. What houses did he mean? He answered, "All of them, of course." Adding, "Oh, my good mother, all hearts here are yours, all are very devoted to you."[7] Julie could not believe her ears. She wrote finally, "Really, without showing it at all, I believed those were things of another world; I thought he was having his joke with me. At last I realized that he was serious about it."[8] For an hour and a half he went on talking about a reunion, refusing to hear Julie tell him gently that it was impossible. "...Seeing that he was driving me to extremes, I gave him an answer he understood clearly: 'Father, the good God has led us to Namur; we believe that we are there by his holy will. I shall never come back to Amiens unless the bishop of Amiens calls me back. We were here, and we would never have left, but when one has been sent away, one has to be asked for again. When a king exiles someone, the king must bring him back.'"[9]

Undaunted, de Sambucy kept insisting that there be a reunion. Finally Julie spoke straight to the point. She stressed that she was asking for half of the sum he owed her now, and that the reason he wanted the reunion was because he needed the money for the house in Amiens. She was aware that Père Varin had counseled Madame de Franssu to give to the Sisters of Notre Dame the money she had originally intended for that purpose. The remaining amount would have to be paid at another time. De Sambucy said he would pay half the sum, but he wanted the promissory note. But Julie, aware of his intentions, answered firmly, "No, I shall give you a receipt for the sum you give me, and when the promissory note is fully redeemed we shall put it in the fire—that is how it stands."[10]

Père de Sambucy sent half the money with Monsieur Leonard who asked for the promissory note again. Julie refused to give it to him, so he threatened to take the money back. Perhaps he thought that seeing the money, Julie would change her mind; but he underestimated her. Julie replied, "Take it back, for I shall certainly not give you the promissory note."[11] His anger was useless; Julie reminded him that the matter was not his concern.

Next Père de Sambucy arrived with Père Bicheron demanding that Julie give them the promissory note in exchange for half the money. Julie stood firm again, and the priests left, going directly to Madame de Franssu. This time Madame summoned up her courage to face the priest. She told de Sambucy that she never had any intention of entrusting her endowment fund to anyone but Julie. The case was settled, and the priest handed over 11,500 francs to Julie telling her that he had not clearly understood Madame de Franssu's intentions.

Once again Julie forced herself into Lempence's cart for the homeward journey, carrying a basket filled with coins. When she had to take public conveyances she tried to look casual about the basket she was carrying, and became nervous when some people appeared to be curious about its contents. She stayed a few days at Ghent, and then, with the assistance of two kind gentlemen who were on their way to Namur, she reached home safely.

During the years of expansion of the congregation, Julie never had much time to spend in Namur. The longest period,

prior to her last illness, was three months. When she saw that all
was well in Namur, she started out for St. Hubert to see how the
community was faring there. She had an opportunity to get a
ride in the carriage of a gentleman, who was sending his two
sons to a boarding school, and was grateful to have Julie look
after them on the trip.

The boys were nine and eleven. The task seemed easy enough
to Julie who loved children, but even she could not control these
two, who were undisciplined and lacked any semblance of manners. Neither her threats nor her kind persuasion did any good.
As soon as the boys were out of sight of their father they
"...climbed on the horses' backs, ran between their legs, in and
out among the wheels."[12] Julie warned them that they could be
killed, but they answered her back and would not listen. Julie
appealed to the young driver to do something, but he refused.
The inevitable occurred! The younger boy was run over by the
wheel of the cart. Although he was not seriously injured, Julie
was shaken. She left the boys at their uncle's house, and walked
ten miles back to St. Hubert.

The sisters were delighted to see her. Being young and inexperienced, and facing new situations that puzzled them, Julie
brought them comfort and a better sense of security in the many
decisions they had to make about the school and community.
They wanted her to stay longer, but when she sensed that she
had provided them with enough support to carry on, she was on
the road again.

Travel was not easy for anyone at this time. Françoise was
always a bit concerned about Julie on her many trips, and looked
forward to hearing from her to know that she had arrived at her
destination safely. We read in her journal:

> To go alone on such journeys at her age and in her frail state of
> health, in public conveyances where she had to hear so much
> cursing, swearing, raillery, and familiarities, she needed courage
> and the maturity and religious bearing that were hers. She was
> over fifty when she began these journeys; her face, though bright
> and animated, was that of a much older person, and this often
> protected her from insult. Ordinarily while traveling, she met nei-

ther raillery nor disrespect because she knew when to say nothing, how to speak to the point, and how to use her gift of repartee without wounding anyone's feelings. In the company of cultured travelers, she usually inspired a certain reverence.[13]

On her return trip from St. Hubert, Julie had yet another adventure. This time she could tell the story with a twinkle in her eye, and made her audience laugh. She had not been able to find any conveyance to take her back to Namur, so some good person lent her a horse to use. A small boy with a large whip was to run alongside the horse and bring him home at the end of the journey. At one point, Julie allowed the horse to drink from a deep pond and take a rest. As she remounted, the boy cracked the whip, frightening the horse, which backed into the deep water carrying Julie with him. She almost lost her balance, but suddenly the horse lunged forward bringing the half-soaked Julie back to solid ground.

When she returned to Namur she found a letter from Madame de Franssu explaining that she had not made her wishes known to Père de Sambucy sufficiently, and blaming herself for his stubborn insistence. Not long after, Julie returned to Amiens to settle the exchange of property that Lempence wanted, and to sell another small piece of property. The business transactions went quickly.

Once again Julie had to walk several miles carrying the money she obtained from the sale of the land. She stayed at Ghent on her return trip, but had one of the most frightening of all her experiences. Julie had boarded the stagecoach in the evening, and found herself in the company of five or six men, one of whom was quite intoxicated. He was a very large man, and in a terrible mood. At midnight he got out of the coach and called to the driver to stop, but the driver did not hear him. Thinking the driver's whip was for him, the man threw himself onto the driver, pulled him off the carriage, and beat him mercilessly, clubbing him with his fists.

The coach kept going without the driver, and the passengers heard the assailant running alongside. Finally, one of them called out, "What have you done with the driver?" He replied, "I have thrown him in the ditch."[14] When some of the men got out to try to find the poor victim, Julie was left alone with the drunken brute, who was obviously disturbed. The horses were still moving on. Julie prayed for God's protection as she knew how easily the coach could be overturned. At last the horses stopped of their own accord.

The men found the driver covered with blood and his leg badly broken. Fortunately at that moment, a mailcoach came by, and the men convinced the mailman to take the wounded man to an inn, where he died two days later. When they informed the assailant that their driver was badly wounded, the intoxicated man showed indifference, and only complained of his swollen thumb. None of the passengers were sympathetic. When they reached the next town the police arrested him. Julie was able to continue her journey without any more disturbances. Reaching Namur, she confessed to Françoise that she was exhausted. The memory of that terrible ordeal haunted her, filled her with pain. Even though the following day she appeared to be quite herself again, she confided that she wondered how she had ever survived the horrifying experience.

Meanwhile the sisters in Ghent had started a lace-making school, since there had been resistance by the civil authorities to allow them to open a regular one. With the help of someone whose authority was greater than the local leaders, Julie received permission for the lace-making school to begin, as it would provide the sisters an opportunity to teach religion as well as to keep some of the poor girls off the street. For Julie, "The true and solid science is the science of Christian doctrine, the most excellent of all sciences. The other sciences are of very little value in my eyes, I assure you.... But as we must also learn them so that we can use them as a hook for catching souls we must not neglect them...."[15] So, if lace-making could be a "hook," lace-making it would be. But almost as soon as the school was opened, Baron de Coppens began looking for someone to buy the house the Sisters were using.

Eventually Julie heard of a former Cistercian abbey that had been bought by Monsieur Pycke de Peteghem for a modest sum, in order to save it from complete destruction during the French

Revolution.[16] The intention behind the sale was that the monastery would be restored to the Cistercians when it was possible to do so; but since there were only two elderly Cistercian sisters living in one part of the building, there was no hope of restoring the community.

The buildings were in a deplorable condition. The chapel was especially damaged as it had been used as a barn, a powder magazine, and later, a forge had been set up in it with a chimney built for that purpose. During the seventeenth century its walls had been decorated with paintings done by "Roose" (Nicholas de Liemacker) who was a pupil of the master of the great painter, Rubens.[17] One part of the monastery was being used as a school, but the schoolmaster, Monsieur d'Hont, let it be known that he was considering relinquishing his lease.

When Julie and Monsieur Lemaire, the legal adviser for the business, came to the abbey, they found the two Cistercian nuns, who had survived the suppression of their order, living in one part of the abbey as guests of the owner. When they saw Julie's poor appearance, one of them laughed out loud. But when the gentleman explained who Julie was, they changed their attitude, and became more cordial. While inspecting the Abbaye aux Bois,[18] Julie saw its possibilities for a school. Her heart ached when she saw the chapel, and the idea of restoring it as a place of worship, moved her to want to lease the monastery. After some negotiating, and having obtained Bishop de Broglie's consent, Julie signed a contract with Madame Pycke, the heir of the property, to lease part of the Abbaye aux Bois on December 1, 1809.[19] The owner was delighted to have the building used by religious again, as were the Cistercian nuns.

Meantime, Père Milingie had leased a house in Ghent for the Sisters because he wanted them in his parish, St. Peter's. When Julie was apprised of the fact that there was a house on the Rue des Femmes, a poor district, she rejoiced in the good that could be done for the people. She saw one hundred thirty-two children pour into the school which opened shortly after the sisters moved there November 21 of the same year. The superior of St. Peter's wrote this brief description to Namur, "I find myself in the midst of a troop of wretched little creatures, their ignorance is lamentable, and that of the parents still worse."[20] For Julie, serving the poor was the work of the congregation, as she stated, "We exist only for the poor, absolutely only for the poor."[21]

The bishop of Ghent was pleased with the arrangements at the Abbaye since he agreed that another school was needed in Ghent. And so it was that when the door closed on the Sisters of Notre Dame at St. Nicolas, two doors opened in Ghent, allowing them to begin the work of education there, and which continues today.

On one of her trips Julie went to Breda where there had been a request for sisters to take over a school. But conditions were not suitable, and Julie had to leave after making a long, tiresome journey. However, on her return to Namur she had a rather lengthy wait in Brussels. Something told her to visit the Countess de Ribaucourt, one of the heirs of the Namur property which the sisters were renting, and which they hoped to purchase one day. It just happened that the property of the Countess' family had been divided just the day before, and the Namur property was her share. The Countess warned Julie that the property was worth 15,000 francs and that her husband would not take anything less for it; but then she whispered, confidentially, that she would reimburse Julie 3,000 francs. Returning to Namur to discuss the negotiations with Françoise, she said, "The good God let me go to Breda where I accomplished nothing, but he was waiting for me in Brussels."[22]

When Julie consulted Bishop Pisani de la Gaude, he advised her to take Mère Blin with her and return to Brussels immediately to pay the entire amount before anything happened to discourage the sale. So Julie and Françoise counted out 15,000 francs, put them in two baskets, and carried their treasure to Brussels where they obtained the deed to the Namur property on December 12, 1809. When they returned to Namur two days later, the whole community sang the "Te Deum" in gratitude to God for giving them the first convent of their own.

Shortly after this trip, Julie and Françoise went to Ghent together to see to the opening of the Abbaye aux Bois. There were many things needed in the old abbey. At first, the sisters had to sleep on the floor on straw mattresses since they had no bedsteads, and had the use of but two rickety chairs left by the former schoolmaster. Julie went out to search for bargains, and little by little outfitted the community, quickly spending the 1400 francs she had set aside for the abbey. She appointed Sister Catherine (Daullee) as the superior.

Now she realized another trip to Amiens was in the offing in an attempt to recover the rest of the money owed to them by Père de Sambucy. She went to Bishop de Broglie to seek advice regarding the trip, and found out he was visiting his aunt, Madame de Metz in her home, just fifteen miles from Amiens. Père Van Schouweberghe, the bishop's secretary, wrote a letter to Bishop de Broglie on her behalf, and directed her to the Chateau Henancourt, the home of Madame Metz. When she arrived there, the bishop was just leaving to take care of some business, and he asked her to wait for him. He invited her into the chateau to meet his aunt. The elderly woman greeted Julie cordially, and showed her to a room which she put at her disposal.

In one of those rare occasions in her life where she found herself with nothing to do but wait, Julie was delighted when the child of one of the servants wandered into the room. She spoke to the child about God, and soon forgot her fatigue. Julie made Christianity so clear and appealing to the little girl, that the child began to pray for rain so that her teacher would have to stay. But finally the bishop returned and Julie had a chance to speak to him about retrieving the money from de Sambucy. Bishop de Broglie told her she should make an effort to get it from the priest, but he warned her it would not be easy.

When she reached the inn not far from the Faubourg convent, Julie once again sent a message to Madame de Franssu, who came immediately for a long visit with her friend. Julie stated that she was hoping for the rest of her money, but Madame de Franssu could not bring herself to discuss it with Père de Sambucy. When the priest arrived, he spoke only of reunion again. It took some time for Julie to ask for the money, which had to be paid by Madame Beaudemont of the Sisters of Christian Instruction. At last de Sambucy agreed to speak to

Madame, and Julie realized disconsolately that she would have to return to Amiens yet again.

Julie stopped at Ghent on her return trip to see Père Van Schouwenberghe who had been appointed the ecclesiastical superior of the abbey as well as of the sisters there. She arrived at the secretary's office shortly before noon. When the priest asked her to join them for dinner, she was persuaded to stay and dine with the bishop. She noticed that Bishop de Broglie was somewhat distant, and less cordial than he had been in the past, but thought it was probably due to some pressing business of his. He had been to see Napoleon in Antwerp, and had sensed tensions developing between the emperor and the church. There was much talk at the table among the priests of their growing concern.

A few days later when she was speaking to Père Van Schouwenberghe, the bishop came along looking very cross and said, "Well, well! Mère Julie with Father Van Schouwenberghe again! Take care, Father, she may deceive you; she has already deceived Sister Saint Joseph, for she's a kind of schemer, and the bishop of Namur knows it....Do you know what she does, this Mère Julie? Well, it isn't really seen, but it is felt just the same."[23]

This last point was referring to an accusation that Père de Sambucy had made against Julie when he heard of a young sister who was too severe in her acts of mortification. In her fervor, the sister had been excessive, and had injured herself. Someone had reported it to de Sambucy. In truth, Julie had been upset by the sister's overly zealous practice of penance, and corrected her. Père de Sambucy wrongly surmised that the superior required extremely harsh penances from her sisters. Actually, Julie often cautioned them to abstain from fasting and penances when she considered it harmful to their health.

Both Julie and the priest were taken aback by the abrupt manner and unexpected treatment of Bishop de Broglie who had been so supportive of her. The bishop said that he was going to replace Père Van Schouwenberghe as ecclesiastical superior of the abbey, and would not assign another. The priest protested, "But Monseigneur, if things are as you say, why is Father de Sambucy anxious to have Mère Julie back in Amiens?"[24] Bishop de Broglie had to admit that he did not know why, but he insisted, "...I do not understand what it is all about. I have been told all sorts of things, all sorts of things. But she is a mischief-maker; she does only what pleases her."[25]

Père Van Schouwenberghe had always liked Julie and could not believe what was happening. When Julie asked the bishop for an ecclesiastical superior, he told her he had no one to give her. When she inquired about Père Van Schouwenberghe, he refused. At last, the bishop said he would appoint a superior before he left for Paris. "And so it went, a mixture of contempt, raillery, joking and serious talk. The whole, (as Françoise tells us) was well calculated to detach a person from the world and lift her to the only faithful friend, the only solid support of the soul."[26]

When Bishop de Broglie withdrew, Père Van Schouwenberghe turned to Julie in surprise and said, "Now where do you suppose that storm blew in from?"[27] Julie guessed that it came from the bishop's visit to Amiens. Père Van Schouwenberghe was angry; were it not for the presence of the Religious of Christian Instruction in Ghent, who were so influenced by Père de Sambucy, he said he would write him a stinging letter. Françoise could not resist the comment: "So much for the fickleness of the human heart."[28]

Between 1809 and 1812 Julie traveled seven times to Amiens. Once she was told by Père de Sambucy that he had the rest of the money he owed the congregation. She went immediately to pick it up, only to find out that he did not have the money after all. But on October 15, 1810 Julie, greatly relieved, wrote to Françoise, "All is finished, by the grace of God."[29] Père de Sambucy had sent Leonard to the inn where Julie was staying to give her the 10,400 francs he owed. In addition, another 4,500 francs were given to her by the notary for the sale of a piece of property belonging to the Blin de Bourdon estate.

Two baskets, one large and one small, were filled with the silver coins. They were very heavy, so Leonard helped Julie load them onto the carriage. The landlady of the inn expressed her surprise that Julie would travel with so much money on a public conveyance. Julie was hardly reassured, but she put her trust in

God and prayed for the protection of the angels on her trip. She kept the small basket on her lap while travelling, and the larger one between her knees. The other passengers looked curiously at the two bundles. They observed that she did not leave the coach whenever they stopped for lunch or dinner, but partook of some bread and provisions she had brought with her. When night fell and the passengers were to stay at an inn, she waited until all were off the coach, then she dragged the baskets as far as the steps leading to her room. Fortunately, one of the waiters came along just in time, and she asked his help up the stairs with her precious bundles. She said, "I have a very heavy basket here. Would you please carry it for me to the room where I always stay? It has books in it and it is really very heavy."[30] She could say that honestly as she had put books on top of the money. The young man dragged the large basket to her room where it was safe for the night.

The next day she was unable to get a coach to Lille. She learned that a carriage was leaving for a place close to Lille the following day, so she decided to take it. When the time came to board the coach, she found a servant girl to help her with the baskets. The two women struggled to get the baskets in place on the carriage, and once that was managed, she would not move. She was, "...as it were, nailed to the seat."[31] Before starting on their way, a soldier appeared who was to make the trip with her. He was in full uniform, complete with a large saber, that could easily have been used as a weapon against her, but he proved to be a trustworthy gentleman, and the journey was a pleasant one.

When they arrived at their destination, the soldier went off and Julie was left with the baskets she was unable to move. The driver came to assist her, but when he went to lift the baskets, he commented, "Well, little lady, you have got some mighty heavy eggs in here."[32] This time, Julie had put eggs on top. She tried to say something distracting like, "Underneath, it is heavy." To which he replied, "Eggs, I'd like to have some of those eggs."[33]

Julie was worried, as they had stopped at an inn where she had never stayed on previous trips. The innkeeper went out of his way to be of service, and was so deferential that Julie was alarmed. The innkeeper's wife brought in her best linens and treated Julie as if she were someone of importance. By the time she got to bed that night, Julie was in such a state that she offered the sacrifice of her life to God, and prepared for death. She did not sleep very well in spite of all the fine linens.

Somehow, she was able to get the baskets onto the coach the next day without anyone's help. She continued her journey as far as Lille, where she knew Monsieur Malingie. She asked him to meet her at the inn where the coach stopped. The good man aided Julie onto the next coach headed for Courtrai, where she hoped to stay with her friend, Madame Vercruysse. When Julie asked some of the passengers where a gentleman named Vercruysse lived, one of them replied that at that moment the coach was just opposite his front door. She asked the driver to stop; and when Monsieur and Madame Vercruysse heard that she was there, they and their household came out to greet her. Several of them carried the baskets this time, Madame Vercruysse expressing alarm that the passengers must have guessed the contents of the baskets. She was certain that someone would be back that night to rob Julie of her treasure. But the night passed without incident, and the next day Julie set out for Ghent. This time one of the young women who worked at the inn helped Julie carry her baskets across town where she was to board the coach. The poor girl was suffering from sores under her arms, and must have experienced a great deal of pain helping with the heavy load. When Julie offered her some money for her trouble, she insisted she was performing this service for the love of God, and that was reward enough.

Finally Julie reached the Place d'Armes in Ghent where the coach stopped. It was late afternoon, and darkness was beginning to fall. She knew she would be unable to carry the two loads across town by herself. Françoise's observation of Julie might well apply here. "It was in such darkness and uncertainty that God generally led her. She tried, in all she undertook, to judge what was God's will: this was the light of her path, though seldom was she sure in advance of the next step she should take."[34]

Suddenly three girls from the school saw Julie standing over the baskets in the courtyard of the inn. To her relief, they ran over to Julie who greeted them warmly, then bade them to go to

St. Peter's Convent and have one of the sisters come to her. When the sister arrived, Julie explained her predicament. Picking up the loads they started slowly towards the convent. They tried to walk upright, and not draw attention to themselves, but several times the young sister stumbled under the weight of the larger basket, finally putting it down, saying she was unable to carry it a step further. Looking about, Julie noticed they were in front of the home of Monsieur Lemaire, the business man who assisted in the negotiations for the abbey. Making her presence known to him she requested to leave the baskets with him for the night. Monsieur Lemaire was happy to accommodate Julie, and insisted that when she came to retrieve her money the following day that she count it out with him.

When she returned the next day, and while counting the money with him, she thought she would ask him if he could use some of the money for his business; in which case she would be glad to lend it to him, and receive interest on his use of it. The kind man agreed, and Julie was well satisfied with her business transaction.

Financially, the ordeal of Amiens was over. Julie was able to use the money she had retrieved to pay the expenses in Namur and some of the secondary houses. She sensed a certain amount of relief that she was free of the problems at the Faubourg, but she also experienced pain when she met people who wanted her to return to the place where the congregation had begun. The people of Amiens had not forgotten Julie; their attachment and devotion was obvious by the many letters she received begging her to come back to Amiens.

Chapter XI

AWAY FROM FRANCE
1811–1813

Père de Sambucy had involved himself in politics in Amiens during the year 1811, for which the Imperial Police carted him off to a prison in Paris. To some of his followers, he appeared to be a veritable martyr, but to Bishop Demandolx he was an embarrassment. The bishop's eyes were opened to the impulsiveness of the young priest, and he began to lose confidence in his judgment. A year later, Père Sellier was speaking to Père Fournier about some diocesan business and casually mentioned the name of Mère Julie, suggesting that perhaps it was time to ask her to return to Amiens. To his great surprise, Père Fournier, who only two years before was adamant about Julie leaving France, eagerly agreed that she should be invited back. But he wondered whether Julie would be willing to return after being treated so harshly. Père Sellier was sure she would, so they decided that they would approach the bishop on the subject.

In September of 1812 Julie received a letter, first from Père Sellier, and another from Père Fournier, asking her—in fact, begging her—to return to Amiens. It was the letter from Bishop Demandolx that most impressed Julie, as it contained his humble apology, and acknowledgment of his misjudgment of her. In his letter, the bishop wrote:

> ...I wish to see you back in Amiens, to resume the office of superior of the Sisters of Notre Dame in my diocese, from which you

were dismissed through an error of judgment on my part because I relied on a person whom I thought I could trust. I am wiser now and I do not hesitate to admit that I was deceived in your regard. I beg you, then, my dear daughter, to return as soon as possible, if not to remain here permanently, at least to make whatever changes are needed to establish a new order of things. You will be heartily welcomed by Sister Marie and the other Sisters, who will be happy to submit to your authority; they have, one and all, assured me of this. In short, there will be no obstacle in your way.[1]

The letter ended with assurances of the bishop's good will and paternal affection.

Julie answered Bishop Demandolx's letter with gratitude for his proof of his confidence in her. She replied, "...had I the ready means of responding to your kindness, how happy I should be to find again the precious benefit I always truly appreciated in spite of the troubled times we passed through, both you and I."[2] However, she made it clear in her letter that she could not live permanently in one place; she had to visit the secondary houses that had already been set up in Flanders, and that there would be one motherhouse where the new members of the congregation would be educated. Julie wrote that she would gladly cooperate with his plan of reunion if these conditions made it possible to do so. Bishop Demandolx hastened to reply, writing to her:

Either I must have explained myself badly, my dear daughter, or you must have misunderstood me. It was in nowise my design to make you quit Namur and establish yourself at Amiens; but looking on you as the Superior General of your institute, I would simply ask you to come here to visit your convent, and to make all the reforms in it you think advisable, so that the same spirit may reign amongst you all. Come, then, as soon as possible, so as to consolidate by your presence an establishment which ought to be dear to you as the birthplace of your Congregation, and which I would fain consider its Motherhouse (though I do not insist on this).[3]

Bishop Demandolx also wrote to Bishop Pisani de la Gaude asking him to intervene with Julie, and encourage her to consider the reunion. In his letter he told his friend, "I cannot help acknowledging that I have severely reproached myself for following the harmful advice of banishing the good Mère Julie from my diocese.... Everything has not yet been settled; but I have begun by recognizing Mère Julie as superior general of all the houses, not forgetting her position as foundress. I entertain the well-grounded hope, that under the leadership of this virtuous religious, her congregation will spread in my diocese and enjoy a resurgence, a fuller life."[4]

Julie's intuition told her not to hurry to Amiens. When she was in Ghent, she met a merchant, the nephew of Monsieur Duminy, Curé of the Amiens Cathedral, who had just returned from Amiens. He told her that the house at the Faubourg was in debt. After hearing his account, Julie could not help but wonder if perhaps there were some hidden motive for her to be invited back. Although the gentleman assured her that the superior in Amiens would "suit her," she wrote to Françoise. "...But, my good friend, what does not suit me in advance are debts of 3,000 francs... They would perhaps like to saddle me with that. Then I shall explain my meaning, asking for time to think it over a little at leisure, telling them that the house has already cost us 5,000 francs. Not having created these debts, I do not consider myself obliged to take them on."[5] So Julie waited, and prayed about the situation, confiding in her friend, "I do not know at all what I am going to do. The good God will show me moment by moment what I have to do."[6]

Julie pondered a long time before deciding on the next step. The kind gentleman from Amiens urged her to take a companion with her in order to better understand the spirit of the convent at the Faubourg, since the scope of her knowledge would be far wider than his. "Seeing that what he told me was not without foundation, I began to think of it a little within myself with the good God. (Sister) Catherine was with me; I said to her, 'Well, my daughter, come with me.' In fact we had thought and prayed about it, and assembled the councils of the two houses."[7] The sisters agreed; Julie should go to Amiens and find out what God had in store for them.

The two sisters left Ghent on November 17, arriving in

Amiens at midnight: they were quite exhausted. Their journey had been extremely dangerous as they came over appalling roads; the carriage almost overturned several times while it swung mercilessly on its leather braces. When they reached the city in the middle of the night, they had to go to three inns before finding a room. They were so tired they "...fell on (the bed) without sheets."[8] The next day Julie sent a message to the superior, Sister Marie Prevost, who lost no time in coming to the inn to get the two sisters. Julie wrote to Françoise later that as she walked into the house in the Faubourg, she was given the words in her heart, "'Look at me and follow me.' Nothing else."[9] In a letter that was later destroyed at her request, Julie confided to Françoise that she saw Christ carrying his cross away from Amiens. It was a vision she could not easily forget.

The next day, she and Sister Catherine visited Bishop Demandolx, who greeted them kindly, and repeated his confirmation of Julie as Superior General who had all the rights of visitation to the secondary houses of the congregation. The day after, the bishop sent Julie a formal declaration of these points, as well as a letter to Sister Marie Prevost explaining what he had done.

At first, Julie found the fourteen sisters very edifying. They were simple and open. But gradually she sensed that they were "...a little too stiff. That is nothing; (she wrote) I think it comes from the superior; not that she is stiff herself, oh no! She belongs to the number of those persons who are lifted out of their place before they are ready. She has shown the greatest possible submission since I have been in the house, but in spite of that it can be seen that being a superior has harmed her very much... This superior was only eight months in the Oratory; enough to catch its spirit, not enough to receive a solid formation."[10]

Then, too, Julie was disturbed by what she found regarding the regularity of the house. She reflected, "We two, (Sister) Catherine and I, are at meditation with four other Sisters out of fourteen people in the house. As the light grows stronger true colors can be better seen. I need only prayers, my good friend, and many of them. I told you that I had met our good Jesus when all in me wanted to flee from Amiens. He saw very well that I felt a great repugnance. The thing is so much the more difficult in that the most complete devotedness appears in all the subjects as also in the superior."[11]

Julie recognized that the sisters must get out of the large house at the Faubourg. There were only ten boarders, and they were getting deeper in debt. She was still puzzled as to the reason she was asked to return, and once again confided to her friend, "I make no promise for the debt of 3,000 or 4,000 francs which they owe. I could not say that this was the only motive for which they asked for a reunion. But I should not like to guarantee that it did not play a great part in their request. The good God knows."[12] She spent many days searching all over for another suitable house.

When people heard that Julie was looking for one, there were some who offered to sell her a house for about 10,000 francs. She teased Françoise that it was all her fault that people thought she was so wealthy. "My dear, everybody thinks I arrived with a load of money to buy the most beautiful house in town. It is incredible nonsense, all this agitation. It has all created a sensation in this town that I cannot describe."[13] She quickly tried to dispel the idea that she could rent or buy a house.

Julie was aware that the people of Amiens were beginning to worry about losing the Sisters of Notre Dame, and began offering houses free of charge. Several men came to see her about houses that were available. With her keen sense of humor she wrote to Françoise, "I do not do anything any more but see gentlemen, no ladies. Their number is as large as my self-love. Poor granny Julie, do you like it?"[14]

Finally a part of a factory was offered to her *gratis* if the sisters would also agree to teach the young women who worked there. When Julie consulted Sister Marie she was satisfied, and the sisters moved into their new quarters in November. In addition, the Count de Rainneville was asking for sisters for his village to open a school there. He promised to provide a suitable lodging for two or three sisters, and that, too, seemed to be a promising community since the Count offered to provide a small income for the sisters. While she was in Ghent, before going to Amiens Julie had been told by Père Duminy's nephew that he wished to purchase the Faubourg, and had offered 3,000 francs to reimburse the sisters for the improvements on the house. That amount of money would have paid off their debts. Once things seemed to be settled, Julie returned to Namur. On the way, she reestablished Sister Catherine as superior of the Abbaye aux Bois in Ghent.

She was not home long before she had several letters from Sister Marie. Everything seemed to be going in reverse. The gentleman who said he wanted the house at the Faubourg found another one that was much more suitable for him. The owners of the factory no longer thought they could give the sisters the use of the building rent-free; and Sister Marie decided that it was time for her to return to the Sisters of Christian Instruction, since she had only been on loan to the Sisters of Notre Dame.

Julie believed that these were the signs by which God was leading her. It was evident that the house in Amiens needed to be closed, and Bishop Demondolx agreed, as he could not support the house himself. He knew nothing of Sister Marie's intentions. With the sale of the furnishings in the house, and with some help from the bishop, the debts were paid. Julie requested the tabernacle that Madame Franssu had donated to the sisters, and it was returned to her. With the closing of the house in Amiens, some of the sisters went to the smaller houses in France, others went to Namur, a few returned to their families, and the rest followed Sister Marie to the Sisters of Christian Instruction. The previous June, Madame Franssu had left Amiens because of her health, both of mind and soul.

Julie, meanwhile, had another problem with the lace-making school in Ghent, where she returned after a short stay in Namur. Since the parish priest was supporting the school at St. Peter's, he felt that he had the right to oblige the sisters to accept eight or ten troubled young women of questionable character into the school, and to teach them manual labor. Julie was worried about the effect their presence might have on the children, but the priest could see no difficulty. However, the sisters had more work on their hands than they could handle.

One of the women threatened to hang herself, and had to be watched day and night. In fact, she was found in the attic where she was in the process of putting a rope around her neck, "...nor could she be dissuaded from her intention," Françoise wrote, "I pass over in silence mention of a second."[15] The sisters were exhausted, and did not know how to deal with the women. When she failed to convince the pastor that the sisters could no longer handle such cases, Julie withdrew them from the school. They all moved to the abbey in December.

In March of 1813, Julie decided to visit the small houses that were near Amiens. The trip brought her to Rubempre, where Victoire was superior. By this time it was clear to Julie that Victoire had "...lost the spirit of her vocation. In the convent she governed there was neither order, right method, nor religious observance; nothing but bustle and loud talking...."[16] Although the pastor had observed the situation, Julie was hesitant to approach the bishop, remembering her former encounters with him over Victoire.

However, one day while she was speaking to Bishop Demandolx, Victoire appeared. The bishop himself had observed what had happened to Victoire, and asked Julie to speak to her. She tried her best, but Victoire would admit to no faults on her part, and only complained about the way she was being treated. When Julie realized that all the talking was leading nowhere she returned to the bishop, who asked, "How did you find her?" Julie answered, "Like bronze." The bishop admitted, "Yes, I saw it in her face. I would not call her an open person; but that is the way with some women. You find out the reason only when they die."[17] Julie did not visit the Rubempre house after that encounter. As soon as Victoire left religious life, the house was suppressed.

During her visits to the houses in France, Julie learned that Napoleon had recently imprisoned Pope Pius VII at Fontainebleau, and she longed to call on him. The pontiff had suffered greatly at the hands of his captors in Savona, where he was kept under house arrest for three years. Because he had excommunicated Napoleon for confiscating the Vatican States, and would not accept the civil changes that had been initiated in France, Napoleon ordered his garrison to restrain the pope, remove his temporal powers, and let it be known that he was only the "Bishop of Rome." However, a young officer took it upon himself to storm the Quirinal during the night, kidnap the pope, and take him to Savona.

By 1812, when Napoleon's army was annihilated in the Russian campaign, the British were getting uncomfortably close to Savona where they hoped to rescue the pontiff. It was then that Napoleon ordered his men to move Pius VII to Fontainebleau. The journey across the Alps in the June heat was excruciating for the pope who was deathly ill. He barely survived the ordeal of the trip, and had been near death's door several times after arriving at the palace outside Paris.

The pope's loyal cardinals had been banished, forced to remove their robes (and were called the "Black Cardinals"), and threatened with imprisonment if they contradicted the emperor. Pius VII was cut off purposely from any of the advisors he trusted, and he worried about his good friend, Cardinal Pacca, who was imprisoned in an icy fortress of the Frenestrelle. He too had refused to take an oath of allegiance to the emperor who demanded it of all the priests of Italy. "Though Rome had been incorporated into the French empire, the braver priests, the braver monks, and the braver nuns had refused the oath, and in consequence had been dragged from their presbyteries, their monasteries, their convents, and imprisoned or driven into exile; in large part the religious houses were closed and their treasures confiscated."[18] It was not safe to be friendly with Pius VII at that time, but there were many who gladly took the risk.

Père LeBlanc managed to keep in touch with the pope even though the Fathers of the Faith were still suppressed in France. It was he who managed to arrange a meeting for Julie with Pius VII. On February 16, 1813 she wrote to Sister Jeanne Godelle, "I have to go to Paris, and please God I shall obtain the blessing of the Holy Father for all my good daughters."[19] She chose as her companion for the journey a novice, Madeleine Quequet. Leaving from Ambleville, the two travelers took turns riding on a donkey Julie had borrowed for the forty-five mile trip outside Paris. She had not explained to Madeleine the purpose of going to Fountainebleau and when they arrived, the novice was told to stay in the courtyard of the palace and mind the donkey.

His Holiness Pope Pius VII.

After what seemed to Madeleine a very long time, Julie appeared, her face bathed in tears. She confided to the novice, "My daughter, I have seen the Holy Father; we have wept together over the troubles of the Church."[20] The pope had given Julie a crucifix[21] which she held reverently throughout the long journey back to Ambleville. She could scarcely speak. Pius VII had been suffering from bitter remorse for having given permission to the bishops to take the oath of loyalty to Napoleon. They were appointed by him to consecrate new bishops for dioceses in need, without the pope's approval. He felt he had betrayed the church.

It is not clear whether the pontiff had been comforted by Julie, or whether Julie was encouraged by him in continuing the work of the congregation. Clearly, the visit was a comfort as well as a sorrow for Julie. She wrote to Françoise, "If the good God grants us the grace of meeting again, we shall have a lot to say about all sorts of places, Paris as well as elsewhere. I do not attempt to speak to you about it; I have no time. My God, what is earth? A real place of exile, of banishment from one's own dear homeland! You do not know anything any more, my good friend, you would have to go and hear and see."[22] The cross memento given her by the pope was reminiscent of the one she had received from the Knight of Malta when she was thirteen years old. In her early life, and toward the end, Julie was gifted with a cross.

Eventually all the houses in France had to be abandoned. At the suggestion of Bishop d'Aviau in Bordeaux, Mlle. Vincent wrote to Julie that it would be more practical for her community to establish itself independently from the Sisters of Notre Dame since communication and travel between Namur and Bordeaux was extremely difficult. Julie recognized the wisdom of the decision, even if a painful one for both communities. The two congregations continued to have very cordial relations afterwards, and the bishop always spoke with great admiration of Mère Julie.

Each of the other houses in their turn, had good reasons to close. The three sisters from Montdidier were in Namur for vacation and retreat when they received word that their convent had been given to the Sisters of Charity in their absence. At Bresles and Rainneville, the benefactors were insisting that the sisters be employed in works other than with the education Julie wished for her congregation, so these, too, had to be withdrawn.

Julie's frustration can be detected in her earlier report to Françoise, "I have just come from Rainneville, and found the little community going on fairly well. May God preserve it, if it be his will that it should last; thorns will not be wanting to it. I saw M. de Rainneville, who speaks as founder; and I, on my side, spoke as foundress, not for the temporal prosperity of the house, but in order to uphold the spirit of our institute in opposition to his demands. My God! what one has to put up with in treating with these gentlemen and ladies, however good they may be! What a large heart one must have to be a Sister of Notre Dame! What strong medicine one must be able to swallow! This is the grace I ask for all my daughters—that they may be very courageous, very generous."[23]

Throughout the time that Julie was making her visitations to the secondary houses, France was in great turmoil. The early enthusiasm of Napoleon's "Grande Armée" was waning, as the emperor began to experience defeat after defeat. Napoleon was constituting his "Children's Army" by conscripting teenage youths to fight a man's war. Nearly every family had lost a brother, son, husband or father, and yet the emperor said on June 26, 1813, "I grew up on a battlefield and when one has done that one cares little for the lives of a million men."[24] He was determined to maintain his empire, no matter what the cost to France or to the French people.

Two years prior to this, Julie was walking back to Namur from St. Hubert through the Ardennes. She left in the evening, hoping to cover seven miles before nightfall in order to have only thirty miles for the next two days. The hills were endless, and travel along the roads alone was dangerous in good times, not to mention the current unrest. Along the road, she fell in with two members of Napoleon's army, one a captain and the other a sergeant. She thought it wiser to be accompanied by these men who were courteous to her and, when she thought about it, accommodated their pace to hers. The weather was hot; Julie was wearing the only clothes she had, her woolen habit. She carried her traveling bag in one hand and a cloak in the other.

The men talked of little else but the battles that were ahead and how devoted they were to their emperor since it was the time when Napoleon was experiencing his initial successes. One had just received a promotion and exclaimed, "I would give the last drop of my blood for my emperor." Julie thought, "And I, should I not give all to my God.?"[25] When she arrived in Namur she was dripping with perspiration, and was so exhausted she was unable to greet all the sisters who had come out to welcome her.

There is no way of knowing whether Julie's soldier companions were alive at the end of 1813; with the loss of over a million men, most likely they were not. Julie too had given most of her life to her beloved country, France. She too was willing to "give her last drop of blood" in that country, but now, she and her sisters had to withdraw to Belgium. Years later when the cause for her beatification was introduced, there were no official records left in the Archives of the Amiens Diocese of Julie ever having been there.

Cross given to Julie by Pius VII.

Chapter XII

SOLDIERS ALONG THE ROAD
1813–1815

Julie seemed to be everywhere after returning to Namur from Picardy. There were requests to have Sisters of Notre Dame open a school in Andenne, about twelve miles east of Namur, as well as in Gembloux, twelve miles to the west. As a result, four sisters were installed in Andenne on October 6, and four in Gembloux on October 11, 1813. Julie went to the towns first to see that there were suitable houses for the sisters, and then accompanied them to their convents when they were ready. She would remain with the sisters until she considered them able to be on their own, but her letters after she left them were filled with inquiries of how things were going, and what they might need.

Attention to the smallest details are found throughout her letters written to the sisters in the secondary houses during any precious moments she could find. For instance, on October 16, 1813, Julie wrote to the new superior of Andenne, Sister Angèle, "On Tuesday I shall send you some flour and a sieve. I think you wish very much to eat homemade bread. Have a kneading-trough made for the dough."[1] In other letters she would advise them when and where to plant, what types of vegetables they should start, and where they could go to get what they needed. In return, she wanted the sisters to keep her informed, and asked them to write regularly to let her know how things were progressing. In the same letter she wrote, "The oftener you write to me the more

165

pleased I am."[2] Her love for her sisters made her heart want to be with all of them at once; often it seemed that she tried to do just that, physically urging her body to make journeys in all kinds of conveyances and weather, for very long distances.

Then too, many of the sisters had experienced serious deprivations during the years of the Revolution, when there was a dire scarcity of food. Now some suffered from ill-health, and Julie worried about them. She wrote to Sister Jeanne at Zele, "I hope, my good friend, that you take care of your health; otherwise, the good God will not be pleased with you. You have fatigue, work and health to look after. It is the love of the good God, not in order to make an idol of the health of your body...take a sensible care for the love of the good God and for his greater glory. Moreover, our health does not belong to us. The good God gives it and takes it away when it pleases him."[3] So her letters were filled with homey advice about resting when they had colds, not fasting while they were teaching, and ordering some to stay in bed a little longer until they felt well again. She longed to be with them when they were ill, and care for them. Often her letters ended with, "I do not wish to leave you."

But it was 1813, and Emperor Napoleon was fighting for his life and his crown. Movements of troops all over France and Belgium were becoming a more frequent sight as armies jostled for positions back and forth in one engagement after another. Following the devastation of one "Grande Armée" in Russia, the emperor lost another one during the Battle of Leipzig in October of 1813. When the French retreated from Germany only about "...eighty thousand men were left (not counting stragglers), and a large fraction of these were wiped out by a typhus epidemic after reentering France. In fifteen months Napoleon had lost two armies totaling close to a million men....Within the space of two months the Napoleonic Empire had crashed to the ground like a great city in an earthquake."[4] In November the Austrian Ambassador Klemens von Metternich, in the Allies' name, offered Napoleon's representative a reasonable peace settlement, proposing to restore France to its borders of 1797, which included Belgium. But the emperor hesitated, and three weeks later the Allies changed their minds and invaded what

Napoleon considered "French territory." Soldiers were everywhere, but especially in the cities.

On January 31, 1814 Julie wrote to Sister Anastasia at Jumet,

> My good friend, we pray to the good God with all our hearts to
> preserve us from having people like (those troops) in our house.
> They run after women and girls like animals. You do not have to
> face anything like that because you are living in the country. But
> we have all of them coming through Namur. Unite with us in
> prayer as much as possible. We say five times a day five Our
> Fathers and five Hail Marys with extended arms, to ask the good
> God for mercy. Each hour of the day a good Sister is before the
> Blessed Sacrament; we cast ourselves into the bosom of the good
> God. I can see, my dear daughter, that even if you do not do what
> we do, you do something else by means of the sacrifices you make
> every day, with the sickness you have in your house. I ask the good
> God please to give you patience.
>
> I feel how much we need to see each other, my good daughter,
> but we must wait for the moments of the good God. This is not
> the time for going out. We have so many foreign troops in Namur.
> They say 40,000 are to come through. The Sisters would not like
> me to leave them for anything in the world. The new arrivals
> are so afraid; the older Sisters are more sensible. I must go to
> everybody to find out what is happening. People keep frightening
> one another. It is enough for the troops to be foreign, for them
> to fear the worst.[5] The troops helped themselves to any supplies
> of food they could find. When they looked for quarters, they
> commandeered any house they wanted and the people could not
> resist them.

Julie had the main entrance to the convent in Namur reinforced,
"...there was need for the precaution, for often, day and night,
heavy blows were rained upon it. The excesses committed here
and elsewhere by the soldiers were of the sort to cause the greatest anxiety."[6] As a result, Julie could not travel to her sisters. She
was confined to Namur for five months; but her anguish for the
sisters was intensified by the fact that for weeks at a time, mail
was not getting through because of the movement of troops on
the roads.

By February, food was getting more scarce as whatever supply the people had, it was taken to feed the enormous numbers of troops passing through. Julie's heart went out to everyone who was suffering. She had seventy sisters and students to feed and care for in Namur. Somehow God provided that none in her care went hungry, and there were those who were sure God intervened on behalf of Julie. An eyewitness gave the account of a sister who had been sent to get provisions from the cellar. When she told Julie that there were none to be found, she was told, "Go back again, my daughter, the good God will make you find what we need."[7] And she did.

Julie wrote to Sister Angèle at Andenne in February, "I counted on sending you a sack of flour today. I went to the market to buy some. So little of it comes for the poor people who hold out their sacks. So much is needed to feed the soldiers. It is the greatest pity in the world. In our town the trouble makes people weep. Most of these soldiers have to be provided with brandy, bread and meat. Ah, how we must thank the good God for preserving us from having these men quartered on us! We guard our gate very carefully, for if any were to come in, it would be impossible to get them out again."[8]

On February 27, 1814, Julie wrote to Sister Anastasia in Jumet warning her about the Cossacks. In her letter to the young superior, she mentioned that she hoped there would be no more Cossacks, even though she had heard a rumor that there were thirty thousand of them still to come. She warned, "Above all, guard your doors well. If a Cossack once enters your house, he will settle in it without your having the right to say a single word. We must observe the greatest vigilance. On our street door there are thirteen protective boards and a very strong bar for fear of their breaking it down. It has been shaken a lot because they wanted to enter, by night and by day. But with due care we hope to be able to protect ourselves."[9] Having caused enough concern, she follows immediately with words of encouragement. "I am confident the good God will let you draw great advantage from all these trials. Nothing causes trees to be more strongly rooted than great winds.... Ah, my God, please grant the grace that it may be for the strengthening of your work, which is always supported only by crosses."[10]

While she comforted and encouraged the sisters, Julie herself could not help but worry about them, fearing for them and the children under their care. She spent long hours in prayer, sometimes throughout the night, begging God to protect and keep them from harm. She asked the sisters to pray with the whole church for the protection of the country, as she believed that religious had a duty to pray in times of emergencies for everyone affected by them. There were times when she could hear the troops pounding on the door below as she was praying in the chapel.

The last battle of that time was fought near Paris, as the Prussians and Austrians closed in on the city. "On March 31, 1814 Czar Alexander and the king of Prussia rode down the Champs-Elysées at the head of their victorious troops. It was the first time since the Hundred Years' War that a foreign army had entered the French capital."[11]

After much debate, the urging of the Provisional Government, and with the defection of an obscure French general and a part of the emperor's army, Napoleon agreed to abdicate. The Bourbon Louis XVIII was to be restored to the throne of France. Napoleon was invited to accept the island of Elba to rule as a sovereign principality. He unsuccessfully attempted suicide by poisoning, though he became violently ill. On April 13, 1814, Napoleon signed the Act of Abdication. For a short while France seemed to be having a period of peace, after almost twenty-five years of revolution and war.

As soon as Julie sensed it safe enough to travel again, she was on the road. She risked going to Andenne on April 12, and from there visited Gembloux, Jumet, Fleurus, Ghent and Zele. With all the turmoil in the country, it is remarkable that Julie was able to open another school in Fleurus in June of 1814. Soon that foundation was flourishing.

In the midst of her concern for the communities, Julie was especially worried about Sister Catherine Daullee, superior of Ghent, whom she knew was seriously ill. She had requested the whole congregation to pray for Sister Catherine, who had imposed very severe mortifications upon herself the previous Lent as part of her prayer for peace and reconciliation in the church. However Catherine's condition worsened, and her lungs began to fill with fluid. When Julie reached Ghent, she found Sister Catherine in the last stages of her illness. When she left Ghent, Julie thought that Sister Catherine was a little better, but she died on July 1, 1814 at the age of twenty-nine. Julie felt the loss deeply; after all, Sister Catherine was one of the first Sisters of Notre Dame. She wrote to the sisters at Nouveau-Bois, "She was ripe for heaven and I am convinced that from her happy eternity she will be our protectress."[12]

For the rest of that year Julie and Françoise were kept busy visiting the houses to ensure that all was well, and negotiating for another abbey in Gembloux even though costly repairs would be required. The Congregation was expanding, and new members had to be trained while it was a time of new growth and enthusiasm. It was also a period of a very shaky peace in spite of outward appearances.

Napoleon had been brooding on the island of Elba for nearly a year. He saw an opportunity of coming back to France for another attempt to wrest the throne from the Bourbons when Louis XVIII began showing signs of restoring absolute authority to the monarchy. The king had made the mistake of "granting" a charter to the nation in which he alone would appoint the Chamber of Peers; the constituents would elect the Chamber of Deputies, following the English model, but reserving the right of legislative initiative exclusively for the crown.

What was worse was that the returning aristocratic émigrés resented having a constitution at all, and also that Napoleon's officials were holding offices that they considered their right. As though that was not enough, the émigrés saw that their lands had been sold, and there was no provision in the charter for them to be returned. "Since several million Frenchmen had purchased national property, any other solution to the problem would, beyond a doubt, have immediately precipitated another revolution; but as Talleyrand put it, the émigrés had forgotten nothing and learned nothing, and they continued to clamor for their property."[13]

The Allies, meanwhile, were haggling over territorial boundaries and kingships, and the Congress of Vienna, which opened in September, 1814, dragged on until June of 1815. The "Big Five," Prussia, Russia, Austria, Germany and France, attempted to design a stable Europe on the ruins of the Napoleonic Wars. The members of the Congress were shocked when they heard that Napoleon had landed in France early in March, 1815, and was heading for Paris. Stunned by the former emperor's peace offers which they would not even consider, the European powers, including the king of France, declared war on Napoleon, not on the country. They outlawed him for breaking the treaty he had signed at Fontainebleau only ten months before. The pressure of completing the tasks of the Congress of Vienna intensified as the Allies prepared to confront Napoleon.

Among the other settlements, Belgium was included in the Kingdom of Holland, along with the Netherlands, under the House of Orange. Napoleon was facing an enormous foe; he had counted on splitting the nations, instead he brought them together. When the "Emperor" announced that he was the "Son of the Revolution," the unexpected occurred. Thousands of men came under his command, and with incredible speed, Napoleon's army crossed the Belgian frontier on June 15, and drove back the Prussian forces. In two brilliant moves, Napoleon defeated the Prussians at Ligny, while the French General, Ney, held back Wellington at Quatre Bras, forcing him to retreat to Brussels. But when faced with the task of keeping the Prussians and the Anglo-Dutch forces from joining against them, Napoleon's army found themselves divided and exhausted. They pursued Wellington and found him at Mont St. Jean, near the village of Waterloo.

Once again troops stormed across Belgium, only this time *it* was the scene of the war; "...it was the towns of Fleurus, Jumet, and Gembloux that were overrun. There was fighting at Fleurus, and skirmishes in the surrounding cantons. From the sisters' windows could be seen the bombarding cannons, and ranks of soldiers falling under fire."[14] There was no time to recall the sisters from the convents closest to the battlefields. On June 18, the fateful day of the Battle of Waterloo, after Napoleon was defeated, scores of soldiers from all the armies involved, roamed the cities and countryside looking for provisions, or for a place to heal their wounded.

A band of soldiers broke into the convent at Fleurus, one of the closest towns to the battlefield. They were searching for something to eat, but when they heard the sisters who had fled to the top of the house, they raced up the stairs after them. They stopped suddenly on the landing, when they saw a statue of Our Lady through a doorway. They looked at each other; then just as suddenly turned, quietly walked down the stairs, and out of the house.

Terrified, the sisters quickly gathered together the boarders in order to run to a house of a trusted neighbor. They had to climb over a fence to reach safety; after scaling it, they discovered one of their number was missing. In spite of their fear they returned to the house to search for the missing person. Once they had found her, they scurried to the neighbor's house where they thought they would be safe. But once again soldiers stormed through the doorway. Quickly the sisters fled to the attic, but not fast enough; one of the soldiers caught the arm of a sister, who was able to shake herself free. Another sister managed to escape and run for help. Fortunately a group of policemen was nearby, and they ushered the soldiers out of the house. But, "...even before the police came, one of the soldiers, who was more humane than the rest, cried out, 'Let us leave these poor devils alone, and get out.'"[15] The sisters had removed their white capes, and were huddled together in the attic, hoping they would not be seen, when the group leader gave word for the soldiers to leave, and no one was harmed.

However, the sisters stayed in their neighbor's refuge for four weeks before they could return to their convent. At their arrival they found that the soldiers had used the convent for a field hospital, and had taken all the mattresses, sheets, and curtains with them when they departed. The convent was in shambles; there was evidence all over of the many crude surgeries performed there. The sisters offered heartfelt prayers of thanksgiving for being safe at home again.

The Gembloux convent was not as fortunate. Soldiers climbed through the windows, pillaged and destroyed everything. When the regiment of Cossacks stormed into the abbey, nineteen-year-old Sister Theresia, the youngest member of the Steenhaut family, was terrified. A Prussian officer arrived just in time to spare the sisters any harm, but Sister Theresia never recovered from the shock of the experience. Julie sent her to Ghent to be close to her parents, hoping she would recover, but Sister Theresia died on February 7, 1815.[16]

Jumet, too, was threatened, but because of the kindness of a Prussian officer, they were spared any insult. However, the sisters gave what food they had to the soldiers, whether they were Prussian or French. The sisters were grateful that the Prussian officer stayed in the convent for several days to protect them and the boarders there from harm. They never forgot his kindness.

Following the Battle of Waterloo, Namur felt the brunt of the retreating armies; French soldiers entered the city on June 19. The townspeople did not know if the fighting was over, or what the defeat of the army meant. Napoleon had escaped to Paris, and the troops had to fend for themselves. The next day the Prussians were firing their cannons at the gates of the city, but there was no response from the French for the "Grande Armée" was without ammunition. When the general of the Prussians realized how kind the townspeople had been to the soldiers, and that there was no resistance coming from them, he ceased the firing to spare the city. The Prussians entered Namur through one gate while the French soldiers left through another, and the fighting ceased.

In describing these events, Françoise ends with, "This is not a story of the war.... It is merely an account of the providence of God, and a tribute of thanksgiving, which we wish to pass on to the Sisters who will come after us."[17] The townspeople erected a special altar in the Namur cathedral in honor of Our Lady in thanksgiving for the town having been spared utter destruction.

The suffering Julie experienced during this time took a toll on her health. Surrounded with the violence of war, her heart went out not only to her prime concern, the sisters and boarders, but to the people suffering all around her. It is said that she and some of the sisters helped to tear sheets to make bandages for the wounded. She had to keep up the courage of all those in her care, yet sometimes she did not hear from the sisters for weeks, as no road out of Namur was safe. She hid some of the precious objects that had been given to the congregation, and took every precaution to keep the sisters and students free from danger.

Françoise recalled, "She (Julie) was all solicitude for the daughters God had confided to her, considering them as a precious charge; and seeing the dangers to which they were exposed, she suffered anguish in body and soul in her anxiety for their safety. This was especially true of the Sisters who lived in the small houses near the scenes of conflict. She knew they were surrounded by war; she heard frightful stories of what was going on, or was even more distressed by getting no news at all. It was with great strength of soul that she listened to the alarming reports, and she encouraged us who were with her, inspiring us with trust in God."[18]

While she was urging those around her to have confidence in the good God as she did, Julie's appearance began to change. Worn out by the enormous stress of the days of war, and allowing herself very little sleep, Julie became very ill shortly after the fighting ended. Her mother's heart withstood the strain while the danger was imminent, but when relief came, her body rebelled.

Chapter XIII

THE LAST JOURNEY
1815–1816

A month after the Battle of Waterloo, July 20, 1815, Julie wrote to Sister Angèle at Andenne, "Let us expect all kinds of vicissitudes as long as we are in this life, for it is nothing but change. Everything ends, everything ends and so do we. Life is sometimes so short...."[1] She had seen seven of her sisters die already, and all but one had been in her twenties or younger. Julie herself had had a close brush with death shortly before she wrote the letter. It happened after most of the hoards of troops had passed, but there were always "...laggards who come at the end and who are not the best characters. They hurl insults."[2] They stole whatever means they could to return to their homes, which were often at great distances from the battlefields. Quite suddenly a farmer would be attacked, and his horses and wagon taken. Not surprisingly, carriage drivers were somewhat reluctant to use any roads they thought might still have soldiers on them. But apparently, Julie found one driver willing to take the risk.

As she was leaving Ghent, a "laggard" jumped on the carriage Julie was using, and holding a huge stone over the head of the driver, threatened to kill him unless he turned over his carriage. "But," Julie commented, the stone "...would have hit me instead. He had climbed on the back of the carriage and the driver told him quite simply to get off. I was greatly astonished to see him with a big stone in his hand, ready to throw it at François (the

175

Monseigneur Pisani de la Gaude.

driver). François would not have been hit by it, but I would have been. That is how calamities happen. But that won't prevent me from visiting you as soon as I see that there are no longer so many troop movements."[3] Somehow both Julie and the driver escaped with their lives.

Apart from the terrors the citizens still experienced at the end of the fighting, there was the devastation left by the pillaging and destruction of property afterwards. Gembloux lay in ruins. Julie's heart ached at the thought of what the sisters experienced there. She wrote, "In Gembloux they left nothing of the Sisters' provisions of beer, wheat, flour, butter—in short, nothing at all! I sent them money to buy some wheat to start with. With the help of the good God, they shall not be in want as long as there is a soul in the Motherhouse. Everything is in common. If it pleases the good God, their children will return after the holidays. But everybody is ruined; all the farms have been sacked. Well, let us abandon everything to God. Let us lean on him. Woe to the man who leans on man, who has only an earthly arm to offer; he will fall with him."[4]

This last comment was prophetic, even if Julie was not referring at all to what was to come. The final great trial of her life, and the one which caused her the greatest sufferings came from the very persons she had loved and trusted all through the agonizing days in Amiens. While there was yet no indication of unrest among the sisters, nor any hint of suspicion regarding her, Julie said to Françoise, "Daughter, there is still one more trial I must endure." Her devoted friend admitted that she reacted just as Peter had done to Christ, replying, "No, Mother, that cannot be; you went through enough at Amiens. It was predicted (Julie) said, that I should be persecuted by bishops, priests and the Sisters. All is not over yet."[5] Ironically, it was Père Enfantin who had been the instrument to bring about her cure, who had predicted this last suffering for Julie.

In order to comprehend the magnitude of the accusations against Julie, it is necessary to go back to 1806 when Napoleon was enjoying enormous power all through Europe. Having signed the Concordat with Rome in 1801, reestablishing the Catholic Church in France on the condition that there would be freedom of religion, and a recognition of France as a Republic, Napoleon went on to decide that he, rather than the church, knew best what should be taught in France. By 1806, Napoleon had conquered Italy, had a medal struck with his image under which was written, *Rex Totius Italiae*, and took upon himself the task of reorganizing the Italian church as he had done the French, without any reference to the pope.

In addition, he would introduce the French Civil Code in Italy by which the whole family cycle—birth, upbringing, marriage and death—was henceforth supervised by the state, not the church as it had been for centuries. The final blow was the fact that divorce, now rampant in France, was to be allowed in Italy. The young secular ruler decided that there were too many cate-chisms in Europe, and there was a great need for a "Universal Catechism" to be used in all classrooms of the entire empire. This, he reasoned, would be a source of unity. Too, he thought it not without merit that it could be an opportunity to instill respect for his authority, which he deemed essential for good governance. Fortunately for Napoleon, he had an ally in Cardinal Caprara, who represented the pope as well as all of the French bishops loyal to him, who agreed on the need of such a catechism. So by May of 1806, it became obligatory to teach the young in their Sunday schools, the "truths" that the emperor found very useful for them to learn. Among the lessons con-tained in the "Universal Catechism" were the following ques-tions and answers which were to be memorized by all students of the empire:

Q.: What are the duties of Christians towards the princes who govern them, and what in particular, are our duties toward Napoleon I, our Emperor?

A.: Christians owe to the princes who govern them, and we in par-ticular, owe to Napoleon I, our Emperor, love, respect, obedience, loyalty, military service, and the taxes ordered for the preserva-tion and defence of the Empire and his throne; we also owe him fervent prayers for his safety, and for the spiritual and temporal prosperity of the state.

Q.: Why are we bound in all these duties towards our Emperor?

A.: First, because God, who creates Empires and apportions them according to His will by heaping His gifts upon him, set him up as our sovereign, and made him the agent of His power and His image on earth. Thus it is that to honor and serve our Emperor is to honor and serve God Himself. Secondly, because our Savior Jesus Christ taught us both by example and by precept what we owe to our sovereign; for He was born under obedience to Caesar Augustus, He paid the prescribed taxes, and in the same breath as He said "Render to God that which belongs to God," He said, "Render to Caesar that which belongs to Caesar."

Q.: Are there special reasons why we should have a particular loyalty to Napoleon I, our Emperor?

A.: Yes, there are; for God raised him up in difficult times to reestablish the public practice of the holy religion of our ancestors, and to protect it. He restored and preserved public order by his deep and active wisdom; he defends the state by the strength of his arm; he has become the Lord's Anointed by the consecration he received from the Sovereign Pontiff, the head of the Church Universal.

Q.: What ought one to think of those who fail in their duty towards our Emperor?

A.: According to the Apostle St. Paul they are resisting the order established by God Himself and making themselves worthy of eternal damnation.[6]

Rome never did approve of the catechism even though Cardinal Caprara said it did. Nor did Rome approve of introducing August 16 as the "Feast of St. Napoleon"—an effort to eclipse the traditional feast of the Assumption on the previous day. No one seemed able to confirm that there *was* such a saint as Napoleon, but even if there were, the church reserved the right to designate a new feast day. It is small wonder that tensions grew between Pius VII and the emperor. With Napoleon continuing to interfere in church affairs, insisting that he had the right to appoint bishops and to rearrange dioceses at will, the bishops were increasingly alarmed by the erosion of church liberties.

In June of 1811, when the emperor invited all the bishops to the National Council of Paris, it had become clear that Napoleon intended to rule the church as he would rule the entire empire; after all, he had taken the Papal States and had the pope under guard. Bishops de Broglie of Ghent, Hirn of Tournai and d'Aviau of Bordeaux made up the committee that was to draw up a response to the emperor. They clearly expressed their refusal to accept Napoleon's terms. The emperor was outraged and immediately dissolved the council. He arrested Bishop de Broglie and sent him into isolation at Vincennes. After demanding de Broglie's resignation as bishop of Ghent and sending him to Beaune under police surveillance, the Cathedral Chapter in Ghent refused to elect a vicar in protest.

Napoleon's response to that act of insubordination was to imprison Bishop de Broglie on the Island of Marguerite for a year and appointed a new bishop of Ghent whom the Flemish priests refused to accept. By 1814, when Napoleon was forced to abdicate the first time, Bishop de Broglie was given assurance by Pope Pius VII that his appointment to the See of Ghent was valid, and Napoleon's had no canonical validity. When Bishop de Broglie returned to Ghent, the Sisters of Notre Dame rejoiced to see him vindicated.

While all these events were taking place, and bishops were watched carefully by the imperial police for any signs of resistance to the emperor, Bishop Pisani de la Gaude was left free in his diocese, and seemed to be immune from persecution. Rumors started to circulate that the bishop of Namur must be one of "Napoleon's men." He had been appointed by the emperor, but his appointment had been approved by Rome in 1804. In fact, it was through *his* efforts that the government finally gave up the idea of introducing the "Universal Catechism" for the country. But while his fellow bishops were hunted down and imprisoned, Bishop Pisani was relatively free, partially due to the influence of one of Napoleon's ministers, Jean Etienne Portalis, who was a loyal friend of the bishop, and a confidant of the emperor. Besides, Napoleon was inclined to protect his own appointments.

But in such times of unrest and change, suspicions abounded of anyone who seemed immune from interference from the government. Good people of Ghent began to whisper that Bishop Pisani *must* be supporting Napoleon. How else could anyone explain his apparent immunity, while their bishop was condemned to exile?

Although Bishop Pisani was the prime target of their attack, Françoise related that "...the blows rebounded upon our Mother, who was grieved beyond measure over the controversy. Some acted as if she were a party to the conflict, or a person not to be trusted—she, who was so simple and upright, so tenderly devoted to the Church; who, as I say, would have sacrificed her life a thousand times to preserve the integrity of the faith.... Her charity was able to find excuses for them, though they were the cause of her suffering. 'Their motives are good' she would say."[7]

The fact that her own sisters began to question her loyalty to the church, and that they brought their complaints to the bishop, caused Julie intense suffering. Françoise was at a loss to describe the sorrow Julie felt when she wrote, "No, I could never give an adequate idea of what Mère Julie was made to suffer during this time: the harassments, the anxieties, the alarms of conscience she endured, about which time and experience have shown she had no part."[8] "The last trial she underwent was probably, for one with as tender a heart as hers, the most painful of her life."[9] Julie felt the condemnation so much that she wrote to Père le Surre, Vicar General of the Ghent diocese:

You are aware, Monsieur, of the difficulties which have arisen concerning religious opinion regarding the *Universal Catechism*. M...has put into the minds of the young Sisters of Ghent some fears that I might follow the views of my bishop, to whom he attributes suspect opinions. For several years I have been attacked in the most extreme manner about him. I have nothing against my bishop, whom I regard as my superior, and I am not concerned with all these matters. But that is what has turned these gentlemen of Flanders against me. They have managed to prejudice the Sisters in my regard, saying that sooner or later I would be likely to draw them into error. In fact, I have suffered the most violent attacks without giving any occasion for them.[10]

In the second letter to Père le Surre, Julie addresses the other complaint the sisters brought against her. The young sisters in Ghent, who defined strict observance of the rule as a measure of perfection, began to question Julie's adherence to the tentative rule that was being used by the congregation until one could be written that suited the needs of the community. The rule that the sisters were using was originally written for a group of religious in Rome, and was entitled, "Rule of the Institute of Mary." It had been given to the sisters as an experiment, in order to inspire a religious spirit, but was not intended to be the final rule of the Sisters of Notre Dame. Julie had a freedom of spirit regarding it, and would often change the time of instructions if she thought that necessary to prepare the new members for their teaching. There was an apparent misunderstanding by some well-meaning persons about the origin of the rule being used at the time. In explaining herself to the vicar general, Julie said, "...there are some articles which it is not possible for us to follow exactly. The bishop (of Namur) and his vicar general know about this. We have a great number of children. Besides, our house being the motherhouse, and receiving subjects who need the most basic formation in regard to everything, it is of a totally different sort from that of Ghent. The house at Namur is a school for our young people, of whom at present we have a large number; they must be instructed from morning until evening...."[11] She would say to Françoise, "I do not adhere slavishly to a regulation when I see a greater good to be done, because for us nothing is yet really settled."[12]

Julie shed many tears over the mistrust of her sisters, especially the ones who had been with her from the beginning of the congregation, Ciska and Marie Steenhaut, and Catherine Daullee who fortunately was reconciled with Julie before her death. But some continued to be critical of her until after the foundress died, and only then did they realize their mistake. Sister Gertrude wrote:

At the present day, writing after the death of our revered Mother, I see things in another light; what I thought exaggerated and extraordinary in her conduct now appears to add fresh lustre to her life by wonderful examples of virtues which are rarely seen.... Notwithstanding all the pain she must naturally have felt in being thus judged by her own daughters, she preserved the most perfect calmness of mind; she never tried to vindicate herself but having at heart the glory of God and the propagation of her Institute, she employed with great prudence the means which would lead her children to love not herself, but Truth alone. The more I consider her life, the more persuaded I am that she was guided by the Spirit of God.[13]

What was more alarming was that some of the clergy in Ghent and Tournai went so far as to suggest that the congregation ought to be divided by dioceses in order to separate Namur from Flanders and Hainault.[14] But Bishop Pisani intervened and appointed Abbé Minsart, the good friend of Julie and Françoise, as the ecclesiastical superior of the congregation. It was he who defended the foundress to the other clerics, and protected the congregation from division.

Julie had known rejection many times, but this was the most difficult. At one point in her life, whenever her good friend, Père Thomas seemed to question her integrity for not immediately returning some of his possessions, she teased Françoise saying, "You are the only one left—you will fail me too, one day—it will come." But her faithful friend hastily added, "That day did not come."[15] "God willed to draw her closer to Himself by allowing her to pass through a trial that would wound her heart and bring to perfection all her virtues; it was the last brush-stroke of the Divine Artist on a soul that would soon receive the sweet reward of her bitterest trial."[16]

Françoise faithfully stood by her friend, trying to console her, but even Julie came to a point of questioning herself. She said to Françoise, "It is possible sometimes to be at fault without realizing it. You must go to the bishop to ask his pardon for me."[17] When Françoise went to see Bishop Pisani, he was astounded that Julie felt she was at fault; the only "fault" he would accuse her of was that she was killing herself, since she had not taken care of her health.

A couple of incidents occurred before she became ill that appeared to hint of her approaching death. On one occasion after the evening meal, Julie noticed a piece of meat that was left on a platter, shaped like a death's head. She commented that this did not occur by chance. During recreation at another time, she related an interesting dream she had.

> I was walking down a little road...that ran the length of a narrow strip of land and ended at the water's edge. Deep water lay to left and right and ahead where the road ended, and I was frightened. From across the water, on a distant shore, voices called to me, "Come over to us," but I was afraid. I sat down in the middle of the road and called back, "I would rather someone came to bring me."[18]

Julie laughed when she related her dream to the sisters, but shortly afterwards they noticed the signs of her last illness.

Intuitively, Julie knew her life was ebbing away from her. On November 27, 1815, she wrote to Sister Anastasia at Jumet: "I am growing so old. Every day I fear to be suddenly overtaken by death. I go on as if I were twenty, but that will pass like many other things. My good friend, let us work with all our hearts at purifying our intentions ever more in all we do. Let us never lose sight of the eye that sees all, the ear that hears all, the hand that writes it all down. A short time hence and we shall no longer be."[19]

In December, she had a terrible fall. The pain was so intense that she fainted, and had to be carried to her room. In spite of a severe headache, as soon as she came to herself she resumed her work. Some days later she wrote to Sister Julienne at Fleurus, "I fell backward on the big staircase, which was being washed....I hope it won't be anything. Two Sisters picked me up. My head is a bit heavy, (from a bad cold) but I am confident it won't be anything, if it pleases the good God."[20]

Shortly afterwards, in a letter to Sister Anastasia, death was on her mind. While expressing a wish to visit the sisters in Jumet at the "first possible moment," Julie went on to say, "I think that soon you and I shall see things we should never have thought possible. Patience, the good God has his plans; let us adore them with all our hearts! My God, we are willing to feel that we are still in this land of exile, so that we may not be attached to it! Oh no, no, our abode is not here below. My good daughter, let us sigh for our dear homeland, heaven."[21] Gradually her health declined and by the middle of January, 1816, Julie was unable to leave Namur.

Françoise was amazed at Julie's endurance of suffering. She claimed that if proof of her sanctity were needed for her friend, watching Julie in her last illness would be sufficient. For three months the foundress experienced agonizing pain, accompanied by sudden changes that would cause the sisters to vacillate between periods of hope for her recovery and fear for her death. Françoise expressed her confusion when she said, "It was impossible to discover whether she wished to live or die."[22]

Eventually Julie lost her appetite, and became so nauseated that she could tolerate only a few drops of water at a time. As a result, her body slowly diminished until she looked emaciated. She suffered from extreme fatigue. Françoise wrote, "The nerves of her neck became at times so rigid that she seemed about to strangle; there was no way of giving her relief except to put her in a warm bath, which helped a little. The slightest noise was a torment. "We spoke to her in as few words as possible."[23]

Throughout her remaining months, Julie's confidence in God remained steadfast. She asked the sisters to arrange for her to receive the last sacraments which were administered to her the next day. Once again, as in her youth, she lay helpless on her bed. Françoise visited and read to her as she had done when they first met in Amiens. At Julie's request she would read a few lines from her favorite book, *The Imitation of Christ*. Even though Julie could not see the words, Françoise described "...how she would put her finger on a passage and say, 'That is the part; read that;' ...the verse was always appropriate."[24] One day the passage was, "If you carry the cross willingly, it will carry you and bring you to your wished-for end; where there will be an end of suffering, though here on earth there will not be."[25] The words seemed to comfort both of them.

At Namur, the community still hoped for a cure. Parish priests asked their congregations to pray for her recovery; the pupils in the schools joined their supplications to those of their teachers; large sums were given in alms for this intention. And as his feast approached, the sisters began novena after novena to Saint Joseph for Julie's cure. When Julie asked Françoise to see to it that three poor children were dressed in honor of Saint Joseph, she answered that she would if the Saint granted them the favor they requested of him. Suspecting something, Julie replied, "Oh, go quickly and promise the Blessed Virgin you will."[26] Françoise promised.

In the end, Saint Joseph did answer the prayers of the community, even though it was not the response they had hoped for: Julie had a happy and peaceful death. Françoise described it, "Never once, right up to her last breath, did she show by word or sign any anxiety, desire, or fear; and this was not at all the effect of her malady. She remained fully conscious right to the end. Her peace was the effect of grace and virtue."[27]

By the end of March, Julie's condition had taken a serious turn for the worse. The sisters had moved her to Françoise's room, as there was no fireplace in her own. On the wall at the foot of the bed there was a picture of Christ being taken down from the cross. Julie could not look at the picture without weeping. She asked Françoise to remove it. Convinced that she was unworthy to continue leading the congregation, she told her friend, "God is taking me out of the world because I am not worthy to carry on His work."[28] With genuine love and humility she begged Françoise's forgiveness for any pain she may have caused her. She, in turn, could only remember the love and goodness she experienced from Julie for over twenty years.

When she was convulsing in her illness, the sisters would look fearful but Julie would comfort them, saying, "Come now, it will be over in a minute; do not be alarmed." It was anguish for Françoise to watch Julie suffer. She nursed her devotedly until, worn out by fatigue and sorrow, she herself was afflicted by an epidemic fever, complicated by pleurisy. Françoise's condition became so serious that a priest was called to administer the last sacraments to her. The following day holy Viaticum was carried to Julie and Françoise. The sisters were grief-stricken by the possibility of losing both of them.

Word began to spread that Julie was dying. The older boarders begged for the privilege of receiving her last blessing; many of the priests in Namur came to visit the holy woman who had so deeply moved them. Having heard that one of the poor girls, Therese Tasset, was heart-broken at the thought of losing her, Julie sent for the child, drew her close to the bed, and gently reminding her of the good God, gave her comfort and blessed her. On April 2 she sent a message to the teachers. "Tell your little girls that I bless them with all my heart; tell them to remember the good God in every circumstance of their lives, and to seek first in all things what will make their salvation secure; the rest shall be added to them."[29]

Bishop Pisani, who had done so much to assist Julie establish her congregation, was struck by the fever and confined to bed. It seemed that those who were closest to her during her life, were kept from being with her in her last hours. But on the sixth of April Françoise dragged herself out of bed and went to Julie. She sank into a chair where she could see her, and Françoise was startled by the change in Julie's face. She could not hold back the tears; she knew the end was near. Julie, noticing the tears, asked Françoise where her confidence had gone. When she was leaving the room, overcome by emotion she could not bring herself to go to Julie's bed, as was her custom, and say goodnight.

The next day when Françoise returned to visit the patient, weak as she was, Julie shook her finger at Françoise and scolded "God was not pleased yesterday."[30] Françoise knew the cause of Julie's displeasure. Humbly Julie looked at her friend and asked, "Will you come back again tonight?" Françoise was too ill; she had to say, "No, my fever has gone up again."[31] She kissed Julie goodnight; feeling very weak, she barely made it back to her own room where she fell upon the bed. The sisters were not sure that Françoise would live through the night. So after all they had been through together, supporting one another during the difficult times, Julie was deprived of her friend's presence at the moment of her death. At the close of the account of her last encounter with Julie, Françoise wrote, "When I saw her again, she was dead."[32]

Many of the sisters had been afflicted by the epidemic, and were confined to bed; while the rest, exhausted by the care of the students and the sick, were sent to their rooms to get some rest. A few sisters sat with Julie as they noticed her breathing became more difficult, and her color changed. She asked that her funeral be simple as that of a poor person, and taking off a little reliquary that she wore, she gave it to Sister Eulalie as a remembrance of her.

The sisters sat by quietly in order to let their patient rest, when suddenly they heard Julie's weak voice begin to sing gently her favorite hymn, the "Magnificat." Her soul, indeed, seemed to "magnify the Lord." As she finished the hymn, she slipped into unconsciousness; it was about seven o'clock in the evening. The sisters sent for Canon Renson, who came and sat by Julie during the night to give her the last blessing, and to pray with the infirmarian and other sisters present at her bedside. At two o'clock in the morning Julie breathed her last breath so gently that they had to hold a mirror to her face to see if she were still breathing. She was finally released from her suffering on Monday, April 8, 1816. Her last words described what was in store for her: "My spirit rejoices in God my Savior."

Françoise was notified immediately. Although she was very weak, she insisted on being brought to Julie's room. She sat for a long time, tears streaming down her cheeks. She felt so alone now, bereft of her trusted confidante and superior. There was no rule yet; the congregation was still in its infancy; and tensions between the motherhouse and Ghent were not resolved. While she shed tears of grief at so great a loss, no longer able to sense encouragement and love from that wonderful smile of Julie's, she was confident that Julie would be their protectress in heaven.

Early in the morning all the sisters who were able, gathered around Julie's bed to pray. They had dressed her in her religious habit, and placed two burning candles on either side of her cross which had been placed on a table next to her bed. They were very startled to see her face, the features were rejuvenated, and all traces of suffering were gone. People who came to pay their respects remarked on how beautiful and peaceful she looked, as though she were flushed with health. Her color was natural, and many commented that she appeared to be smiling. They were reassured that she was watching over them from her place in heaven.

Word spread through Namur that Julie had died, and people meeting each other exclaimed, "The saint is dead." Before long hundreds of people were coming to the convent asking for some token of the "saint." When Bishop Pisani was told that Julie wished a simple funeral, he would not hear of it. It was Holy Week, so the funeral had to be celebrated on Wednesday, April 10, since the Sacred Triduum was to begin on Thursday.

The bishop appointed the Vicar General, Père Medard, to represent him as the presider for the mass. Bishop Pisani was still too ill to attend the funeral, but he wrote to Sister Eulalie on the very day of Julie's death, expressing his regret at being unable to be with the foundress at the hour of her death. The seventy-three year old prelate assured the sisters of his prayers for Françoise's recovery; he feared she might "sink under this terrible blow." At his own expense Bishop Pisani obtained a walled vault at the local public cemetery for Julie. Suddenly, all over the city were seen notices that "Mère Julie Billiart, the saint, is dead."

The funeral was celebrated with the full solemnity given to persons of great importance. The parish church of Saint Joseph was crowded for the requiem mass. As soon as the liturgy ended, all the bells of Namur tolled their sorrowful message. Over four hundred people joined in the procession behind the casket that had to be carried on a circuitous route around the town to accommodate the devotion of so many people; most of the shops were closed. The elderly Père Medard walked directly behind the coffin, immediately followed by eighteen torchbearers; next in turn came the sisters and children from the school all bearing lighted candles, and hundreds of townspeople. Strangers passing through Namur on April 10, seeing the procession testified later that they were told, "The saint is dead! We have lost a saint!"[33]

Letters came from Bishop Demandolx, Père Thomas, Père

Varin and countless others who testified again and again to Julie's holiness and her apostolic zeal. When Bishop Pisani finally recovered, he came to the motherhouse to console Françoise and the sisters, telling them that Julie "...was one of those souls who do more for the church in a few years, than hundreds of others, good though they may be without her apostolic spirit, can do in a century."[34]

The epitaph which was to be placed on Julie's tombstone was composed by Père Medard. On it he had etched a brief summary of her founding of the Sisters of Notre Dame, a list of the houses she had established, and added "...after having exhausted her strength by her excessive labours for the glory of God, she fell asleep in the Lord, as much regretted by those who survived her, as admired by those who knew her."[35] When it was ready, Sister Anastasia Leleu, who had rushed to Namur after Julie's death and was immediately transferred there, wished to direct the erection of the tombstone herself. Taking a couple of sisters with her and two trustworthy workmen, she went to the cemetery and removed the four walls surrounding the grave. Unable to resist the intense desire to look once more on the face of her closest friend, she gave some money to the sexton, and asked him to remove himself from the location for a while. The two workmen pried open the coffin and to the amazement of those there, Julie appeared just as healthy and fresh as she had appeared in life; her limbs were flexible when they moved them and there was no stiffness in her fingers.

Tears of joy and sorrow together poured down the faces of the sisters as they knelt in prayer around the grave. Sister Anastasia gently removed the ivory crucifix that had been placed in her hands; the one she had so often held when she was praying, and kissed so reverently. She also took her large rosary, and some of the cloth that had covered Julie, then quickly had the workmen replace the cover of the coffin.

Returning to the convent, the sisters went immediately to Françoise to give her the precious items they had recovered. The new Superior General, Françoise, knelt, her eyes filling with tears as she gazed at the crucifix. As so many times in the past,

Mère St. Joseph Blin de Bourdon
Co-Foundress of the Sisters of Notre Dame de Namur.

the cross was the symbol of Julie's life, and that ivory crucifix brought the two friends together again for a brief moment.

Sisters and pupils regularly visited Julie's tomb to pray for her intercession. Many remarked of experiencing a keen sense of her presence with them as they prayed. Others claimed they were cured by her intercession.

When William I, king of the Netherlands, began his rule in 1815, a new wave of fear gripped the people of Belgium. Once again Catholics began to worry that they would be persecuted for practicing their faith, for the king was a Protestant, and determined to rid the country of Catholicism.

By 1817, Françoise had a vault built in the garden of the motherhouse in the crypt of a little oratory, planning to remove Julie's body and place it there to protect it from any desecration that might occur in the public cemetery. So on July 27, 1817, Sister Anastasia and her companions went to the cemetery as if to pray there. Once again they gave some money to the grave diggers to uncover the coffin and then go away for a while so they could "pray in private." The sisters found Julie's body still incorrupt. Quickly they wrapped her body in a cloth they had hidden under their cloaks; closed the coffin again, and had the grave diggers bury it. They carried Julie's body home to the motherhouse without anyone knowing what they had done. Bishop Pisani knew of their plans but never asked any questions regarding them. As far as he was concerned, he knew nothing about what happened.

For the next few years only the sisters and a few priests knew of the location of Julie's body, for fear of the government. When some of the sisters came to Namur for retreat during the holidays and learned that their foundress was buried near the little chapel in the garden, Sister Jeanne, Superior of Jumet, and Sister Gertrude, Superior of Gembloux, remembered that one day when Julie was walking with them in the garden during recreation, and looked at the spot where the chapel now stood, she said to them, "This is the place in which my miserable body will rest one day."[36] Neither of them had ever quoted Julie's comment to anyone.

Chapter XIV

GOD'S WORK
1816–ON

Julie often told Françoise, "It is God's work, not ours." Then she would wait with confidence to see God act, and believed that it was divine Providence that kept the congregation going. Françoise believed Julie, but when her dearest friend died, time seemed to stand still. After Julie's death, Françoise was still seriously ill, to the point where the sisters did not know if she would survive. There was no approved rule, and within the year Montdidier, the last house in France, was closed. There were at that time fifty-eight Sisters of Notre Dame, and twenty-five novices needing formation. Françoise was grateful that Sister Anastasia Leleu had come from Jumet immediately after hearing of Julie's death; Françoise felt the need of Julie's "petit conseil," and was deeply touched to have her come to her side so quickly. She had greeted Sister Anastasia in a voice broken with emotion, saying, "My dear child, this is just like you; take care of your Sisters."

The community instinctively turned to Françoise for direction, and earnestly prayed for her recovery. Père Varin wrote to her from Paris:

...I am sure that the work of which she (Julie) has been the instrument in the hands of God, far from suffering from her loss, will receive fresh prosperity through her intercession, for who could help having recourse now to her prayers? If they were so power-

ful over the Heart of God when she was in this place of exile,
surely they will be more powerful now that she is in her heavenly
home....[1]

Although Françoise prayed to Julie for guidance and strength
her physical condition worsened. One evening Sister Eulalie
gathered the boarders together to make the Way of the Cross in
the chapel to pray for Françoise's recovery. Gradually her body
gained strength, but it was not until the twenty-first of May that
she was able to meet with the whole community. They unani-
mously voted for her to replace Julie as Superior General on
June 2, 1816, in the presence of Père Medard, the Vicar General,
and two other clerics. Sister Anastasia was appointed her
Assistant, and became Françoise's greatest support.

While the others rejoiced, Françoise recognized in a more
profound way than ever before, that if the congregation were to
continue, it would have to be "God's work." She confided her
fears about her own competence to Père Medard, who had no
doubt that she was the right choice of the sisters, and encouraged her with his confidence in her ability. Although she was in
her sixtieth year, once physically revived, her energy and
courage took on the spirit that Julie had tried to instill in her sisters. Often Françoise would begin her words with, "Mère Julie
wished us to..." and in this way, she kept alive the memory of
Julie's personal influence.

Her first major task was to complete the provisional rule that
had been used during the fifteen years of the existence of the
congregation. By September, 1818, Françoise had a rule that the
sisters had approved, and one to which Bishop Pisani gave his
approbation, proclaiming himself its protector. This official
recognition greatly heartened the sisters who had undergone so
much from the misunderstandings and confusion surrounding
the rule during the last months of Julie's life. Now Françoise
could devote her time to the education of the novices, and the
development of the teachers in the secondary houses.

Julie had always predicted, beginnings would be marked by
the cross which was the sign of God's blessing on any work of
the Sisters of Notre Dame. This time the suffering came from

events occurring in the government. William of Orange, though King of Holland, had been given the rule over Belgium as well, following the Battle of Waterloo. The two countries, separated by language and religion, were very distinct in character. Holland had kept an educational system going even during the worst years of the Napoleonic Wars. Belgium on the other hand, had a dismal record when it came to education. Some of the villages had been fortunate enough to hire a literate teacher, but many others hired the cheapest person they could find to "look after" the small children, while the rest of the family worked in the fields during harvest time. Many places had no pretense of educating the children at all. William, once his rival Napoleon was out of the way, decided to institute schools throughout Belgium, and bring them all under the control of the government. He recognized that such a system could work decidedly to his advantage. For awhile, schools conducted by religious were not subject to much scrutiny, but gradually, the government began to require rigorous examinations of the teachers in all the schools, frequently marking down those conducted by religious. Françoise countered the trend by exacting more study and preparation from the sisters, and would not allow any of the novices into the secondary houses until they were well prepared.

Whatever the sisters tried to do to meet the demands of the government, it was not enough. Patterning himself after Napoleon, William envisioned establishing a church of Belgium with himself as ruler, and completely independent of Rome. Once again the sisters faced the challenge of standing against a schismatic church. In May, 1818, two ordinances appeared from the Minister of Worship relative to religious communities:

> Henceforth there were to be no houses of contemplative religious. These were of no use in the kingdom, and they must disappear. As for the teaching congregations, they would be tolerated until the day when the Department of Public Instruction should be ready to function throughout the kingdom.[2]

Restrictions multiplied, and it became more apparent that William and the Ministers of Worship and Education wanted to rid themselves of religious orders. The only ones who escaped this kind of persecution were the nursing communities. The reason for their exemption was the simple one that the government had no trained persons to replace them. The government went so far as to dictate how many sisters could be in each convent, and made exact recording of the number a strict requirement. During this period, Françoise was receiving numerous requests for sisters to open new schools. She had to refuse several dioceses as it was becoming more and more difficult to receive subjects at the motherhouse.

Yet even during this worrisome time, the reputation for excellence of the Sisters of Notre Dame spread throughout Belgium and Holland. In 1819, Father Wolff who was the Provincial of the Jesuit missionaries in Holland, approached Françoise to ask a favor of her. Two of his penitents showed signs of a religious vocation, and he was anxious to begin a congregation in Holland in order to establish religious schools to preserve Christian ideals there. He wanted his foundation to be modelled after the Sisters of Notre Dame, and requested that his subjects be trained in one of their convents.

Françoise was enthusiastic about the idea. After the first two subjects arrived in Ghent, she recommended to Father Wolff that he try to find at least six women who wished to begin his foundation. This would provide him with a solid group who could start a house in Holland, and be prepared to train new subjects. The priest welcomed the suggestion and consequently, from 1818 to 1824, seven Dutch postulants were trained at Ghent and Namur. Once they were thoroughly prepared, Father Wolff recalled them to Holland where they established the Congregation of the Sisters of Notre Dame of Amersfoort,[3] using the same rule as that of the sisters in Namur. Political and historical circumstances forced them to become a separate congregation but the sisters considered Julie their Foundress and Protectress, as they do today.

In a series of exasperating edicts, the Minister of Education harassed the sisters with a series of decrees which further convinced everyone that the government was trying to rid the country of religious schools. When all of the establishments of the

Brothers of the Christian Schools were suppressed in 1823, Françoise wondered how long it would be before the Sisters of Notre Dame suffered the same fate. When women wanted to join the congregation, Françoise had them dress as seculars even though they were preparing to make vows in the institute.

In March, 1823, a royal decree was issued to the effect that all houses which had not received official authorization before August 1, would be suppressed. Fear gripped the sisters in all of the seven houses outside the Namur diocese which had been denied authorization. Françoise worked tirelessly on the petitions to a reluctant government for approval of all the houses.

In the midst of these trials, Françoise suffered the loss of her closest confidante, Sister Anastasia Leleu, who died at four in the afternoon of February 9, 1823. She was only forty-three years of age, but typhoid fever claimed her life. She had been with the congregation from the beginning, and it was three years before Françoise could compose the notice she was accustomed to write following a sister's death. Her last words reflected the essential teaching of Julie: "It is good to be with God."[4] Heartsick at the loss of one so dear to her, Françoise said, "The first year (after she died) my feelings were too keen, after that I was held back by the difficulty of describing her virtues in a way which would satisfy either the Sisters or myself."[5]

The next blow to the institute was the demand that all French teachers either return to their country, or renounce their French citizenship and become a Belgian subject. Françoise prepared to have another sister replace her, but the King, himself, signed her naturalization papers. So on December 27, 1824, Françoise became a Belgian citizen but other French sisters were not so fortunate. Some of them were dismissed from their classes even while in the midst of teaching them. When a French sister returned to Namur, one of the novices had to be dismissed since the government kept such strict account of the number of sisters at the motherhouse.

Each new attempt to destroy the congregation brought with it more anxiety to many of the sisters about its future. But Françoise's confidence did not waver. In spite of all the evidence to the contrary, she believed that the Sisters of Notre Dame would flourish, and that God would provide for them. Thus she continued to initiate programs of growth, building new buildings to accommodate the large number of students wishing to come to the schools, and even providing sisters for a new foundation that was requested by a very influential woman of Verviers, who promised them protection.

In June, 1829, King William decided to tour his kingdom to find out what the people thought of him. Françoise encouraged the sisters in the non-approved houses to ask for approval from the king. At Fleurus, the king himself presented the request for approbation to the local authorities. When William arrived at Namur, Françoise, trained in courtly manners, received the royal visitor with such exquisite grace and charm that when he was leaving, the king turned to her, and exclaimed, "Madame, a woman like you should live forever."[6]

For a few more months the persecutions continued toward all religious schools; but by the end of July, 1830, Paris was again in a state of revolution, and the spirit spread to Belgium. By August, Belgium was fighting its own revolution, and out of that struggle came a new constitution and their own king. The Catholics greeted the change with great relief. Since none of the Sisters of Notre Dame houses had been closed during the time of King William's reign, Françoise saw this as a sign of God's affirmation of the work of the congregation.

Once the sisters were able to accept new members again, no less than fourteen ex-boarders from Namur presented themselves for admission into the congregation. With their addition, the number of novices rose to forty, and Françoise was able to answer the many invitations she received to open more schools.

The congregation entered into a burst of growth that was but another sign of Julie's promise, "If God wishes it, we will flourish." Françoise wrote in 1832, "It is a little vine which the saintly Mère Julie has planted, which I have watered as well as I could, and to which God has given such an increase that now its branches extend throughout almost the whole of Belgium...."[7] By then, the twenty sisters who accompanied Julie and Françoise to Namur had multiplied tenfold; God's work was obviously being done.

There were many more trials and painful circumstances that Françoise, like Julie, had to undergo before her death. She was asked to accept another term as Superior General, even though she was considered to be in advanced age. But by February, 1838, the co-foundress had finished the work God had called her to. During the previous October, 1837, Françoise's health began to fail her. She chided the sisters who prayed for her cure, telling them, "If God were to listen to you, I should still be here a hundred years hence."[8] Then on the anniversary of her first consecration and formal beginning of her religious life, February 2, 1838, she received the last sacraments. After Françoise had renewed her vows and asked pardon of the sisters for any offence she may have inflicted, they filed by her bed one by one to bid her farewell. As weak as she was, she managed to smile at each sister, and wave her goodbye. The older members came at the end, and when she saw those who had suffered so much with her, and supported her through good times and bad, she could not hold back the tears—tears of gratitude as well as loss, for she loved them very much.

At four o'clock in the afternoon of February 8, after the priest recited the psalm, "I rejoiced in the things that were said to me, we shall go into the House of the Lord," a radiant smile lit up Françoise's face, and she took her last breath. The following night the body of Françoise was carried to the chapel garden, and laid beside the tomb of Julie. They were together in death as they had been in life.

During the years following her death, devotion to Julie extended beyond the walls of the motherhouse. Not until 1842 was it publicly known that Julie's remains were contained in a vault under the garden chapel, where the sisters made frequent visits to ask the foundress to pray for them. In that year, the flood waters of the Meuse and Sambre Rivers penetrated the vault and broke through the coffin. What was left of Julie's remains were placed in a smaller chest. In 1880, following another flood, the chest was placed above ground in the chapel, where the tombs of both Julie and Françoise remain today.

When the chapel was finally opened to the public, many people in the area came to the shrine, praying to Julie in their time of need. Gradually the call to start the Process for Canonization began to be heard from many parts of Europe. Evidence of the power of her intercession came pouring in from near and far, and in some unexpected places. Former pupils claimed her power was working in their lives. When the first steps towards canonization, the Process of Beatification, began in earnest, one of the formal witnesses of the Process in Namur, said:

> I have in my possession, and I have read, more than two hundred attestations concerning favours obtained by the intercession of the Venerable Mère Julie, given by persons who have been the object of them since her death, but especially during the last twenty years: sickness healed, help granted in temptations, or other difficulties, protection in case of fire, vocations obtained or strengthened, conversions....[9]

The rapidity with which the congregation spread was taken as an even greater sign of the presence of God in the work of Julie's sisters, and a testimony to her genuine holiness. By 1896, the Sisters of Notre Dame had opened convents in England, Scotland, North America, and two in the Belgian Congo.[10] Julie's vision and conviction that her sisters were meant to "Go out to all the world" was being realized. Wherever they went, they spread the message Julie had given them of the goodness of God, and told the story of the woman of Cuvilly.

Julie's Beatification was declared on May 13, 1906. The first step toward official recognition of her holiness brought great joy to all the members of her congregation and their pupils. Immediately, the sisters made every effort to continue the process towards canonization. In order for the church to declare the sanctity of a person, three authentically documented miracles are required as proof of the individual's power of intercession. Although there were many stories relating to Julie's help, two of the incidents that were accepted occurred in two different parts of the world.

The first miracle was reported by a Monsieur Homer Rhodius who was born in Namur in 1850, and grew up hearing stories of Julie, and the work of the Sisters of Notre Dame. In November

1919, he was suffering from a condition that caused intense pains in his stomach, accompanied at times by nausea and migraine headaches. Two doctors examined him and declared him suffering from incurable uremia. As his condition worsened, the last sacraments were administered to the dying man, and later he fell into a deep coma. The doctors gave him twenty-four hours to live; but his family could not accept the fact that there was no hope for him. They began a novena to Julie, and obtained a relic of her which they placed on the sick man. The following morning, Monsieur Rhodius began to improve; the second day, he regained consciousness, and on the fourth day he was able to take nourishment. On December 12, 1919, he was pronounced out of danger, and a few days later he returned to work. No symptom of the illness ever reappeared. The doctors could give no medical explanation for his recovery.

The second miracle was the result of the prayers of the Sisters of Notre Dame of Coesfeld. Their congregation began at the request of Abbe Elting of Coesfeld, Westphalia, Germany. He had asked the Sisters of Notre Dame of Amersfoort to instruct two teachers who had opened their home to orphans and abandoned children, and were assuming the responsibility of their education. Both women desired to dedicate their lives to God in religious life. Two Sisters of Notre Dame from Amersfoort began the formation of the two women in the spirit of Julie, providing them with a copy of their rule, which was patterned after the Sisters in Namur. Upon the completion of their novitiate, the two women pronounced vows in 1852.

Within three years, however, the government of Protestant Prussia, which had taken over Catholic Westphalia in 1814, would not tolerate the dependence of German religious under the authority of "foreigners," and the Amersfoort Sisters were expelled from Germany. Once again, historical and political circumstances forced another group of religious to establish an autonomous congregation. However, the Sisters of Notre Dame of Coesfeld consider their foundress to be Saint Julie. Their congregation flourished as well, and eventually, sisters were sent to Holland, England, Italy, the United States, Brazil, Indonesia, India, New Guinea, and South Korea.

It was the Coesfeld Sisters in Campos Novos, Brazil who were instrumental in the second instance accepted as an authentic miracle during the Process of Canonization for Julie. On September 29, 1950, Senor Otacilia Ribeiro, age 29, was brought from Marombas, an impoverished area in the State of Santa Catarina, to the hospital in Campos Novos conducted by the Sisters of Notre Dame. He had been shaking badly, and was suffering from abdominal pain. Dr. John Martins Ribeiro was sent for immediately. The physician declared that if they were to save his life they would have to operate at once. The surgery revealed a very rare tumor, which the doctor described as follows, "I noted the tumor inaccessible, and it would be fatal if such intervention (to excise it) was practiced."[11] He closed the incision, told the sisters that the poor man would probably not last the night, and that is was hopeless to think of removing such a large, hard and invasive tumor. He told them to send for the man's father, who had brought him to the hospital and was waiting for word of his son's condition. The sisters sent for the priest and Otacilio received the last sacraments.

The next morning Sister Maria Ludvine suggested that the sisters begin a novena to Blessed Julie. They invited Senor Ribeiro to join them and had to explain to one who had never heard of Julie, who she was, and what a novena entailed. Together they said a prayer to Julie and the sisters placed a relic on the patient's wound. On the second day, Senor Ribeiro said that he felt a little better, and when Dr. Ribeiro arrived to see his patient, he noted what he saw, "...I found Mr. Otacilio Ribeiro completely cured, the abdomen (wound) in normal state."[12] The doctor could hardly believe his eyes; there was not even a sign of the incision he had made the day before. The patient promised that if he ever had a daughter, he would name her Julie. Once again, there was no medical explanation for the patient's cure.

At last there was sufficient proof that Julie was indeed, a powerful intercessor, and a woman of extraordinary virtue. Finally the day that all the sisters had been waiting for arrived, the canonization took place June 22, 1969. Senor Otacilio Ribeiro, his sixteen-year-old daughter Julie, and Dr. John Martins Ribeiro attended the ceremony together. By that time, Sisters of Notre

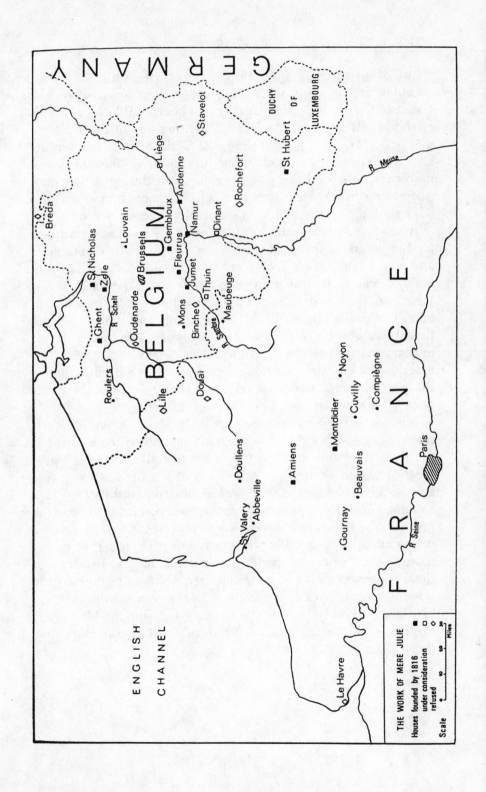

THE WORK OF MÈRE JULIE

Houses founded by 1816 ■
under consideration ◻
refused ◇

Scale

ENGLISH CHANNEL

GERMANY

BELGIUM

FRANCE

DUCHY OF LUXEMBOURG

◇Stavelot

•Liège

◇Andenne

◇Rochefort

■St Hubert

R. Meuse

◇Breda

•Louvain

Namur

◻Dinant

•Brussels

◇Gembloux

•Fleurus

•S.Nicholas
■Zele

Ghent■ R. Schelt

◇Oudenarde

•Jumet
◻Thuin
•Mons ◇Binche R. Sambre
•Maubeuge

•Roulers

◇Lille

◇Douai

•Noyon

■Montdidier •Cuvilly
•Compiègne

•Doullens

•Beauvais

■Amiens

•Abbeville

S.Valery

•Gournay

R. Seine

Paris

◇Le Havre

Dame of all three congregations were serving on nearly every continent in the world where they continue to serve today. The vision of the woman from Cuvilly had been fulfilled. Hundreds of thousands of people had heard the message of the one-time paralytic, "Ah, how good is the good God." Sisters representing all three congregations claiming Julie as their foundress and patroness, attended the joyous celebration during which magnificent testimony was given of the holiness of the woman who once signed her letter, "A Very Unworthy Sister of Notre Dame."

Julie speaks to us from another century. As she was conforming her life to the image of Christ, she mirrored Mary, her model and her sister. Julie's love for and devotion to Our Lady of Sorrows was as natural and fitting as her own experience of life. Her own purity and simplicity made her especially fond of Mary's title, the "Immaculate Conception," and it is no wonder that she called the congregation "Sisters of Notre Dame." It was in Mary that she saw her greatest advocate and protectress. The magnificent tapestry that hung over Saint Peter's Basilica during the canonization mass showed Saint Julie in glory, where her good God received her in her triumph of joy.

It is not difficult to imagine Our Lady, "Notre Dame," eagerly reaching out to her faithful daughter, anxious to share with her the final revelation of what Julie's life was all about. Now Julie sees the whole picture, the other side of her life's tapestry. She knows, and rejoices that she was an instrument of grace to a countless number of people in her day, and continues to be in the present. She began in France a whole movement toward the education of girls, especially the poor; one that has grown and spread throughout the world. It can be claimed justifiably that there is no sweeter voice, no greater joy, no more profound gratitude in any Sister of Notre Dame who ever was or who ever will be, than in Julie Billiart, as she continues to sing the Magnificat she began at the moment of her death, and continues to pray throughout eternity.

NOTES

I. On the Road to Flanders (1751–1787)

1. The family genealogy was supplied by M. Prache of Versailles who is related to the Billiart family by way of a female ancestor who married a Lanvin, the maiden name of Julie's paternal grandmother, Madeleine Lanvin. The genealogy was sent to the Namur Archives only a few years ago. In 1739 Jean François was twenty-two years old and Marie Louise Antoinette de Braine, twenty-four. Besides the children mentioned, they had a son on November 11, 1759, but the baby died unnamed the same day.

2. Langlois, Claude. *Le Catholicisme au feminin; les congrégations françaises à supérieure générale au xixe siècle*. Paris: Les Editions du Cerf., 1984, p. 273.

3. Blin, Françoise. *The Memoirs of Mother Frances Blin de Bourdon*. Sr. Thérèse of the Blessed Sacrament Sullivan, ed. Westminster, Maryland: Christian Classics, 1975, p. 1.

4. Testimony of Fr. Trouvelot, *Mémoirs*, pp. 220–221.

5. "The 18th century French priest was not only more educated and better trained than his 17th century predecessor, but also was probably the most overworked person in pre-Revolutionary France. His influence pervaded every facet of life in his parish. Not only was he responsible for every aspect of the spiritual life of the parish, but he also functioned as an unpaid quasi-civil servant, obligated to register the births, marriages and deaths within the parish and to provide economic information to the civil authorities of the province; he also served as an informal police watch within the village, as a monitor to the local midwife, and as a superintendent for the village schoolmaster." Olwen H. Hufton, *The Poor of Eighteenth-Century France, 1750–1789*. Oxford: The Clarendon Press, 1974, p. 24. Quoted in "The

Life and Times of Saint Julie Billiart," by Mary Hayes, S.N.D., presented at the Julie Conference, Namur, Belgium, 1987.

6. *Mémoirs,* op. cit., p. 221.

7. Ibid., p. 206.

8. Partridge, Sr. Mary Xavier, S.N.D., James Clare, S.J., ed. *Life of Blessed Julie Billiart: Foundress of the Institute of the Sisters of Notre Dame.* London: Sands & Co., 1909, p. 11.

9. The cardinal had been asked to bless a special chapel built in honor of St. Barnabas by the Knights Hospitallers of St. John of Jerusalem on their estate at Bellicourt near Cuvilly. The Knights were men of means and some had returned from a pilgrimage to the Holy Land shortly before the confirmation at St. Eloi. Partridge, p. 14.

10. The reliquary is now in the Museum of the Congregation of the Sisters of Notre Dame de Namur at the motherhouse in Namur, Belgium.

11. Hufton, Olwen, op. cit., p. 259.

12. *Mémoirs,* p. 1.

13. Ibid., p. 222. Testimony of Père Trouvelot at the time of Julie's beatification process.

14. The banner is in the museum at Namur.

15. "The diet of the mass of people was meagre and lacking in nutrients necessary for adequate sustenance, especially since most of the poorer members of society were engaged in long hours of hard manual labor, whether in the fields, or in the workshops, docks and markets of the cities. The normal peasant diet can be briefly summarized as consisting of cereals, usually in the form of bread, though often supplemented by various forms of gruel. The basic hot dish of the day was "la soupe," of which, once again, bread was the staple component with the result that bread was the basis of every single meal the peasant consumed. It was, of course, variously supplemented by milk products, some fruit and vegetables, sometimes by fish which supplied the bulk of the protein since meat was very rare indeed." Forrest, Alan. *The French Revolution and the Poor.* New York: St. Martin's Press, 1981, p.6.

16. *Mémoirs,* p. 207.

17. This was a copy of a painting that allegedly had been made from the veil of Veronica offered to Christ to wipe his face as he made his way to Calvary. The traditional belief was that Christ rewarded this act of kindness by causing an imprint of his face to remain on the veil.

18. After Julie had begun her congregation, she had an occasion, while waiting for a benefactress, to meet two little girls, one of whom was suffering from a disease of the eyes. Julie, remembering her own

experience, made the sign of the cross over the child's eyes and she was cured. (Cf. Partridge, op. cit.,p. 356.) It is interesting to note that in the 1909 account of Julie's life, the author describes the pilgrimage to Montreuil as being a "double favor" for Julie and Marie Madeleine. In a 1932 account, (Sister Cuthbert of St. Joseph) we find reference to two pilgrimages, Marie Madeleine's first, followed by one for Julie. In either case, the point is made that both were cured.

19. *Mémoirs,* p. 1.

20. Hufton writes of the violence in the eighteenth century, especially in the villages. She says, "Families avenged infractions upon their property such as the pasturing of a cow, the inevitable straying of a scraggy, but voracious goat, or the misuse of ponds and streams, not by litigation, but by beating and threats.... Shepherds on lonely mountainsides (who) would while away the hours in violent quarrels with their handful of companions, would beat up a lonely traveler, not with theft in mind but because they had a genuine taste for violence." Op. cit., p. 363.

21. Julie's symptoms beginning with the blurring of vision that prompted the trip to Montreuil, and the gradual loss of the use of her muscles resembles the symptoms of multiple sclerosis. Sister Jean Bunn, S.N.D. (British Province) gave a list of the symptoms Julie presented to a medical doctor. Without telling the doctor who the patient was, she asked him what diagnosis he would give on the evidence given to him. His response was, "That's simple; it's a case of multiple sclerosis." (Interview, March 5, 1991, Woolton, Liverpool, England.)

22. Bishop Francis Joseph de la Rochefoucauld had never met Julie since he succeeded the cardinal who had confirmed her in 1764. It was this bishop of Beauvais, much beloved friend of his people, who perished in the massacre of the Carmes, September 2, 1792. (Partridge, op. cit., footnote, p. 23).

23. Ibid.

24. Forrest, Alan, op. cit., p. 6.

25. Ibid.

26. *Mémoirs,* p. 2.

27. Partridge, p. 23

28. *Mémoirs,* p. 2.

29. Ibid.

II. Confusion and Fear (1788–1794)

1. Stewart, John Hall. *A Documentary Survey of the French Revolution;* New York: The Macmillan Co., 1951, p. 6.

2. Ibid., p. 7.

3. *Mémoirs*, p. 207.

4. Hayes, op. cit., p. 15.

5. Ibid.

6. Ibid.

7. Partridge, p. 24.

8. Hayes, p. 16.

9. Partridge, p. 24.

10. Tackett, Timothy. *Religion and Regional Culture in Eighteenth-Century France;* The Ecclesiastical Oath of 1791. Princeton, Princeton Univ. Press, 1986, p. 346. Quoted in Hayes, p. 18. She adds, "Of the 137 old regime dioceses, only five had an incidence higher than 88 percent, while three others in addition to Beauvais stood at 88 percent."

11. Ibid.

12. *Mémoirs*, p. 201.

13. Partridge, p. 29.

14. Ibid.

15. Bernet, J. *Récherches sur la Dechristianization dans le District de Compiègne*. Univ. of Paris; Sorbonne, Institut d'Histoire de la Revolution Française: Thèse de doctorat de III'ème Cycle, 1981, quoted in "The Prophetic Influence of Julie on Yesterday": by Sr. Colette Valschaerts, S.N.D., Julie Conference, Namur, 1987, p. 167.

16. *Mémoirs*, p. 3.

17. Ibid.

18. Partridge, p. 32.

19. Ibid., p. 34.

20. Ibid., p. 35.

21. Ibid., pp. 35–36.

22. It is interesting to note that the Carmelites of Compiègne were beatified one month after Julie was given that honor on May 13, 1906.

23. Partridge, p. 37.

III. Amiens (1794–1803)

1. Hayes, Mary. SND. "The Life and Times of St. Julie Billiart," Julie Conference, Namur, 1987. Unpublished., p. 23.

2. Forrest, Alan. *The French Revolution and the Poor*. New York: St. Martin's Press, 1981, p. 174.

3. Ibid.

4. Ibid.

5. Cobb, Richard. *The Police and the People; French Popular Protest,* 1789–1820. New York: St. Martin's Press, 1970. Quoted in Hayes, p. 23.

6. *Mémoirs,* p. 4.

7. Ibid.

8. Ibid., p. 5.

9. Ibid.

10. Françoise's mother died in 1784 after a serious carriage accident left her crippled and in great pain. Françoise nursed her mother through the year before she finally succumbed to her injuries.

11. Letter 8, January, 1797, in *The Letters of St. Julie Billiart,* trans. by Sr. Frances Rosner, S.N.D. and Sr. Lucy Tinsley, S.N.D., Rome: Gregorian Press, 1974, p. 80.

12. Ibid., p. 81.

13. Ibid., Letter 5, (Sept. 15, 1795), p. 30.

14. Ibid., Letter 1, p. 19.

15. Ibid., Letter 10, (Dec. 2, 1795), p. 46.

16. Ibid., Letter 29, (Feb., 1797), p. 82.

17. Ibid., Letter 6, (Oct. 21, 1795), p. 32.

18. Ibid.

19. Ibid.

20. Ibid., Letter 6, p. 31.

21. Ibid., Letter 7, p. 34.

22. Ibid.

23. Ibid., Letter 11, (Dec. 23, 1795), p. 48.

24. Ibid., Letter 3, (Aug. 16, 1795), p. 25.

25. Ibid., Letter 16, (Feb. 1, 1796), p. 58

26. Forrest, op. cit., p. 6.

27. *Mémoirs,* p. 286.

IV. Return to Amiens (1803–1804)

1. *Mémoirs,* op. cit., p. 7.

2. Ibid.

3. Forrest, Alan, op. cit., p. 7.

4. Ibid.

5. *Mémoirs,* p. 8.

6. Ibid.

7. Ward, Margaret. *Life of Saint Madeline Sophie: Foundress of the Society of the Sacred Heart,* 1779–1865. Second Ed.; Roehampton, Convent of the Sacred Heart, 1925, p. 127.

8. Ibid., p. 97.

9. *Mémoirs,* p. 9.

10. Ibid.

11. Ibid.

12. Ibid.

13. Partridge, op. cit., p. 96.

14. Ibid.

15. Ibid., p. 103.

16. *Vie de Julie Billiart Par Sa Première Compagne Françoise Blin de Bourbon.*

17. Ibid., p. 103.

18. Letter 34, p. 92.

19. Ibid.

20. Letter 35, p. 95.

21. Ibid.

22. Document of Sister Marie Francine (South Belgium), citing pp. 32–45 of the record.

23. Letter 37, pp. 99-100

24. Ibid.

25. Letter 38, p. 102.

26. Ibid.

V. To Go Out to All the World (1804–1806)

1. Hales, E. E. Y. *Napoleon and the Pope: The Story of Napoleon and Pius VII.* London: Eyre & Spottiswoode. 1962. p. 71.

2. Bishop Demandolx died in August, 1817. His heart was deposited in the chapel in the cathedral of Amiens and his body was buried in the cemetery of the Madeleine in Amiens. In 1937, the cemetery was abandoned and his remains were transferred to the bishop's vault in the cathedral in Amiens. Cf. French translation of the *Mémoirs.*

3. *Mémoirs,* p. 11.

4. Following is the Formula of the Vows pronounced by the first Sisters: "I, ..., promise unto God Almighty, before the Blessed Virgin, His Mother, and the whole court of heaven, and in (the) presence of you, Father, holding the place of God, perpetual poverty, chastity, and obedience, and conformably to this obedience, an especial care of the instruction of children, understanding the whole according to the constitutions, the conditions, and the dispositions which have been manifested to me, at Amiens, in the chapel of the House of Orphans, October 15, 1805." The formula is in the handwriting of Sister Anastasia Leleu. Cf. Partridge, op. cit., p. 103-104 footnote.

5. The Society of Jesus was restored in 1814, two years before Julie's death but she used the name St. Ignace, only a few times.

6. *Mémoirs,* p. 11.

7. Partridge, op. cit., p. 104

8. Quoted in the end notes of the *Mémoirs,* p. 278. The religious was Madame Geneviève Deshayes.

9. Ibid.

10. Partridge, p. 517.

11. Ibid.

12. *Mémoirs,* p. 12. Note: The sister who attended her was Françoise. She had ample opportunity to practice heroic sacrifices as well. Raised by her grandparents in a household where every need was attended and where she was surrounded by adoring adults, she now found herself "...amongst a group of young persons who, however excellent their dispositions and however fervent their desires of perfection, must frequently have been uncongenial to her from their narrower mental outlook and even by their very exuberance."

A passage from her spiritual journey reads, "Uncultivated manners, awkwardness, stupidity, the ridiculous behavior and tactlessness of people arouse in me impatience and contempt. What a commotion is set up in my heart! If anything clashes with my taste or my views, I can scarcely hold my tongue about it. O my God, tear me away from myself. I will wage a continual warfare, until I succeed in separating myself from the life of the senses." Cf., Tomme, *The Life of Mère St. Joseph* p. 79.

13. *Mémoirs,* p. 211.

14. "light of revelation to the Gentiles."

15. *Mémoirs,* p. 211.

16. Ibid., p. 12

17. Memoirs of Sister Marie Steenhaut quoted in Partridge, op. cit., p. 114.

18. Ibid., p. 116.

19. Ibid., p. 15.

20. Ibid., p. 13.

21. Ibid., p. 109.

22. Ibid., p. 14.

23. Letter 41, p. 107.

24. Ibid.

25. Ibid.

26. Ibid.

27. Ibid.

28. Letter 43, p. 112-113.
29. Letter 43, p. 111.
30. Ibid., p. 111-112.
31. Partridge, p. 119.
32. Letter 45, p. 114.
33. Ibid.
34. Letter 44, p. 113.
35. *Mémoirs,* p. 16.
36. Ibid.
37. Ibid., p. 17.

VI. Congregation Marked by the Cross (1806–1807)

1. *Mémoirs,* p. 228. However, in another work the date given was June 17, 1806. Cf. Tomme, *The Life of Mère St. Joseph.* London: Longmans, Green and Co., 1923, p. 93. The first approval was provisional. There was a second approval by Napoleon on March 10, 1807. The series of approvals was another sign of the confusion of authority over the religious communities in France. The Bishops assumed they had the greater authority; the Emperor assumed he had the last say, and the municipal authorities thought they controlled the establishment of all schools in their cities.

2. Ibid., p. 90.

3. Cf. Ward, Margaret. *Life of Saint Sophie Barat,* op. cit., p. 142.

4. *Mémoirs,* p. 19-20.

5. Ibid., p. 23.

6. Ibid.

7. Ibid., p. 24.

8. Tomme, op. cit., p. 99.

9. Ibid., p. 22.

10. *Mémoirs,* p. 22.

11. Ibid.

12. Tomme, p. 104.

13. Letter 55, p. 138. This letter had the distinction of being the first written from Namur at a time when no one, including Julie, knew that this city would become so important for the Institute.

14. Ibid., p. 139.

15. *Mémoirs,* p. 18.

16. Tomme, p. 105.

17. Ibid.

18. Letter 56, p. 140

19. Ibid.

20. Ibid., p. 141.

21. Ibid., p. 142.

22. McCarthy, Sr. Mary Frances, S.N.D. *Selected Letters of Mother Saint Joseph Blin De Bourdon.* Maryland: Christian Classics, Inc., 1990. #1, p. 1.

23. Letter 57, p. 144.

24. McCarthy, Letter 1, p. 3.

25. Ibid., Letter 3, p. 7.

26. Letter 62, p. 166.

VII. Fogs of the Somme (1807–1809)

1. *Mémoirs,* p. 38.

2. Letter 74, op. cit., p. 201.

3. *Mémoirs,* p. 29.

4. Ibid., p. 31.

5. Ibid., p. 36.

6. Ibid.

7. Letter 72, p. 192.

8. Ibid., p. 196.

9. Ibid.

10. Ibid., p. 197.

11. Ibid.

12. Quoted in *Mémoirs,* p. 41.

13. Ibid., p. 42.

14. Julie and Françoise always considered Père Varin and Père Thomas the "founders" of the community. The priests did not think of themselves as such.

15. *Mémoirs,* p. 42

16. Ibid., p. 48. Both priests were Fathers of the Faith and were well versed in the spirit of St. Ignatius.

17. Ibid.

18. Ibid., p. 49.

19. Ibid., p. 52.

20. Ibid., p. 53.

21. Ibid.

22. Ibid., p. 51.

23. Partridge, p. 173.

24. *Mémoirs,* p. 60.

25. Ibid., p. 62.

26. Ibid.

VIII. Refugees (1809)

1. *Mémoirs,* p. 51
2. Ibid., p. 67.
3. Ibid.
4. Ibid.
5. Ibid., p. 69.
6. Ibid., p. 72.
7. Ibid.
8. Ibid., p. 73.
9. Norbert had been under the tutelage of Père Bicheron who had him in a boarding school. Julie had to see that Norbert had sufficient clothes, but when she was leaving Amiens, she had to take him with her as no one would have been in Amiens to look after the needs of the boy.
10. Letter 93, p. 242.
11. *Mémoirs,* p. 82.
12. Quoted in Partridge, op. cit., p. 191.
13. Ibid., p. 192.
14. Letter 94, p. 245.
15. *Mémoirs,* p. 65.
16. Letter 96, p. 248.
17. Letter 95, p. 247.
18. *Mémoirs,* p. 78.
19. Ibid.
20. Ibid., p. 83.
21. Ibid., pp. 87-88.
22. Ibid., pp. 89-92
23. Letter 96, p. 248.
24. *Mémoirs,* p. 94.
25. Ibid., p. 100.

IX. Center of the Spirit (1809)

1. Letter 112, p. 298.
2. Now called Rue Julie Billiart.
3. Carroll, Malachy Gernard. *The Charred Wood: The Story of Blessed Julie Billiart.* London: Sands & Co., Ltd., 1950. p. 150.
4. Letter 111, p. 297.
5. Linscott, *The Fourth Essential,* p. 29.

6. *Counsels of Perfection,* for the use of the Sisters of Notre Dame de Namur. Baltimore, Maryland, 1947. pp. 10–11.

7. Letter 204, p. 541.

8. *Counsels of Perfection,* p. 2.

9. Ibid., p. 28.

10. Ibid., p. 29.

11. Ibid., p. 44.

12. Ibid.

13. Ibid., p. 63.

14. Ibid.

15. Ibid., p. 62.

16. *Mémoirs,* p. 162.

17. Letter 121, p. 324.

18. *Mémoirs,* p. 208.

19. Letter 58, p. 151.

20. Ibid., p. 204.

21. Cf. Burns, Camilla, S.N.D. "The Spiritual Influence of Julie on Forever," unpublished paper given at the Julie Conference, Namur, Belgium, July 31, 1989. Reference is made to *Bérulle and the French School,* New Jersey, Paulist Press, 1989.

22. The original statue on the facade of the great cathedral of Amiens is now in the Louvre Museum in Paris. Another statue made in the exact likeness of the first, stands at the entrance of the cathedral where the other stood when Julie passed it on her way to the church.

23. "Conferences of Ven. Mère Julie," written by Sister Gertrude Steenhaut, Conference No. 21. Quoted in Partridge, op. cit., p. 208.

24. *Mémoirs,* p. 103.

25. Letter 116, p. 308.

26. Partridge, p. 223.

27. Letter 117, p. 310.

28. Ibid.

29. Letter 114, p. 305.

30. Letter 121, pp. 322–323.

31. Sophie Barat had a difficult time in the beginning of her congregation to give it a name that would not antagonize the government which was opposed to any group that resembled the Jesuits whom they had banished. Mother Barat's sisters were determined to promote devotion to the Sacred Heart and wanted their title to reflect that devotion, but they had to wait until a more favorable time.

32. Quoted in Williams, Margaret, R.S.C.J., *Saint Madeline Sophie: Her Life and Letters.* New York: Herder and Herder, 1965. p. 120.

33. *Mémoirs,* p. 106.
34. Ibid., p. 108.
35. Ibid.

X. *Journeys to Amiens (1809–1810)*

1. *Mémoirs,* p. 110.
2. Ibid.
3. Ibid., p. 111.
4. In 1809, Madame de Franssu had written to Françoise that she had made "certain plans" which she hoped would come to pass the next spring. However, due to her illness, she was not able to carry out her plan of founding yet another religious congregation to serve the needs of the poor. In 1813 at Crest, under the guidance of her "angel," Père Enfantin, she began the Congregation of Sisters of the Nativity, which exists today. Her story parallels some of the difficulties Julie had in beginning the Sisters of Notre Dame. Cf. Cristiani, L. Madame de Franssu, Fondatrice de la Congregation de la Nativité de Notre-Seigneur (1751–1824). Avignon: Aubanal Freres, 1927. Quoted in *Mémoirs,* p. 298.
5. *Mémoirs,* p. 112.
6. Letter 132, p. 355.
7. Ibid.
8. Ibid.
9. Ibid.
10. Ibid., p. 356.
11. Ibid.
12. *Mémoirs,* p. 115.
13. Ibid., p. 110.
14. *Mémoirs,* p. 117.
15. Letter 138, p. 372.
16. There is some contradiction here. Françoise discusses a woman who had bought the monastery, while in Partridge's biography this gentleman is named as the owner. (Cf. *Mémoirs,* p. 127 and Partridge, op. cit., p. 233.
17. The story of the chapel continues into the twentieth century. At the end of the Second World War when the German army was being expelled from Ghent by the Allied troops, a group of young German soldiers burst into the chapel and machine-gunned the paintings and the altar. A visitor today can see these famous paintings where artists have made repairs of the bullet holes.

18. Also known as "Nouveau-Bois," or its derivation, "Nonnen-bosch," the Flemish title meaning, "Nuns' Wood."

19. *Mémoirs,* p. 127.

20. Partridge, p. 234.

21. Letter 86, p. 225.

22. *Mémoirs,* p. 130.

23. Ibid., pp. 142-143.

24. Ibid.

25. Ibid.

26. Ibid.

27. Ibid.

28. Ibid.

29. Letter 157, p. 424.

30. *Mémoirs,* p. 154.

31. Ibid.

32. Ibid.

33. Ibid.

34. Ibid, p. 157.

XI. Away From France (1811–1813)

1. *Mémoirs,* p. 179.

2. Ibid., p. 180.

3. Partridge, op. cit., p. 248.

4. *Mémoirs,* p. 180.

5. Letter 226, p. 585.

6. Ibid.

7. Ibid., p. 586.

8. Letter 227, p. 589.

9. Letter 228, p.; 593. See also *Mémoirs,* p. 181. Julie most likely had a "locution" at this time; that is, the spiritual gift of an interior message that the person recognizes comes from God, not herself. Many persons have had such spiritual experiences.

10. Ibid., pp. 592–593.

11. Letter 230, p. 599.

12. Ibid.

13. Letter 228, p. 595.

14. Ibid.

15. *Mémoirs,* p. 186.

16. Ibid., pp. 186–187.

17. Ibid., p. 187. When the house at Rubempre was closed, Victoire returned to secular life, and that is the last that was heard of her.

18. Hales, E.E.Y. *Napoleon and the Pope: The Story of Napoleon and Pius VII.* London; Eyre and Spottiswoode, 1961, p. 143.

19. Partridge, p. 263.

20. Ibid., p. 254.

21. Presently it is in the museum of the Congregation in Namur.

22. Letter 252, p. 647.

23. Ibid., pp. 260–261.

24. Glover, Michael. *The Napoleonic Wars.* New York: Hippocrene Books, 1978, p. 188.

25. *Mémoirs,* p. 151.

XII. Soldiers Along the Road (1813–1815)

1. Letter 274, p. 694.

2. Ibid.

3. Letter 262, p. 674.

4. Herold, J. Christopher. *The Age of Napoleon.* New York: Harper and Row, 1963, pp. 372-3.

5. Letter 307, p. 750.

6. *Mémoirs,* p. 193.

7. Partridge, op. cit., pp. 308–309.

8. Letter 310, p. 755.

9. Letter 318, p. 770.

10. Ibid., p. 771.

11. Herold, op. cit., p. 377.

12. Partridge, p. 310.

13. Herold, p. 382.

14. *Mémoirs,* p. 196.

15. Ibid., p. 197

16. Ibid., p. 272.

17. Ibid., p. 198.

18. Ibid.

XIII. The Last Journey (1815–1816)

1. Letter 415, p. 943.

2. Ibid., p. 942.

3. Ibid., p. 943.

4. Ibid., p. 944.

5. *Mémoirs,* p. 211.

6. Hales, E.E.Y., *Napoleon and the Pope;* London: Eyre and Spottiswoode, 1962, pp. 88-90.

7. *Mémoirs,* p. 213.

8. Ibid., p. 212.

9. Ibid., p. 211.

10. Letter 340, p. 811.

11. Letter 431, p. 812.

12. *Mémoirs,* p. 213.

13. Partridge, op.cit., p. 331.

14. Ibid.

15. Rooney, Sr. Lucy. "The Memoirs Reprinted: The Missing Pages." Unpublished, p. 8.

16. *Mémoirs,* p. 215.

17. Ibid., p. 213.

18. Ibid., p. 204.

19. Letter 440, p. 996.

20. Letter 446, p. 1008.

21. Letter 448, p. 1011.

22. *Mémoirs,* p. 201.

23. Ibid., p. 202.

24. Ibid.

25. À Kempis, Thomas. *Imitation of Christ.* Trans. by Albert J. Nevins, M. M. Huntington, Ind., Our Sunday Visitor, Inc. 1976, p. 76.

26. *Mémoirs,* p. 203.

27. Ibid.

28. Testimony of M. Renson, her confessor, quoted in Partridge, p. 367.

29. Partridge, p. 371.

30. *Mémoirs,* p. 203.

31. Ibid.

32. Ibid.

33. Partridge, p. 381.

34. Ibid.

35. Ibid., p. 388.

36. Ibid.

XIV. God's Work (1816)

1. Tomme, E.C., *The Life of Mère St. Joseph,* London: Longmans, Green & Co., 1923, p. 140.

2. Ibid., p. 172.

3. Under extremely difficult circumstances, the Sisters of Notre Dame of Amersfoort established themselves in Holland, kept the same rule as the sisters in Namur, and were forced by political and historical circumstances to become an independent congregation. However, they flourish today with educational and health care ministries in Holland, Indonesia, Malawi, and Brazil.

4. *Mémoirs,* p. 267.

5. Tomme, op. cit., p. 190.

6. Ibid., p. 212.

7. Ibid., p. 218.

8. Ibid., p. 276.

9. Partridge, op. cit., p. 396.

10. Ibid., p. 397.

11. Quoted from the Medical Affidavit signed by Dr. John Martins Ribeiro, February 16, 1953. This document is in the Archives of the Sisters of Notre Dame in Namur.

12. Ibid.

APPENDIX

When a woman entered a religious congregation in the days of Julie, she would be given a new name as a symbol of her taking on a "new life." To help the reader more easily identify the sisters most often mentioned in the book, the following list includes the baptismal name of the sister and the name given to her in the congregation when she made her first vows. However, in some instances, the sisters did not make vows until they had settled in Namur but were addressed as "sister" almost from the time they entered the institute.

NAME	NAME IN THE CONGREGATION
Angelique Bicheron	Sister Josephine
Marie Rose Julie Billiart	Sister Ignace
Françoise Blin de Bourdon	Sister St. Joseph
Elizabeth-Victoire Boutrainghan	Sister Thérèse and then Sister Victoire
Catherine Daullee	Sister Catherine
Josephine Evrard	Sister Xavier
Justine Garson	Sister St. John
Jeanne Godelle	Sister Jeanne
Victoire Leleu	Sister Anastasia
Elizabeth Leroy	Sister Anne
Elizabeth Michel	Sister Gonzaga
Adelaide Pelletier	Sister Bernardine
Francesca Steenhaut	Sister Gertrude
Marie Steenhaut	Sister Marie

BIBLIOGRAPHY

à Kempis, Thomas. *Imitation of Christ,* Trans. Albert J. Nevins, M.M., Huntington, Ind., Our Sunday Visitor, Inc., 1976.

Billiart, Julie. *Counsels of Perfection;* For the Use of the Sisters of Notre Dame de Namur. Baltimore, Maryland, 1947.

Blin, Françoise. *The Memoirs of Mother Frances Blin de Bourdon*. Trans. Sister Therese of the Blessed Sacrament Sullivan, S.N.D. Westminster, Maryland: Christian Classics, 1975.

Burns, Camilla, S.N.D. "The Spiritual Influence of Julie on Forever," Unpublished. Julie Conference: Namur, Belgium, 1989.

Carroll, Malachy. *The Charred Wood; The Story of Blessed Julie Billiart*. London: Sands and Co., Ltd., 1950.

Cobb, Richard. *The Police and the People: French Popular Protest, 1789–1820,* New York: St. Martin's Press, 1970.

Forrest, Alan. *The French Revolution and the Poor.* New York: St. Martins Press, 1981.

Glover, Michael. *The Napoleonic Wars.* New York: Hippocrene Books, 1978.

Hales, E.E.Y. *Napoleon and the Pope: The Story of Napoleon and Pius VII.* London: Eyre and Spottiswoode, 1962.

Hardner, Sr. Anne of Jesus, S.N.D. *Mere Ignace Goethals.* London: Alexander Ouseley Limited, 1934.

Hayes, Sr. Mary, S.N.D. "The Life and Times of Saint Julie Billiart." Unpublished. Julie Conference, Namur, Belgium, 1987.

Herold, J. Christopher. *The Age of Napoleon.* New York: Harper and Row, 1963.

Linscott, Sr. Mary, S.N.D. *The 4th Essential,* Private Publication, 1971.

Linscott, Sr. Mary, S.N.D. *Quiet Revolution: The Educational Experience of Blessed Julie Billiart and the Sisters of Notre Dame de Namur.* Glasgow: Burns and Sons, 1966.

McCarthy, Sr. Mary Frances, S.N.D. *Selected Letters of Mother Saint Joseph Blin de Bourdon.* Maryland: Christian Classics, 1990.

Partridge, Sr. Mary Xavier, S.N.D., James Clare (ed.). *Life of Blessed Julie Billiart: Foundress of the Institute of the Sisters of Notre Dame.* London: Sands and Co., 1909.

Rosner, Frances, S.N.D. and Tinsley, Sr. Lucy, S.N.D. *The Letters of St. Julie Billiart.* Rome: Gregorian Press, 1974.

Rooney, Sr. Lucy. *"The Memoirs Reprinted: The Missing Pages."* Unpublished.

Schama, Simon. *Citizens: A Chronicle of the French Revolution.* New York: Vintage Books, 1990.

Stewart, John Hall. *A Documentary Survey of the French Revolution.* New York: The Macmillan Co., 1951.

Tackett, Timothy. *Religion and Regional Culture in Eighteenth Century France: The Eccliastical Oath of 1791.* Princeton: Princeton Univ. Press, 1986.

Tomme, Sr. Frances de Chantal, S.N.D. *Julie Billiart and Her Institute.* London; Longmans, Green and Co., 1938.

Tomme, Sr. Frances de Chantal, S.N.D. *The Life of Mère St. Joseph.* London: Longmans, Green and Co., 1923.

Val Schaerts, Sr. Colette, S.N.D. *"The Prophetic Influence of Julie on Yesterday."* Unpublished. Julie Conference, Namur, 1987.

Ward, Margaret. *Life of Saint Madeleine Sophie: Foundress of the Society of the Sacred Heart, 1779–1865.* Second Ed.: Roehampton, Convent of the Sacred Heart, 1925.

Williams, Margaret, R.S.C.J. *Saint Madeleine Sophie: Her Life and Letters.* New York: Herder and Herder, 1965.

INDEX

225